n or before

A BOOK OF
RAILWAY JOURNEYS

By the same author:

Naval
    Sub-Lieutenant: A Personal Record of the War at Sea
    Nelson's Captains
    Pursuit: The Chase and Sinking of the Bismarck
    Menace: The Life and Death of the Tirpitz

Crime and the Law
    10 Rillington Place
    The Trial of Stephen Ward
    A Presumption of Innocence
    The Portland Spy Case
    Wicked Beyond Belief

Travel and Diaries
    One Man's Meat
    Very Lovely People

Play
    Murder Story

A BOOK OF
RAILWAY
JOURNEYS

Compiled by

LUDOVIC KENNEDY

COLLINS
St James's Place, London
1980

William Collins Sons & Co Ltd
London • Glasgow • Sydney • Auckland
Toronto • Johannesburg

First published 1980
© in the compilation and introduction Ludovic Kennedy 1980
ISBN 0 00 216197 4
Set in 11 point Waverly

ACKNOWLEDGMENTS

The author and publishers are grateful to the copyright holders for their permission to reproduce extracts which appear here.

A. Philip Randolph: A Biographical Portrait, copyright © 1972, 1973 by Jervis B. Anderson. Reprinted by permission of Harcourt Brace Jovanovich, Inc. Daisy Ashford: The Young Visitors, published by Chatto & Windus Ltd. Acknowledgment is also due to Mrs. Margaret Steel and Mrs. Clare Rose. ''Night Mail'' by W. H. Auden, from W. H. Auden: Collected Poems. Copyright © 1938 by W. H. Auden. Reprinted by permission of Random House, Inc. and Faber and Faber Ltd. From Journey to a War by W. H. Auden and Christopher Isherwood, copyright © 1939 and re-newed 1967 by W. H. Auden and Christopher Isherwood. Reprinted by permission of Random House, Inc. and Faber and Faber Ltd. Excerpt from The Big Spenders by Lucius Beebe. Copyright © 1966 by Doubleday & Company, Inc. Reprinted by permission of the publisher. British publisher and copyright holder Hutchinson Publishing Group Ltd. Patricia Beer: ''Mr. Dombey.'' Hutchinson Publishing Group Ltd. John Betjeman: ''Pershore Station'' or ''A Liverish Journey First Class'' from Collected Poems. John Murray (Publishers) Ltd. Christabel Bielenberg: The Past Is Myself, published by Chatto & Windus Ltd. Published in the U.S.A. under the title Ride Out the Dark by W. W. Norton & Co. Inc. Edmund Blunden: ''Railway Note,'' published by Macmillan London Ltd. Permission granted by Gerald Duckworth & Co. Ltd. Alan Burgess: The Small Woman, published by Evans Bros Ltd. Anthony Carson: ''Courier's Train,'' first published in Punch magazine. Paul Chavchavadze: Marie Avinov: Pilgrimage Through Hell, published by Prentice Hall, Inc. Copyright © 1968 by Paul Chavchavadze. Reprinted by permission of McIntosh and Otis, Inc.

For Alastair
in the hope that he will come
to enjoy trains as much
as his father has.

ILLUSTRATIONS:

SOURCES AND ACKNOWLEDGMENTS

Jacket: Birmingham Museum and Art Gallery; *Frontispiece:* (Arrival of Christmas Train, drawn by Duncan) Illustrated London News; 6. Mary Evans Picture Library; 13. Dunedin Public Art Gallery Society, Inc.; 28. John Freeman Group; 37. L'Illustration. Mary Evans Picture Library; 42. Birmingham Museum and Art Gallery; 45. BBC Hulton Picture Library; 49. William Collins; 57. National Railway Museum, York; 65. The Illustrated London News; 68. Mary Evans Picture Library; 75. Collins Publishers; 77. Atlas Photo Agency; 82. Popperfoto; 86–87. The Illustrated London News; 92. BBC Hulton Picture Library; 98. The Metropolitan Museum of Art, Bequest of Mrs. H. O. Havemeyer, 1929. The H. O. Havemeyer Collection; 109. Mary Evans Picture Library; 111. The Mansell Collection; 114. Peter Newark's Western Americana; 117. Mary Evans Picture Library; 120. The National Gallery of Art, Washington; 124, 129, 132. All from Peter Newark's Western Americana; 133, 134, 135. All from Mary Evans Picture Library; 135. Peter Newark's Western Americana; 143. The Mansell Collection; 147. Mary Evans Picture Library; 156–157. The Mansell Collection; 159. BBC Hulton Picture Library; 163. The Mansell Collection; 180. ILN Picture Library; 193. Almasy; 199. John Hillelson Agency Ltd.; 207. The Illustrated London News; 213. Mary Evans Picture Library; 219. Snark International; 226, 229. Both from Keystone Press Agency Ltd.; 233. The Wiener Library; 256. John Hillelson Agency Ltd.; 259. Mary Evans Picture Library; 269. The Illustrated London News; 283. Ashe & Grant; 291. The Illustrated London News; 301. S. A. Studio Lourmel 77 Photo Routhier; 319. Mary Evans Picture Library; 325, 335. Both from National Railway Museum, York; 351. Mary Evans Picture Library; 353. Compagnie Internationale de Wagons-Lits et du Tourisme.

CONTENTS

EUROPE

U . S . A .

ELSEWHERE

India

WAR

CRASHES

FICTION

INTRODUCTION

Trains are on the way back; if not in substance, at least in the imagination. Mr. Paul Theroux may be said to have started the revival with *The Great Railway Bazaar*, a fascinating account of his travels by train from London to Tokyo and back. Recently in Paris the French staged a vast railway station exhibition, *Le Temps des Gares*; while in New York and London there have been revivals of the musical *On the Twentieth Century* based on America's former crack express of the same name. The BBC has completed a seven-part series of television documentaries entitled *Great Railway Journeys of the World*, and Britain has also been celebrating the 150th anniversary of the opening of the Liverpool to Manchester railway. Illustrated descriptions of train journeys are now a feature of colour magazines; and railway clubs, private branch lines, special excursions, etc., are, I am told, all in rude health.

For some of us, of course, trains never went away. My own affection for them began as a small boy when travelling to the Scottish Highlands for summer holidays before the war. Then, as now, the delight lay in the unaccustomed break with routine —the bustle of the terminus, porters jostling for the bags; stocking up with literature and chocolate at the platform stalls; then, settled in, the long, sweet wait for the whistle and the slow inching forward to the north. Dinner and a fitful sleep, and in the morning a bedside window on another world: deer on the hillside, wind on the heather, the heart of Scotland at my feet.

Since then I have travelled in trains whenever possible. My favourite was the *Terra Nova*, the private car of the Governor of Newfoundland, whose private secretary and A.D.C. I once briefly was. The Governor and his wife slept in the car's two bedrooms: in the drawing room-cum-observation car the butler and I slung hammocks from the roof. For official visits and fish-

ing holidays the *Terra Nova* was hitched to the rear of the Newfoundland Express, which went at all of thirty miles an hour;
and sustained by the Governor's pink gins (for he was also an
admiral) and by the butler's pepper steaks (for he was also the
cook) and the grandeur of the Newfoundland scenery, we pottered contentedly across the island to wherever duty or pleasure
called.

In the days when train travel was the norm, we were all
rather inclined to take it for granted. After a thirty-year glut of
jet and motorway travel, the novelty of which has long since
worn off, we can see that train travel was—and when you can
get it, still is—comparative bliss. No one who has travelled long
distances on a motorway, chained like a dog to his seat, unable
to read or drink, blocked by juggernauts from the passing view,
deafened by their engines and blackened by their fumes, would
wish to repeat the experience for pleasure.

Air travel is little better. One is cramped and disorientated.
Chains are *de rigueur* here too; and if you happen to find yourself next to a manic child or compulsive chatterbox, there is
little you can do to escape. Airlines attempt to compensate for
these deficiencies with piped music, films, and instant alcohol.
These overload the system and, combined with a swingeing
time-change, lead to total dysfunction; arriving within hours of
setting out, one needs two days to recover.

Train journeys, in comparison, have much to offer. Unlike
sea or air travel, one has a fair notion where one is; and the
countryside, like a moving picture show, unrolls itself before
one's eyes. One is transported in comfort, even style, to the wild
places of earth—forest, mountain, desert; and always there is
the counterpoint between life within the train and life without:

> One scene as I bow to pour her coffee:—
>   Three Indians in the scouring drouth,
>   huddled at a grave scooped in the gravel,
>   lean to the wind as our train goes by.
>   Someone is gone.
>   There is dust on everything in Nevada.
> I pour the cream.*

* William Stafford, *Vacation.*

One can move around in a train, visit the buffet for snacks or a drink, play cards (or, on some American trains, the piano), strike up a conversation, read, sleep, snore, make love. Luggage is to hand too, not as in car or airplane, ungetatable in trunk or belly.

Some trains are designed to satisfy national needs. The American club car, for instance, exists for passengers to bore each other with accounts of business deals, marital problems, extramarital affairs: the price they know they must pay is to be bored in turn later. The English have never gone in for club cars, believing that on long journeys one should not utter at all. When buffet cars were first introduced to British trains, there was a real danger they might lead to social intercourse. Happily they turned out to be so utterly bereft of comfort and style, so perennially awash in soldiers and beer, as to discourage any right-thinking person from staying a moment longer than the time needed for his purchase, which he is then free to convey to the privacy and silence of his seat.

Yet the sweetest pleasure of any long train journey lies in its anticipation. I have never eyed any long-distance train I was about to board (except perhaps in Britain) without wondering, as the old hymn says of Heaven,

> What joys await us there?
> What radiancy of glory?
> What bliss beyond compare?

Even if achievement rarely matches promise, one may still daydream. How green are the vistas, what's for dinner, whom shall I meet? In the end it's the passengers who provide the richest moments of any long-distance trip. For train travel, being constricted both in time and space, magnifies character, intensifies relationships, unites the disparate. Ordinary people become extra-ordinary, larger than life; and in the knowledge that they will not meet again, expansive, confiding, intimate. Let us talk now, you and I: later will be too late.

In the pages that follow, the reader will find many such brief encounters: the Rev. Francis Kilvert and Irish Mary; Harold Nicolson and Arketall; myself and Mr. and Mrs. Pitman; Christabel Bielenberg and the S.S. officer; Paul Theroux and Wendy. In the fiction section the meetings are even stranger: Myatt and Carol in *Stamboul Train*; the general and his companion in *The Very Silent Traveller*; the workman and the wet-nurse in Maupassant's *An Idyll*. No wonder that trains are so often the setting for stories, for the essential stuff of stories—movement and relationships—is also the stuff of trains.

When the first American steam locomotive went chugging across the plains of Nebraska and Wyoming, the Indians called it *The Iron Horse*. Others have also thought of it as a living creature, puffing and panting, groaning and sighing, whistling and clanging through the night. Its successor, the diesel, is altogether more discreet, yet still to be thought of as something more than inanimate steel and wood. But are trains masculine or feminine? We give them brave, heroic names like the *Flying Scotsman*, the *Hiawatha*, the *Yorkshireman*, the *Empire-Builder*—yet there are some, like Fanny Kemble and Stephen Spender, who speak of an engine or even a train as "she"; who find affinity between the womb and the steel cylinder in which they are carried. Perhaps it is this that makes a train crash seem more unexpected and unnatural than a car or air crash; as if a bomb had flattened the family home.

The literature of train travel is huge, and in making selections for this anthology I have followed no other criterion than what has informed, amused, delighted, or amazed me; nothing has been included because of any belief that it "ought" to be. The reader will note that in the section on English train journeys, most extracts are pre-World War I—indeed, some are pre-Boer and even pre-Crimean War. That is because the best accounts that have come my way have been of that period. Outside fiction, there are no outstanding descriptions of modern British train journeys. On the other hand, there are two outstanding writers in English of modern foreign train journeys: Mr. Peter Fleming in the second quarter of the twentieth century, Mr. Paul Theroux in the third. I make no apologies for including so many extracts from their books: these are, in their different ways, what accounts of rail travel should be.

I have also included chapters on train travel in the two most powerful countries in the world today, the U.S.A. and the U.S.S.R. The history of the United States is largely the history of its railroads: from the opening of the West during the 1860s, through the Civil War to the boom years of the late nineteenth and early twentieth centuries and the coming of what has been called the crack varnish—luxury trains like the *Sunset Limited*, the *Southern Crescent*, the Santa Fe *Super Chief*. These, too, were the days of the millionaires' ultimate status symbol, the private coach, about whose often eccentric owners Lucius Beebe (himself a former eccentric owner) writes so wittily.

After the last war, the jet plane and the motorcar almost killed off the American long-distance passenger service; and E. B. White's lament about the run-down of the trains in Maine was echoed elsewhere. However, since the government-financed Amtrak took over the system in 1971, things have been marginally improving. Eight hundred new coaches have been ordered, and with gasoline less plentiful and increasing in cost, the number of train passengers has been steadily rising. In October 1979, for the BBC, I made a trip from New York to Los Angeles by way of the *Broadway Limited*, the *San Francisco Zephyr*, and the *Coast Starlight*. It was a nice, lazy, rather bumpy journey in which I was taken through some splendid scenery, met some unusual people, ate and drank to my satisfaction, and rarely arrived anywhere on schedule. Between San Francisco and Los Angeles, the *Starlight* travels roughly the same distance as does the *Flying Scotsman* between London and Edinburgh; and takes eleven hours for the trip compared to the *Scotsman*'s five.

Train travel in Russia, on the other hand, and particularly on the Trans-Siberian Express, seems to have exerted a powerful pull on the minds of many American and European travellers. The numbers of those who have travelled on the Trans-Siberian and written accounts of it grow year by year. One can see the attractions of journeying by train from Europe to the Pacific, especially when the route takes one through the heart of the most closed society in the world. Yet no account I have read suggests that this eight-day journey, in which the train's clocks are kept rigidly on Moscow time, is other than a nightmare of prolonged discomfort, wretched food, dubious travelling companions, monotonous scenery, and suspicious officials. By way of corrective I have included accounts of two journeys rather more peculiar to Soviet life—those of Marie Avinov in the thirties, and Alexander Solzhenitsyn in the fifties, both adrift in the Gulag Archipelago.

Again because the literature on the subject is so great, I have included a section on various train journeys undertaken during the last war. During those five years, trains were used as perhaps never before, certainly never on that scale. They were deployed to carry troops and ammunition to the front, evacuees to safety from the enemy's bombs, Jews to their deaths in concentration camps, leaders like Churchill and Hitler to conferences on war strategy. Peter Fleming's hilarious account of how he and his colleagues captured an ammunition train in Greece is, in its way, as gripping as James Leasor's story of how Franz von Werra became the only German prisoner of war to escape from an Allied train and find his way back to Germany.

In the fiction section, the biggest problem was what to include and what to omit. Many readers will be sorry not to see particular favourites: *Poisson d'Avril*, perhaps, from *The Further Reminiscences of an Irish R.M.*; Axel Munthe's story of the two coffins; the meeting of Vronsky and Anna; Maugham's *The Hairless Mexican; Alice and the Ticket-Collector;* Max Beerbohm's *A. V. Laider*. Some I rejected because they were too long, some because they made little sense when taken out of context, some, to be blunt, because they did not have the same appeal for me as for those who recommended them. Among the poetry excerpts I shall no doubt have my knuckles rapped for omitting T. S. Eliot's *Skimbleshanks*; but the Cat of the Railway Train has never been for me. What is left is a very small selection from a very large body of literature; but I hope, nonetheless, agreeable.

When I first floated the idea of the book, several hundred people volunteered suggestions for inclusion. To all of them, whether I have followed their recommendations or not, my grateful thanks; particularly to Mr. Benny Green who sent me a tape full of useful tips, and to Mr. Roy Fuller, a most generous guide to poems on railway travel; also to A. K. Astbury, T. A. Shearer, Margaret M. Sherman, John Skelton, Mary Stewart, and Maurice Stewart. My researcher, Annabel Craig, deserves an especial word of thanks. During most of 1979 she kept me

supplied with a steady flow of photostated writings of railway
journeys, culled from a variety of books found in a variety of
libraries; and so steeped in the subject did she become that in
1980 my publishers called on her to make the initial selection
of the book's admirable illustrations.

Finally, my thanks to my editors, Philip Ziegler and Hilary
Davies in London and James Wade and Charles McCurdy in
New York, from whose skills and suggestions the book has
greatly profited.

When I was asked to give three short talks about what the BBC called "my experiences," I said that I would talk about railway trains. I find it difficult, at this moment, to understand why I said this. I suppose I thought that most people had in their hearts the same sort of soft spot for trains that they have for dogs and sailing ships and policemen, and would therefore listen with indulgence to even the most trivial anecdotes about them. But is there anything in this theory? It remains to be seen.

PETER FLEMING

The railroad track is miles away,
  And the day is loud with voices speaking,
Yet there isn't a train goes by all day
  But I hear its whistle shrieking.

All night there isn't a train goes by,
  Though the night is still for sleep and dreaming,
But I see its cinders red on the sky,
  And hear its engine steaming.

My heart is warm with the friends I make,
  And better friends I'll not be knowing,
Yet there isn't a train I wouldn't take,
  No matter where it's going.

EDNA ST. VINCENT MILLAY, *Travel*

Almost anything is possible in a train.

PAUL THEROUX

BRITAIN

The First Railway Journey

The Stockton and Darlington scheme had three times to present itself before it received the sanction of Parliament. The application of 1818 was defeated by the Duke of Cleveland, because the line threatened to interfere with one of his fox-covers. Certain road trustees, also, spread the report abroad that the mortgagees of the tolls would suffer; and to meet this objection, Edward Pease had to disarm opposition by a public notice that the company's solicitors were ready to purchase these securities at the price originally paid for them.

In 1821, however, the Bill passed; and on Tuesday, the 27th of September, 1825, the line was opened. "The scene on the morning of that day," said Mr. Pease, fifty years afterwards, "sets description at defiance." Many who were to take part in the event "did not the night before sleep a wink, and soon after midnight were astir. The universal cheers, the happy faces of many, the vacant stare of astonishment of others, and the alarm depicted on the countenances of some, gave variety to the picture." At the appointed hour the procession went forward. The train moved off at the rate of from ten to twelve miles an hour, with a weight of eighty tons, with one engine—"No. 1"—driven by George Stephenson himself; after it six wagons, loaded with coals and flour; then a covered coach, containing directors and proprietors; next twenty-one coal wagons, fitted up for passengers, with which they were crammed; and lastly, six more wagons loaded with coals.

"Off started the procession, with the horseman at its head. A great concourse of people stood along the line. Many of them tried to accompany it by running, and some gentlemen on horseback galloped across the fields to keep up with the engine. The railway descending with a gentle incline towards Darlington, the rate of speed was consequently variable. At a favourable part of the road, Stephenson determined to try the speed of the engine, and he called upon the horseman with the flag to get out of the way," and Stephenson put on the speed to twelve miles, and then to fifteen miles an hour, and the runners on foot, the gentlemen on horseback, and the horseman with the flag, were soon left far behind. "When the train reached Darlington, it was found that four hundred and fifty passengers occupied the wagons, and that the load of men, coals, and merchandise amounted to about ninety tons."

ANON

THE NINETEENTH CENTURY

Stockton to Darlington, 1825:
Stephenson on the sparkling iron road—
Chimney-hatted and frock-coated—drives
His locomotive, while the Lydian mode
Of Opus 132 may actually be
In the course of making. At twelve miles an hour
The century rushes to futurity,
Where art will be mankind-destroying power.
How can the music fail to bear the dates
And quirks of fashion time must prove
Grotesque? Especially as it celebrates
Avuncular and bust fraternal love.
Yet somehow an anachronistic god
Has lasted beyond his final period.

ROY FULLER

Those in favour . . .

The increasing powers of Steam which like you I look on "half proud half sad half angry and half pleased" in doing so much for the commercial world promise something also for the sociable, and like Prince Houssein's tapestry will I think one day waft friends together in the course of a few hours and for aught we may be able to [tell] bring Hampstead and Abbotsford within the distance of "will you dine with us quietly tomorrow."

SIR WALTER SCOTT

I rejoice to see it, and to think that feudality is gone for ever: it is so great a blessing to think that any one evil is really extinct.

DR. ARNOLD

And those against . . .

I see no reason to suppose that these machines will ever force themselves into general use.

DUKE OF WELLINGTON

Nothing is more distasteful to me than to hear the echo of our hills reverberating with the noise of hissing railroad engines, running through the heart of our hunting country, and destroying the noble sport which I have been accustomed to from my childhood.

MR. BERKELEY, M.P.

Your middle-class man thinks it is the highest pitch of development and civilisation when his letters are carried twelve times a day from Islington to Camberwell, and from Camberwell to Islington, and if railway-trains run to and fro between them every quarter of an hour. He thinks it nothing that the trains only carry him from an illiberal, dismal life at Islington to an illiberal, dismal life at Camberwell; and the letters only tell him that such is the life there.

MATTHEW ARNOLD
from S. LEGG (ed.),
The Railway Book (1952)

Passengers and freight: *The Liverpool and Manchester Railway*, 1831 (S. G. Hughes after I. Shaw)

Liverpool to Manchester, 1830

The opening of the line took place on the 15th of September, 1830, when the Duke of Wellington, Prime Minister, Mr. Peel, Home Secretary, Mr. Huskisson, and a number of other distinguished persons, were to pass in the first train with the directors. A gay *cortège* of thirty-three carriages, accompanied by bands of music, started from Liverpool, amidst the acclamations of a countless multitude of observers, and with all the splendour of an ancient pageant. But soon the enjoyment of the scene was marred. While the engines were stopping to take in water at Parkside, Mr. Huskisson, with some other gentlemen, strolled along the line. As they were returning to their seats, another train of carriages came up. All ran for shelter; but, unhappily, Mr. Huskisson hurried to the side of the train, and, opening the door, attempted to enter; the door swung back at the moment—he fell to the ground, and was in an instant overthrown and crushed beneath the wheels of the advancing carriage. His thigh was fractured and mangled, and his own first expression, "I have met my death," proved too true, for he died that evening in the neighbouring parsonage of Eccles. The train passed on to Manchester without further accident; but the contemplated festivities were forgotten amidst the gloom occasioned by this tragedy.

ANON

Manchester to Liverpool, 1835

6 found all of us in our omnibus on our way to the much talked of railhead. On reaching this office, as soon as you have paid your fare, you are commanded to walk upstairs to the coach rooms—this movement is just like going up the stairs of Queens Street Chapel.

Reaching the top, there you behold a range of coaches of large dimension fastened close to each other. Some are closed like our Leeds coach, and others are open on the sides—in order to have a view of the country, as I thought, and of their manner of proceeding. We all took our place in an open one, which resembles an omnibus. Before starting, I took a survey of all around, first placing my little ones safe. The steam carriage which propels each train is something like a distilling wagon and have each a name of no inviting character, for instance, Fury, Victory, Rapid, Vulcan, Tiger and so on.

A few minutes after 7 we started, not very fast at first, but, in less than five minutes, off we went like a shot from a gun. No sooner did we come to a field than it was a mile behind us, but this was nothing in comparison with meeting a long train of carriages from Liverpool. I was never so frightened in my life than at this moment; I shrank back completely horrified in my seat; I do not think the train was more than 2 seconds in passing, yet it was as long as Holywell Hill. We were then going at a full 34 miles an hour, consequently they passed us at double that time.

It is impossible to form any idea of the rapidity of moving. Several other trains passed us, but as I was aware of their approach they no longer alarmed me as at first. The first 17 miles we went in 32 minutes. I am much disappointed in the view of the country, the railway being cut through so many hills you have frequently for miles only clay mounds on each side of you—consequently no splendid prospect can attract your attention. Even when the railway is on a bridge or at an elevation above the usual track of land, you are not charmed by that diversity of prospect which is to be met with in ordinary stage coach travelling. That has a decided superiority over this new work of man.

I was an hour and a quarter going the 33 miles, the latter part of the journey being performed at the slow speed of 20 miles an hour. Previous to entering Liverpool, you go through a dark, black, ugly, vile abominable tunnel of 300 yards long, which has all the horrors of banishment from life—such a hole as I never wish to go through again, unless my time is as precious as it was the other day.

Charles Young to his sister Jane, written from Castletown, Isle of Man, 6th August, 1835.

FROM A RAILWAY CARRIAGE

Faster than fairies, faster than witches,
Bridges and houses, hedges and ditches;
And charging along like troops in a battle,
All through the meadows the houses and cattle;
And all of the sights of the hill and the plain
Fly as thick as driving rain;
And ever again, in the wink of an eye,
Painted stations whistle by.

Here is a child who clambers and scrambles,
All by himself and gathering brambles;
Here is a tramp who stands and gazes;
And here is the green for stringing the daisies!
Here is a cart run away in the road
Lumping along with man and load;
And here is a mill, and there is a river;
Each a glimpse and gone for ever!

ROBERT LOUIS STEVENSON

Lackadaisical attitude of early passengers

Neither the companies' servants nor the public had yet learned to treat railway trains with the necessary caution. Engine-drivers fancied that a collision between two engines was much the same thing as the inter-locking of the wheels of two rival stage-coaches. Passengers tried to jump on and off trains moving at full speed with absolute recklessness. Again and again is it recorded, "injured, jumped out after his hat"; "fell off, riding on the side of a wagon"; "skull broken, riding on the top of the carriage, came in collision with a bridge"; "guard's head struck against a bridge, attempting to remove a passenger who had improperly seated himself outside"; "fell out of a third-class car-

riage while pushing and jostling with a friend." "Of the serious
accidents reported to the Board of Trade," writes one authority,
"twenty-two happened to persons who jumped off when the
carriages were going at speed, generally after their hats, and
five persons were run over when lying either drunk or asleep
upon the line."

W. M. ACWORTH
from S. LEGG (ed.),
The Railway Book (1952)

FROM MARLBOROUGH TO WEST WALES

       . . . Should we not pause
An instant at regal Badminton? But you
Know of no royal loyalties other than your own
With a derisive whistle hurtle
Past innocent Gloucestershire yeomen
Standing agog on the platform, while the acrid smoke
Of Sodbury's stuffy tunnel almost chokes us . . .
Before the climb out of that three mile slimy hell-hole
To the smugglers marshes with the rude name (Undy)
To glamorous Glamorgan, mile-long Margam, steel
Tensile as your own force. But now (thank God) we turn
And miss out odourous Llansamlet, stinking of sulphur

       . . .
       . . . Rattling through St. Clears
Into that place where alien Celts welcome all tankdrivers
Whatever race, provided they are Anglo Saxon, with
       plenty of cash.
It's raining now—it always is at Whitland, and the dark
       clouds
Press on Prescelly, gather on Maencloghog. And now at
       last
I know the line's end, the right line, like a homing
       pigeon. . . .

H. SANDHAM

Brimstone fumes and Irish Mary

Wednesday, 18 May 1870

Went down to the Bath Flower Show in Sydney College Gardens. Found the first train going down was an Excursion train and took a ticket for it. The carriage was nearly full. In the Box tunnel as there was no lamp, the people began to strike foul brimstone matches and hand them to each other all down the carriage. All the time we were in the tunnel these lighted matches were travelling from hand to hand in the darkness. Each match lasted the length of the carriage and the red ember was thrown out of the opposite window, by which time another lighted match was seen travelling down the carriage. The carriage was chock full of brimstone fumes, the windows both nearly shut, and by the time we got out of the tunnel I was almost suffocated. Then a gentleman tore a lady's pocket handkerchief in two, seized one fragment, blew his nose with it, and put the rag in his pocket. She then seized his hat from his head, while another lady said that the dogs of Wootton Bassett were much more sociable than the people.

Wednesday, 19 June 1872

Left Bockleton Vicarage for Liverpool. At Wrexham two merry saucy Irish hawking girls got into our carriage. The younger had a handsome saucy daring face showing splendid white teeth when she laughed and beautiful Irish eyes of dark grey which looked sometimes black and sometimes blue, with long silky black lashes and finely pencilled black eyebrows. This girl kept her companion and the whole carriage laughing from Wrexham to Chester with her merriment, laughter and songs and her antics with a doll dressed like a boy, which she made dance in the air by pulling a string. She had a magnificent voice and sung to a comic popular air while the doll danced wildly,

A-dressed in his Dolly Varden,
A-dressed in his Dolly Varden,
  He looks so neat
  And he smells so sweet,
A-dressed in his Dolly Varden.

Then breaking down into merry laughter she hid her face and glanced roguishly at me from behind the doll. Suddenly she became quiet and pensive and her face grew grave and sad as she sang a love song.

The two girls left the carriage at Chester and as she passed, the younger put out her hand and shook hands with me. They stood by the carriage door on the platform for a few moments and Irish Mary, the younger girl, asked me to buy some nuts. I gave her sixpence and took a dozen nuts out of a full measure she was going to pour into my hands. She seemed surprised and looked up with a smile. "You'll come and see me," she said coaxingly. "You are not Welsh, are you?" "No, we are a mixture of Irish and English." "Born in Ireland?" "No, I was born at Huddersfield in Yorkshire." "You look Irish—you have the Irish eye." She laughed and blushed and hid her face. "What do you think I am?" asked the elder girl, "do you think I am Spanish?" "No," interrupted the other laughing, "you have too much Irish between your eyes." "My eyes are blue," said the elder girl, "your eyes are grey, the gentleman's eyes are black." "Where did you get in?" I asked Irish Mary. "At Wrexham," she said. "We were caught in the rain, walked a long way in it and got wet through," said the poor girl pointing to a bundle of wet clothes they were carrying and which they had changed for dry ones. "What do you do?" "We go out hawking," said the girl in a low voice. "You have a beautiful voice." "Hasn't she?" interrupted the elder girl eagerly and delightedly. "Where did you learn to sing?" She smiled and blushed and hid her face. A porter and some other people were looking wonderingly on, so I thought it best to end the conversation. But there was an attractive power about this poor Irish girl that fascinated me strangely. I felt irresistibly drawn to her. The singular beauty of her eyes, a beauty of deep sadness, a wistful sorrowful imploring look, her swift rich humour, her sudden gravity and sadness, her brilliant laughter, a certain intensity and power

Waiting for the Train (James Tissot)

and richness of life and the extraordinary sweetness, softness and beauty of her voice in singing and talking gave her a power over me which I could not understand nor describe, but the power of a stronger over a weaker will and nature. She lingered about the carriage door. Her look grew more wistful, beautiful, imploring. Our eyes met again and again. Her eyes grew more and more beautiful. My eyes were fixed and riveted on hers. A few minutes more and I know not what might have happened. A wild reckless feeling came over me. Shall I leave all and follow her? No—Yes—No. At that moment the train moved on. She was left behind. Goodbye, sweet Irish Mary. So we parted. Shall we meet again? Yes—No—Yes.

THE REV. FRANCIS KILVERT,
Diary

Adventures of the Countess of Zetland

A singular accident brought me into communication with Lord Gormanston. Early in November His Lordship, his family, and household were passengers by the up Holyhead express. When nearing Bletchley, while the train was travelling at fifty miles an hour, a young woman, having His Lordship's little boy in charge, by some means fell out of the train. It was surprising that she was not killed on the spot, but such was not the case. She fell so close to the adjoining set of rails that the down newspaper train cut off a lock of her hair. The young woman was not missed at first, but owing to the open door being noticed the train was signalled to be stopped at Leighton, and thence Lord Gormanston returned to enquire after the unfortunate maid. Notwithstanding the scalp wounds and the shock the young woman recovered.

LADY ZETLAND

THE RAILWAY JUNCTION

From here through tunnelled gloom the track
Forks into two; and one of these
Wheels onward into darkening hills,
And one toward distant seas.

How still it is; the signal light
At set of sun shines paley green;
A thrush sings; other sound there's none,
Nor traveller to be seen—

Where late there was a throng. And now,
In peace awhile, I sit alone;
Though soon, at the appointed hour,
I shall myself be gone.

But not their way: the bow-legged groom,
The parson in black, the widow and son,
The sailor with his cage, the gaunt
Gamekeeper with his gun,

That fair one, too, discreetly veiled—
All, who so mutely came, and went,
Will reach those far nocturnal hills,
Or shores, ere night is spent.

I nothing know why thus we met—
Their thoughts, their longings, hopes, their fate:
And what shall I remember, except—
The evening growing late—

That here through tunnelled gloom the track
Forks into two; of these
One into darkening hills leads on,
And one toward distant seas?

WALTER DE LA MARE

An English hobo

Some passengers, we may add, are eccentric in their ideas of locomotion. Not long ago, on the arrival of the 3.15 Irish mail at Chester platform, a man was found lying underneath a carriage He was grasping the brake-rod with his legs and hands, and in order to hold the rod securely, he had some flannel in his hands. He had ridden in this way from Holyhead to Chester, nearly ninety miles. How he escaped death was a marvel. He was sentenced to pay twenty shillings, or to have twenty-one days' hard labour.

Another passenger, of an adventurous order of mind, desired a similarly cheap and airy ride from Euston to Liverpool. His name was John Smith, and he was described as "a seafaring man respectably attired." It appeared from the evidence, and indeed from Mr. Smith's own admission, that on the previous night he left the Euston station by an express train at nine p.m., which, travelling at a high rate of speed, does not stop until it reaches Rugby at eleven p.m., a distance of 82½ miles. "Mr. Smith did not take his seat like an ordinary passenger inside any of the carriages, but he travelled underneath one of them, and would, no doubt, have concluded his journey to Liverpool in safety, but that on the arrival of the train at Rugby the wheel-examiner, seeing a man's legs protruding from under one of the carriages, had the curiosity to make further search, and discovered Mr. Smith coiled round the brake-rod, a piece of iron not above three inches broad, in a fantastic position. Mr. Smith was immediately uncoiled, and being technically in error was detained in custody. The bottom of the carriage was only eighteen inches from the ground, and where the engine takes up water as it travels, Mr. Smith was not more than six inches from the trough; he therefore had not far to fall in case of a casualty; but the bench, surprised at a railway passenger under any circumstances having survived a journey of eighty-two miles, said 'it was a miracle he was not killed,' and let him off with a fine of 2s. 6d. and costs, or fourteen days' imprisonment. Mr. Smith stated that his journey 'was not a very comfortable one,' "—a remark the accuracy of which—however on other matters we may differ from him—may be conceded.

ANON

MIDNIGHT ON THE GREAT WESTERN

In the third-class seat sat the journeying boy,
   And the roof-lamp's oily flame
Played down on his listless form and face,
Bewrapt past knowing to what he was going,
    Or whence he came.

In the band of his hat the journeying boy
   Had a ticket stuck; and a string
Around his neck bore the key of his box,
That twinkled gleams of the lamp's sad beam
    Like a living thing.

What past can be yours, O journeying boy
   Towards a world unknown,
Who calmly, as if incurious quite
On all at stake, can undertake
    This plunge alone?

Knows your soul a sphere, O journeying boy,
   Our rude realms far above,
Whence with spacious vision you mark and mete
This region of sin that you find you are in,
    But are not of?

THOMAS HARDY

A botanical specimen
found on the Great Western

Dr. M'Nab, Professor of Botany in the Royal College of Science, Dublin, says that in a railway carriage on the express between Paddington and Milford, he noticed in the window two tufts of moss, one near each corner of the glass. "There was a little black soil kept moist by the condensation of vapour on the window, and two little bright green patches, consisting of about forty or fifty plants, about one-eighth of an inch in height, and apparently very healthy. The other window had the same moist deposit of soil, but no mosses. I put a small quantity of the soil and moss into my pocket-book, and after my return to the college placed two or three of the little plants under the microscope. The plants have only a few leaves, and probably belong to the genus *tortula*; but along with the moss I could detect an abundance of two species of *oscillatoria* in a very healthy condition, with abundance of *phycochroma* in their cells. On examining the slide with a higher power, I detected a number of diatoms, all belonging to a small species of *navicula*. The soil in which the mosses were growing was very peculiar. It consisted almost exclusively of exceedingly minute black particles, appearing as mere specks with a sixth-inch object glass, and all exhibiting the most active Brownian movements. The moving soil seems a fitting accompaniment to the locomotive habitat of the specimens. I suppose it will be necessary to say the distribution of the plants is remarkable, extending, as it does, from Paddington to Milford and back. You may, therefore, accept this as a small contribution towards the 'Botany of the South Wales Express.' "

ANON

THE WASP

Once as I went by rail to Epping Street,
Both windows being open, a wasp flew in;
Through the compartment swung and almost out
Scarce seen, scarce heard; but dead against the pane
Entitled "Smoking," did the train's career
Arrest her passage. Such a wonderful
Impervious transparency, before
That palpitating moment, had never yet
Her airy voyage thwarted. Undismayed,
With diligence incomparable, she sought
An exit, till the letters like a snare
Entangled her; or else the frosted glass
And signature indelible appeared
The key to all the mystery: there she groped,
And flirted petulant wings, and fiercely sang
A counter-spell against the sorcery,
The sheer enchantment that inhibited
Her access to the world—her birthright, there!
So visible, and so beyond her reach!
Baffled and raging like a tragic queen,
She left at last the stencilled tablet; roamed
The pane a while to cool her regal ire,
Then tentatively touched the window-frame:
Sure footing still, though rougher than the glass;
Dissimilar in texture, and so obscure!

Perplexed now by opacity with foot and wing
She coasted up and down the wood, and worked
Her wrath to passion-point again. Then from the frame
She slipped by chance into the open space
Left by the lowered sash—the world once more
In sight! She paused; she closed her wings, and felt
The air with learned antennae for the smooth
Resistance that she knew now must belong
To such mysterious transparences.
No foothold? Down she fell—six inches down!—
Hovered a second, dazed and dubious still;
Then soared away a captive queen set free.

JOHN DAVIDSON

Escape of a murderer

The murderer and burglar, who was one of the most startling products of modern society, was taken, on January 22, 1879—after his capture by Sergeant Robinson on the lawn in St. John's Park, Blackheath—by train on his way to Sheffield, where he was to undergo examination before the magistrates for the murder of Arthur Dyson, civil engineer, at Banner Cross.

The notoriety of the criminal had become almost the country's talk. His resource and daring were on everybody's tongue. "It would be a funny thing if he escaped," said a spectator, chatting to an official in the Sheffield Police Court, which was crammed with a crowd waiting in eager expectation for the prisoner's arrival. Scarcely were the words uttered than there was an indescribable flutter in the Court, much whispering, and many serious faces. Charles Peace had escaped! All the way down from Pentonville the man, who was restless, savage, and snarling, just like a wild beast, gave the warders continual trouble. When the Great Northern express was speeding through the pastoral country a little north of Workshop, Peace, jibing and sneering at his gaolers, sprang to the carriage window and took a flying leap out of the express. But his panther-like action availed him little. The under-warder seized him by the left foot as he leapt from the compartment, and held on with desperate grasp. The other warder tugged at the communication-cord, but it would not act.

On went the express by field and homestead, the driver unaware of the fierce struggle behind. Peace, suspended head downward, with his face banging now and then against the oscillating carriage, tried with his right leg to kick himself free from the warder's grip. The struggling attracted the attention of the passengers, but they could do nothing to assist the warder, who, with every muscle quivering, was straining with his writhing prisoner. Shout after shout passed from carriage to carriage, only to be carried miles away by the wind; the noise of the clamouring travellers simply made strange echoes in the driver's ears. For two miles the struggle went on; then Peace, determined to end it, whatever the result to himself, wriggled his left foot out of his shoe, which was left in the warder's grasp, and at last he was free. He fell wildly, his head struck the carriage footboard with tremendous force, and he bounded into the six-foot, where he rolled over and over, a curious bundle half enveloped in a cloud of dust.

Still onward sped the train, the warder, helpless to secure his prey, craning his neck as far as he could out of the carriage window, his face a study of rage and concern because he had been outwitted. Nearly another mile was covered before the express pulled up. No time was then lost in chasing the fugitive. The warders, accompanied by several passengers eager for adventure, ran back along the line and found Peace in the six-foot, not far from the place at which he had made his reckless descent from the train. The man was lying near the down track, a huddled heap, unconscious, with a serious wound in his head. He was not merely a person of amazing unscrupulousness but of wondrous vitality, and he soon recovered sensibility, murmuring, as he was lifted into the guard's van of a goods train for removal to Sheffield, "I am cold; cover me up." The warders were only too pleased to cover him up; they took every care of him. When he was conveyed to Armley in readiness for his trial they were armed with revolvers; but the "small, elderly-looking, feeble man, in brown convict-dress," made no further attempt to escape. He was sentenced to death at Leeds assizes and hanged, no one regretting the hardened criminal's doom.

JOHN PENDLETON
from S. LEGG (ed.),
The Railway Book (1952)

Uncertainty of place of birth

Lord Frederic Hamilton records a story of the Indian Census of 1891, when a man gave his place of birth as "a first-class carriage on the London and North-Western Railway, somewhere between Bletchley and Euston; the precise spot being unnoticed either by myself or the other person principally concerned."

ANON
from S. LEGG (ed.),
The Railway Book (1952)

TRAVELLING TO MY SECOND MARRIAGE ON THE DAY OF THE FIRST MOONSHOT

We got into the carriage. It was hot.
An old woman sat there, her white hair
Stained at the temples, as if by smoke.
Beside her the old man, her husband,
Talking of rivers, salmon, yearling trout,
Their dwindled waters.

A windscreen wiper on another engine
Flickered like an irritable, a mad eyelid,
The woman's mouth fell open. She complained.
Her husband said, "I'd like
A one-way ticket to the moon.
Wouldn't mind that."

"What for?" "Plant roses." "*Roses?*" "Roses,
Yes. I'd be the first rosegrower on the moon.
Mozart, I'd call my rose. That's it.
A name for a new rose; Mozart.
That's what I'd call the first rose on the moon,
If I got there to grow it."

Ten nine eight seven six five four three two one.
The old woman, remember her, and the old man:
Her black shoes tapping; his gold watch as he counted.
They'd been to a funeral. We were going to a wedding.
When the train started the wheels sang *Figaro*
And there was a smell of roses.

ROBERT NYE

A lunatic at large

In the month of August 18—, it was incumbent upon me to take
a journey to a town at some distance from my own residence.
Time being no object with me, and the country through which
my route lay very beautiful, I resolved to take it in what was to
me the most enjoyable way; but after diligent inquiry for anything in the shape of a stage-coach, I found that her Majesty's
mail had ceased running the week before; so that "the rail" was
my only chance of getting to the place of my destination.
Whereupon I made a virtue of necessity; submitting, though
with the worst grace in the world; for my habitual dislike to
this mode of travelling was increased by one of those unaccountable fits of reluctance to taking the journey, which sometimes
seizes one, and which is usually set down to the score of nervousness. So I tried to explain mine; which, as the time drew near,
rose to a complete dread of it, to my no small annoyance, for I
had a contempt for omens and presentiments; and zealously, but
vainly, I tried to pooh! pooh! myself out of it.

The morning broke, dull, wet, oppressive, with apparently
half a score thunder-storms in reserve for my especial use; and
at six o'clock I jumped up from an uneasy dream, in which I
was struggling with some nondescript wild beast, to find I had
only half an hour left to make my toilet and get to the station.
Of course, everything went wrong; strings slipped into knots,
buttons flew; never was there such confusion. I could not be
quick, I was in such a hurry. Hastily swallowing a cup of tea
(part of which, to crown my mishaps, went the wrong way), I
ran off; and must own that, important as was my business, I
felt half sorry, as I entered the booking-office, to find myself in
time: for a secret hope had possessed me that I might prove too
late; a hope that had expanded into certainty as I heard the
hour at which I expected the train to start announced from half
a dozen steeples ere I was half way to the station. I reached it;
found the time had been altered; so got my ticket; "snapped" at
the clerk who furnished it (this relieved me a little), and sprang
into a carriage, which tempted me as containing only one occu-

pant; and the huge mass slowly took its noisy way from under, acres surely, of glazed roof, and speedily left it behind.

The rain ceased as we got into the open country, a fine breeze sprang up, which blew away my fidgets, and I began internally to laugh at myself for having been such a fool; not forgetting to congratulate my better self on its having triumphed over the nervous fears that had beset me. It really became almost pleasant. A mail-train, so that I was secure from the plague of frequent stoppages, and their consequent fresh starts. An exhilarating atmosphere: the dark clouds that had spoken of thunder when I rose, now betraying no such obstreperous intentions, but quietly taking themselves off as fast as they could. The weight on my spirits removed;—yes, I began to be susceptible of a modified sort of enjoyment; and in the gaiety of my heart, I told my fellow-traveller that it was a fine day: a remark to which he vouchsafed me no answer, save such might be called the turning on me a pair of eyes that looked vastly like live coals. They almost made me start; but I considered it was no business of mine; the gentleman's eyes were his own, and I doubted not that mine, owing to a short, sleepless night, were as much too dull as his were too bright: so I whisked my pocket-kerchief across them, by way of polishing them a little, took out a newspaper, sank into a cosy corner, and prepared to read, or sleep, as the case may be. In the very drowsiest part of a long speech, I was just going off into the most luxurious slumber imaginable, when I was roused by the restlessness of my companion; who, as I waked up thoroughly, seemed labouring under some strong and inexplicable excitement. He looked agitated, changed his seat frequently, moved his limbs impatiently, borrowed my paper, and in a trice returned it with some unintelligible observation; then peered anxiously out of the window, through which he thrust himself so far, as to induce me to volunteer a caution, which he received pleasantly, stared at the wheels, as though he were calculating their revolutions, and then resumed his seat.

His perturbation was manifest. I could not imagine what possessed the man; but at length, noticing the agitated manner with which he often glanced through the window, as though to see whether we were followed, I determined that he must be some gentlemanly rogue, to whom speedy flight was indispensable; and that his anxiety and excessive disturbance arose from fear of pursuit: a fear that to me seemed one of those vain ones peculiar to the wicked, for we were then nearly at the ultimatum of railway speed, and did not expect to stop before reaching our destination, still at a considerable distance. His whole manner and appearance confirmed this view of the case; I presumed his evil conscience had conjured up a "special engine" at our heels; and after indulging in a few appropriate moral reflections (to myself, of course), I resumed my paper.

The next minute he was opposite to me. I heard a light movement, raised my head—a strong knife, such as is used in pruning trees, was open in his hand; and, with eyes verily scintillating, his startling address, in a tone, the coolness of which strangely contrasted with its import, was—"I'm going to kill you!" The horrible truth flashed upon me at once: he was insane, and I *alone* with him, shut out from all possibility of human help! Terror gave me calmness: fixing my eye upon him, so as to command his movements, and perhaps control him, I answered quietly and firmly, "No, you are not." It was well I was prepared. That moment he sprang on me, and the death-struggle began. I grappled with him, and attempted to secure his right arm; while again and again, as I strained every nerve to accomplish this purpose, did that accursed blade glitter before my eyes; for my antagonist was my superior in muscle and weight, and armed in addition with the demoniacal strength of madness, now expressed in every lineament of his inflamed and distorted countenance. What a sight was that, not *super-*human face! Loudly and hoarsely I called for help:—but we were rushing along thirty miles in the hour, and my cries were drowned amid the roar of wheels and steam. How horrible were my sensations! Cooped up thus, to be mangled and murdered by a madman, with means of rescue within a few feet of me, and yet that help, that communication with my fellows that would have saved me, as utterly unattainable, as though we were in a desert. I quivered, as turning aside thrust after thrust, dealt with exhaustless and frenzied violence, I doubted not that the next must find its way to my heart. My strength was rapidly failing: not so that of my murderer. I struggled desperately, as alone the fear of such a death could enable a man to do; and, my hands gashed and bleeding, at last wrenched the knife from his hold, and flung it through the window. Then I first seemed to breathe! But not yet was I safe. With redoubled rage he threw himself at my throat, crushing it as with iron fingers; and as I felt his whole frame heave and labour with the violence of the attack, for one dreadful moment I gave up all for lost. But, surely then, some unseen Power strengthened me. Half strangled, I flung the whole weight of my body upon him, got him down, and planting my knee on his breast, by main strength held him, spite of his frantic efforts to writhe himself from under me. My hands were bitten, and torn in his convulsive rage, but I felt not —heeded it not—life was at stake, and hardly I fought for it. The bitterness of death was upon me, and awfully clear and distinct, in that mortal struggle, were the past and the future: the human, sinful past, and the dread, unknown, avenging, *eternal* future. How were the joys and sorrows of years compressed into that one backward glance and how utterly insignificant did they appear as the light of life seemed fading from them. Fearfully calm and collected was my mind, while my body felt as though dissolving with the terrible strain to which all its powers were subjected. And yet, consumed as I was with mental and physical agony, I well remember my sensation of *bliss*, for such it was, when the cool breeze for a single moment blew upon my flushed and streaming brow, which felt as though at the mouth of a furnace!

But this could not last long. My limbs shook, and were fast relaxing their grip, a mist swam before my eyes, my recollection wavered, when—thank heaven! I became sensible of a diminution of our speed. Fresh strength inspired me. I dashed my prisoner down as he again attempted to free himself. Then the welcome sound of letting off the steam—the engine stopped, the door opened—and I was saved!

My companion was quickly secured, and presently identified as a lunatic who had escaped from confinement. To it he was again consigned; and I, from that day to this, have never entered a railway carriage with only *one* passenger in it!

Such is a simple recital of my adventure, which I have not sought to heighten by any arts of narration. It is, indeed, utterly

beyond my power to convey any adequate idea of that horrible
encounter. Its most faithful transcript has been found in many a
night-mare and fearful dream, with which it has furnished the
drear hours of night.*

RICHARD BENTLEY,
Bentley's Miscellany (1853)

Cook's first tour

I was an enthusiastic temperance man, and the secretary of a
district association, which embraced parts of the two counties of
Leicester and Northampton. A great meeting was to be held at
Leicester, over which Lawrence Heyworth, Esq., of Liverpool—
a great railway as well as temperance man— was advertised to
preside. From my residence at Market Harborough I walked to
Leicester (fifteen miles) to attend that meeting. About midway
between Harborough and Leicester—my mind's eye has often
reverted to the spot—a thought flashed through my brain, what a
glorious thing it would be if the newly-developed powers of
railways and locomotion could be made subservient to the
promotion of temperance! That thought grew upon me as I travelled over the last six or eight miles. I carried it up to the platform, and, strong in the confidence of the sympathy of the chairman, I broached the idea of engaging a special train to carry the
friends of temperance from Leicester to Loughborough and back
to attend a quarterly delegate meeting appointed to be held
there in the two or three weeks following. The chairman ap-
proved, the meeting roared with excitement, and early next day
I proposed my grand scheme to John Fox Bell, the resident secretary of the Midland Counties Railway Company. Mr. Paget,
of Loughborough, opened his park for a gala, and on the day
appointed about five hundred passengers filled some twenty or
twenty-five open carriages—they were called "tubs" in those

* The above is no mere fiction. It occurred on one of the English railways some years ago, and the facts were communicated to a member
of the writer's family by the gentleman whose life was thus
strangely perilled. It . . . may perhaps induce others to avoid a
railway journey with only one strange fellow-traveller—RB.

days—and the party rode the enormous distance of eleven miles and back for a shilling, children half-price. We carried music with us, and music met us at the Loughborough station. The people crowded the streets, filled windows, covered the house-tops, and cheered us all along the line, with the heartiest welcome. All went off in the best style and in perfect safety we returned to Leicester; and thus was struck the keynote of my excursions, and the social idea grew upon me.

THOMAS COOK
from S. LEGG (ed.),
The Railway Book (1952)

The perils of travelling third class: *Impressions et Compressions de Voyage* by Honoré Daumier

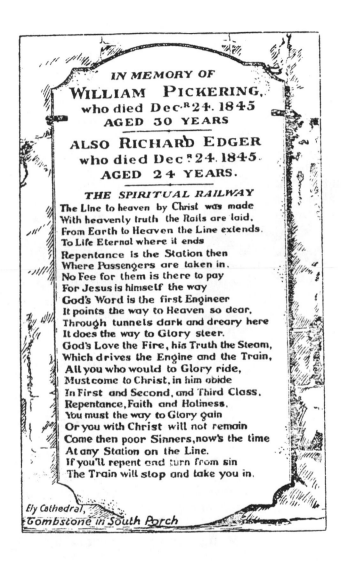

IN MEMORY OF
WILLIAM PICKERING,
who died Dec.R 24. 1845
AGED 30 YEARS

ALSO RICHARD EDGER
who died Dec.R 24. 1845.
AGED 24 YEARS.

THE SPIRITUAL RAILWAY
The Line to heaven by Christ was made
With heavenly truth the Rails are laid,
From Earth to Heaven the Line extends.
To Life Eternal where it ends
Repentance is the Station then
Where Passengers are taken in,
No Fee for them is there to pay
For Jesus is himself the way
God's Word is the first Engineer
It points the way to Heaven so dear,
Through tunnels dark and dreary here
It does the way to Glory steer.
God's Love the Fire, his Truth the Steam,
Which drives the Engine and the Train,
All you who would to Glory ride,
Must come to Christ, in him abide
In First and Second, and Third Class,
Repentance, Faith and Holiness,
You must the way to Glory gain
Or you with Christ will not remain
Come then poor Sinners, now's the time
At any Station on the Line.
If you'll repent and turn from sin
The Train will stop and take you in.

Ely Cathedral,
Tombstone in South Porch

This poem commemorates the deaths of Thomas (not William) Pickering and Richard Hedges (not Edger), driver and fireman of a train which left Norwich on Christmas Eve 1845, and crashed, because of overspeeding, at the bottom of an incline near Thetford. No passengers were seriously hurt. Ed.

PERSHORE STATION,
or A LIVERISH JOURNEY
FIRST CLASS

The train at Pershore station was waiting that Sunday
    night
Gas light on the platform, in my carriage electric light,
Gas light on frosty evergreens, electric on Empire wood,
The Victorian world and the present in a moment's
    neighborhood.
There was no one about but a conscript who was saying
    good-bye to his love
On the windy weedy platform with the sprinkled stars
    above
When sudden the waiting stillness shook with the
    ancient spells
Of an older world than all our worlds in the sound of the
    Pershore bells.
They were ringing them down for Evensong in the
    lighted abbey near,
Sounds which had poured through apple boughs for
    seven centuries here.
With Guilt, Remorse, Eternity the void within me fills
And I thought of her left behind me in the Herefordshire
    hills.
I remembered her defencelessness as I made my heart a
    stone
Till she wove her self-protection round and left me on
    my own.
And plunged in a deep self pity I dreamed of another
    wife
And lusted for freckled faces and lived a separate life.
One word would have made her love me, one word
    would have made her turn
But the word I never murmured and now I am left to
    burn.
Evesham, Oxford and London. The carriage is new and
    smart.
I am cushioned and soft and heated with a deadweight in
    my heart.

JOHN BETJEMAN

A writer's odyssey

On May the 1st, 1912, I went to London Road Station, Manchester, and entered a third-class compartment in the afternoon train bound for Shrewsbury, a lazy county town then. My only luggage was an old black and dented tin box tied round and round for security's sake with a rope. The lock, if I remember, would not lock. Inside this box were a few garments, a suit of cricket flannels, and a hundred books and more, mainly volumes of the new Everyman Library, or the Home University Library, which you could buy at a shilling each. Amongst these volumes was Grote's *History of Greece*, and Walter Bagehot's *Literary Studies*; also there was Descartes' *Discourse on Method* ("Cogito ergo sum"). In this tin trunk, as it lay on the platform of London Road Station, waiting to be put into the luggage van by a porter, reposed all my goods and chattels except the clothes I had on my back, some odd shillings, a pocket comb and two pairs of spectacles, each six and a half diopters strong, for myopia; one pair of which I wore from the moment I opened my eyes in the morning until I closed them at night. The other pair I had procured in case of accidents on the field of play at Shrewsbury. I don't believe that any youth has set forth on a career as a professional cricketer more curiously equipped than this.

I remember opening the door of a third-class compartment after I had seen the tin box safely stowed away. The carriage was unoccupied, only recently out of a siding, where it had stood in the warmth of the day for hours with the windows closed. The compartment was overpowering with that odour of stuffed seats and padding which is peculiar to railways. I remember the refreshment of air when I pulled a leather strap and let down a pane on which was printed "Non-Smoker."

At four o'clock, or thereabouts, the train moved out of the station; I still had the compartment to myself. We passed under the bricks and mortar of Manchester, through a Nibelheim of clanking noises; then we emerged into the sunshine of May day, yellow slanting gleams piercing the miasma of smoke and grime. Looking down through the window in my solitude I saw from the height of a bridge—I saw like one of God's spies—the Manchester that had nurtured me since I was born; rows and rows of dismal houses, with back yards full of old cans and bedsteads and torn oilcloth; long vistas of streets with lamp-posts and corner shops. I saw a council school with an asphalt playground and spiked railings. I was leaving it all; to-night I would sleep out of Manchester, not in a house in one of those endless streets that stretched away in a static lean dreary hopelessness. I was on the way to Shrewsbury, an old town with a marketplace in it.

Out of Manchester into Cheshire ambled the train, and my anxiety about this new life was shot through and through with a sensation strange to me: I was shaking myself free of habit: I didn't know what was about to happen to me. I did not know exactly what setting awaited me in Shrewsbury; I had not even seen a photograph of the place. My life had been bounded by an eggshell; except for a few week-end rambles in Derbyshire, my twenty-one years had been spent within a radius of three and a half miles of bricks and mortar; for the first time in my life I was able in physical fact to run alongside my imagination.

The evening light fell on cows standing still in the meadows. The train came to a halt with an escape of steam, then silence. I stuck my head out of the window and saw the gleaming railway lines, the immaculate tidiness of the permanent way as it stretched and pointed to a distance of green and wooded futurity. I was journeying not the mere fifty miles or so that divide Manchester from Shrewsbury; I was shedding a skin.

When the train reached Crewe I left my compartment and from an unobserved point of vantage watched the porters hauling bags and cases and crates and noisy milk-cans out of the luggage van; I was afraid my old tin trunk might be mixed up with them and lost for ever, even though I had stuck addressed labels on it. Several boys were sitting in the carriage when I returned. They were on the way to Shrewsbury. The new term began next day. They disconcerted me as I sat in my corner pretending to read; I feared they would penetrate to my secret, that I also was travelling to Shrewsbury and was the new "pro." I was aware that I did not look the part at all; I lacked the expected masculinity. I was the thinnest professional cricketer that ever lived, and I fancy I must have resembled Traddles. The charming accents of the speech of these boys gave me my first taste of the good days to come.

NEVILLE CARDUS,
Autobiography

ADLESTROP

Yes. I remember Adlestrop—
The name, because one afternoon
Of heat the express-train drew up there
Unwontedly. It was late June.

The steam hissed. Someone cleared his throat.
No one left and no one came
On the bare platform. What I saw
Was Adlestrop—only the name

And willows, willow-herb, and grass,
And meadowsweet, and haycocks dry,
No whit less still and lonely fair
Than the high cloudlets in the sky.

And for that minute a blackbird sang
Close by, and round him, mistier,
Farther and farther, all the birds
Of Oxfordshire and Gloucestershire.

EDWARD THOMAS

MR. DOMBEY

The whistle blows. The train moves.
Thank God I am pulling away from the conversation
I had on the platform through the hissing of steam
With that man who dares to wear crape for the death of
   my son.
But I forget. He is coming with us.
He is always ahead of us stoking the engine.
I depend on him to convey me
With my food and my drink and my wraps and my read-
   ing material
To my first holiday since grief mastered me.
He is the one with the view in front of him
The ash in his whiskers, the speed in his hair.

He is richer now. He refused my tip.
Death and money roll round and round
In my head with the wheels.
I know what a skeleton looks like.
I never think of my dead son
In this connection. I think of wealth.
The railway is like a skeleton,
Alive in a prosperous body,
Reaching up to grasp Yorkshire and Lancashire
Kicking Devon and Kent
Squatting on London.
A diagram of growth
A midwinter leaf.

I am a merchant
With fantasies like all merchants.
Gold, carpets, handsome women come to me
Out of the sea, along these tracks.
I am as rich as England,
As solid as a town hall.

PATRICIA BEER

On the Footplate:

1. The Scotch Express

In 1897, the American author of *The Red Badge of Courage* visited Britain and rode on the footplate of the London to Glasgow express.

Against the masonry of a platform, under the vaulted arch of the train-house, lay a long string of coaches. They were painted white on the bulging part, which led halfway down from the top, and the bodies were a deep bottle-green. There was a group of porters placing luggage in the van, and a great many others were busy with the affairs of passengers, tossing smaller bits of luggage into the racks over the seats, and bustling here and there on short quests. The guard of the train, a tall man who resembled one of the first Napoleon's veterans, was caring for the distribution of passengers into the various bins. There were no second-class compartments; they were all third and first-class.

The train was at this time engineless, but presently a railway "flier," painted a glowing vermilion, slid modestly down and took its place at the head. The guard walked along the platform, and decisively closed each door. He wore a dark blue uniform thoroughly decorated with silver braid in the guise of leaves. The way of him gave to this business the importance of a ceremony. Meanwhile the fireman had climbed down from the cab and raised his hand, ready to transfer a signal to the driver, who stood looking at his watch. In the interval there had something progressed in the large signal box that stands guard at Euston. This high house contains many levers, standing in thick, shining ranks. It perfectly resembles an organ in some great church, if it were not that these rows of numbered and indexed handles typify something more acutely human than does a keyboard. It requires four men to play this organ-like thing, and the strains never cease. Night and day, day and night, these four

men are walking to and fro, from this lever to that lever, and
under their hands the great machine raises its endless hymn of
a world at work, the fall and rise of signals and the clicking
swing of switches.

And so as the vermilion engine stood waiting and looking
from the shadow of the curved-roofed station, a man in the signal house had played the notes that informed the engine of its
freedom. The driver saw the fall of those proper semaphores
which gave him liberty to speak to his steel friend. A certain
combination in the economy of the London and Northwestern
Railway, a combination which had spread from the men who
sweep out the carriages through innumerable minds to the general manager himself, had resulted in the law that the vermilion engine, with its long string of white and bottle-green
coaches, was to start forthwith toward Scotland.

Presently the fireman, standing with his face toward the
rear, let fall his hand. "All right," he said. The driver turned a
wheel, and as the fireman slipped back, the train moved along
the platform at the pace of a mouse. To those in the tranquil carriages this starting was probably as easy as the sliding of one's
hand over a greased surface, but in the engine there was more
to it. The monster roared suddenly and loudly, and sprang forward impetuously. A wrong-headed or maddened draft-horse
will plunge in its collar sometimes when going up a hill. But
this load of burdened carriages followed imperturbably at the
gait of turtles. They were not to be stirred from their way of dignified exit by the impatient engine. The crowd of porters and
transient people stood respectful. They looked with the indefi-
nite wonder of the railway-station sight-seer upon the faces at
the windows of the passing coaches. This train was off for Scotland. It had started from the home of one accent to the home of
another accent. It was going from manner to manner, from
habit to habit, and in the minds of these London spectators there
surely floated dim images of the traditional kilts, the burring
speech, the grouse, the canniness, the oat-meal, all the elements
of a romantic Scotland.

There had been no fog in London, but here on the edge of the
city a heavy wind was blowing, and the driver leaned aside and

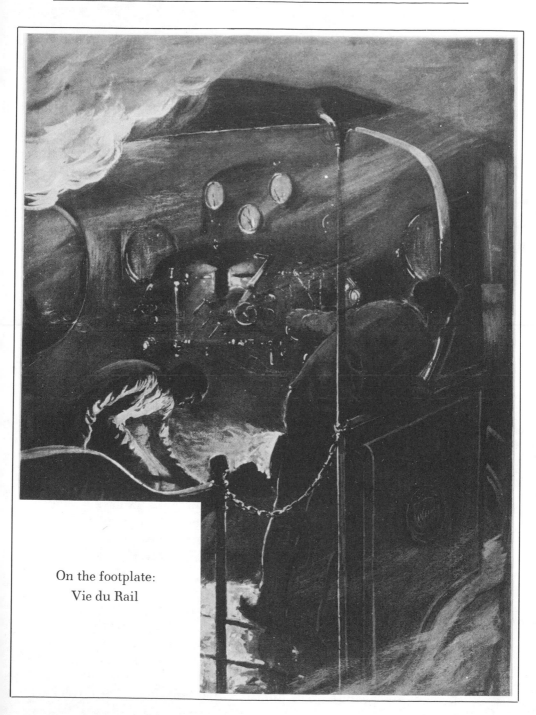

On the footplate:
Vie du Rail

yelled that it was a very bad day for travelling on an engine. The engine-cabs of England, as of all Europe, are seldom made for the comfort of the men. One finds very often this apparent disregard for the man who does the work—this indifference to the man who occupies a position which for the exercise of temperance, of courage, of honesty, has no equal at the altitude of prime ministers. The American engineer is the gilded occupant of a salon in comparison with his brother in Europe. The man who was guiding this five-hundred-ton bolt, aimed by the officials of the railway at Scotland, could not have been as comfortable as a shrill gibbering boatman of the Orient. The narrow and bare bench at his side of the cab was not directly intended for his use, because it was so low that he would be prevented by it from looking out of the ship's port-hole which served him as a window. The fireman, on his side, had other difficulties. His legs would have had to straggle over some pipes at the only spot where there was a prospect, and the builders had also strategically placed a large steel bolt. Of course it is plain that the companies consistently believe that the men will do their work better if they are kept standing. The roof of the cab was not altogether a roof. It was merely a projection of two feet of metal from the bulkhead which formed the front of the cab. There were practically no sides to it, and the large cinders from the soft coal whirled around in sheets. From time to time the driver took a handkerchief from his pocket and wiped his blinking eyes.

In this flight toward Scotland one seldom encountered a grade crossing. In nine cases out of ten there was either a bridge or a tunnel. The platforms of even the remote country stations were all of ponderous masonry in contrast to our constructions of planking. There was always to be seen, as we thundered toward a station of this kind, a number of porters in uniform, who requested the retreat of any one who had not the wit to give us plenty of room. And then, as the shrill warning of the whistle pierced even the uproar that was about us, came the wild joy of the rush past a station. It was something in the nature of a triumphal procession conducted at thrilling speed. Perhaps there was a curve of infinite grace, a sudden hollow explosive effect made by the passing of a signal-box that was close to the track, and then the deadly lunge to shave the edge of a long platform. There were always a number of people standing afar, with their eyes riveted upon this projectile, and to be on the engine was to feel their interest and admiration in the terror and grandeur of this sweep. A boy allowed to ride with the driver of the band-wagon as a circus parade winds through one of our village streets could not exceed for egotism the temper of a new man in the cab of a train like this one. This valkyric journey on the back of the vermilion engine, with the shouting of the wind, the deep, mighty panting of the steed, the gray blur at the track-side, the flowing quicksilver ribbon of the other rails, the sudden clash as a switch intersects, all the din and fury of this ride, was of a splendor that caused one to look abroad at the quiet, green land-scape and believe that it was of a phlegm quiet beyond patience. It should have been dark, rain-shot, and windy thunder should have rolled across its sky.

It seemed, somehow, that if the driver should for a moment take his hands from his engine, it might swerve from the track as a horse from the road. Once, indeed, as he stood wiping his fingers on a bit of waste, there must have been something ludi-crous in the way the solitary passenger regarded him. Without those finely firm hands on the bridle the engine might rear and bolt for the pleasant farms lying in the sunshine at either side.

This driver was worth contemplation. He was simply a quiet, middle-aged man, bearded, and with the little wrinkles of habitual geniality and kindliness spreading from the eyes to-ward the temple, who stood at his post always gazing out through his round window, while, from time to time, his hands went from here to there over his levers. He seldom changed either attitude or expression. There surely is no engine-driver who does not feel the beauty of the business but the emotion lies deep, and mainly inarticulate, as it does in the mind of a man who has experienced a good and beautiful wife for many years. This driver's face displayed nothing but the cool sanity of a man whose thought was buried intelligently in his business. If there was any fierce drama in it, there was no sign upon him. He was so lost in dreams of speed and signals and steam, that one specu-lated if the wonder of his tempestuous charge and its career over England touched him, this impassive rider of a fiery thing.

There may be a popular idea that the fireman's principal function is to hang his head out of the cab and sight interesting objects in the landscape. As a matter of fact, he is always at work. The dragon is insatiate. The fireman is continually swinging open the furnace-door, whereat a red shine flows out upon the floor of the cab, and shoveling in immense mouthfuls of coal to a fire that is almost diabolic in its madness. The feeding, feeding, feeding goes on until it appears as if it is the muscles of the fireman's arms that are speeding the long train. An engine running over sixty-five miles an hour, with 500 tons to drag, has an appetite in proportion to this task.

View of the clear-shining English scenery is often interrupted between London and Crewe by long and short tunnels. The first one was disconcerting. Suddenly one knew that the train was shooting toward a black mouth in the hills. It swiftly yawned wider, and then in a moment the engine dived into a place inhabited by every demon of wind and noise. The speed had not been checked, and the uproar was so great that in effect one was simply standing at the center of a vast, black-walled sphere. The tubular construction which one's reason proclaimed had no meaning at all. It was a black sphere, alive with shrieks. But then on the surface of it there was to be seen a little needle-point of light, and this widened to a detail of unreal landscape. It was the world; the train was going to escape from this cauldron, this abyss of howling darkness. If a man looks through the brilliant water of a tropical pool, he can sometimes see coloring the marvels at the bottom the blue that was on the sky and the green that was on the foliage of this detail. And the picture shimmered in the heat-rays of a new and remarkable sun. It was when the train bolted out into the open air that one knew that it was his own earth.

Once train met train in a tunnel. Upon the painting in the perfectly circular frame formed by the mouth there appeared a black square with sparks bursting from it. This square expanded until it hid everything, and a moment later came the crash of the passing. It was enough to make a man lose his sense of balance. It was a momentary inferno when the fireman opened the furnace door and was bathed in blood-red light as he fed the fires.

The effect of a tunnel varied when there was a curve in it. One was merely whirling then heels over head, apparently in the dark, echoing bowels of the earth. There was no needle-point of light to which one's eyes clung as to a star.

From London to Crewe the stern arm of the semaphore never made the train pause even for an instant. There was always a clear track. It was great to see, far in the distance, a goods train whooping smokily for the north of England on one of the four tracks. The overtaking of such a train was a thing of magnificent nothing for the long-strided engine, and as the flying express passed its weaker brother, one heard one or two feeble and immature puffs from the other engine, saw the fireman wave his hand to his luckier fellow, saw a string of foolish, clanking flat-cars, their freights covered with tarpaulins, and then the train was lost to the rear.

There is a five-minute stop at Crewe. A tandem of engines slip up, and buckled fast to the train for the journey to Carlisle. In the meantime, all the regulation items of peace and comfort had happened on the train itself. The dining-car was in the center of the train. It was divided into two parts, the one being a dining-room for first-class passengers, and the other a dining-room for the third-class passengers. They were separated by the kitchens and the larder. The engine, with all its rioting and roaring, had dragged to Crewe a car in which numbers of passengers were lunching in a tranquility that was almost domestic, on an average menu of a chop and potatoes, a salad, cheese, and a bottle of beer. Betimes they watched through the windows the great chimney-marked towns of northern England. They were waited upon by a young man of London, who was supported by a lad who resembled an American bell-boy. The rather elaborate menu and service of the Pullman dining-car is not known in England or on the Continent. Warmed roast beef is the exact symbol of a European dinner, when one is traveling on a railway.

This express is named, both by the public and the company, the "Corridor Train," because a coach with a corridor is an unusual thing in England, and so the title has a distinctive meaning. Of course, in America, where there is no car which has

To Brighton and Back for 3s 6d: fourth class on
the London, Brighton and South Coast Railway,
c. 1860 (Charles Rossiter)

not what we call an aisle, it would define nothing. The corridors
are all at one side of the car. Doors open thence to little compartments made to seat four, or perhaps six, persons. The first-class
carriages are very comfortable indeed, being heavily upholstered in dark, hard-wearing stuffs, with a bulging rest for the
head. The third-class accommodations on this train are almost
as comfortable as the first-class, and attract a kind of people that
are not usually seen traveling third-class in Europe. Many people sacrifice their habit, in the matter of this train, to the fine
conditions of the lower fare.

One of the feats of the train is an electric button in each compartment. Commonly an electric button is placed high on the
side of the carriage as an alarm signal, and it is unlawful to
push it unless one is in serious need of assistance from the guard.
But these bells also rang in the dining-car, and were supposed
to open negotiations for tea or whatever. A new function has

been projected on an ancient custom. No genius has yet appeared to separate these two meanings. Each bell rings an alarm and a bid for tea or whatever. It is perfect in theory then that, if one rings for tea, the guard comes to interrupt the murder, and that if one is being murdered, the attendant appears with tea. At any rate, the guard was forever being called from his reports and his comfortable seat in the forward end of the luggage-van by thrilling alarms. He often prowled the length of the train with hardihood and determination, merely to meet a request for a sandwich.

STEPHEN CRANE,
"The Scotch Express,"
from *Men, Women and Boats*

RAILWAY NOTE

The station roofs curve off and line is lost
In white thick vapour. A smooth marble sun
Hangs there. It is the sun. An ermine frost
Edges each thorn and willow skeleton
Beyond the ghosts of goods-yard engines. Who
On earth will get the big expresses through?
But these men do.
We ride incredulous at the use and eyes
That pierce this blankness: like a sword-fish flies
The train with other trains ahead, behind,
Signalled with detonation, whistle, shout;
At the great junction stops.
Ticket-collectors board us and fling out
Their pleasantry as though
They liked things so,
Answering the talkative considerate kind,
"Not so bad now, but it's *been* bad you know."

EDMUND BLUNDEN

On the Footplate:

2. The Flying Scotsman

Here we were on an engine of the most powerful kind in the world, attached to one of the most famous of all travelling hotels—the string of coaches called The Flying Scotsman—with its Cocktail Bar and Beauty Parlours, its dining saloons, decorated in more or less credible imitation of the salons of 18th century France, its waiters and guards and attendants of all sorts, its ventilation and heating apparatus as efficient as those of the Strand Palace Hotel, and here we were carrying on as if we were pulling a string of coal trucks.

All the luxury and culture of the world depends ultimately upon the efforts of the labourer. This fact has often been described in books. It has often been the subject of cartoons and pictures—the sweating labourer groaning beneath the weight of all the arts and sciences, the pomps and prides of the world—but here it was in plain daily life.

And what made it even more obvious was the complete absence of connection with the train behind us. The train was there—you could see it if you looked out when going round a bend—but that was all. And just as the passenger very seldom thinks about the men on the engine, so we thought nothing at all about the passengers. They were simply part of the load. Indeed there may not have been any passengers—we weren't aware of any.

And the absence of connection between engine and train was emphasized by the entirely different physical sensations which engine travelling gives you. The noise is different—you never for a moment cease to hear, and to feel, the effort of the pistons. The shriek of the whistle splits your ears, a hundred other noises drown any attempt at conversation.

Though the engine is well sprung, there is a feeling of hard contact on the rails all the time—something like riding on an enormously heavy solid-tyred bicycle. And that rhythmic tune

Approaches to Newcastle-upon-Tyne

which you hear when travelling in the train, the rhythm of the
wheels as they go over the joins in the metal (iddy UMty . . .
iddy UMty . . . &c.) is entirely absent. There is simply a continuous iddyiddyiddy . . . there is no sensation of travelling *in*
a train—you are travelling *on* an engine. You are on top of an
extremely heavy sort of cart horse which is discharging its terrific pent-up energy by the innumerable outbursts of its breath.

And continuously the fireman works, and continuously the
driver, one hand on the throttle lever, the other ready near the
brake handle (a handle no bigger than that of a bicycle and yet
controlling power sufficient to pull up a train weighing 500
tons) keeps watch on the line ahead for a possible adverse signal.
If the signals are down they go straight ahead, slowing down
only for the sharper curves and the bigger railway junctions.
You place absolute trust in the organization of the line and you
know practically every yard of it by sight. You dash roaring into
the small black hole of a tunnel (the impression you get is that
it's a marvel you don't miss it sometimes) and when you're in
you can see nothing at all. Does that make you slow up? Not at
all—not by a ½ m.p.h. The signal was down; there *can't* be
anything in the way and it's the same at night. I came back on
the engine from Grantham in the evening, simply to find out
what they *can* see. You can see nothing but the signals—you
know your whereabouts simply by memory. And as for the signals: it's surprising how little the green lights show up compared with the red. It seemed to me that they went more by the
absence of a red light (in the expected place) than by the presence of a green one. You can see the red miles away but the
green only when you're almost on it. And if it seemed a foolhardy proceeding to rush headlong into tunnels in the day time,
how much more foolhardy did it seem at night to career along
at 80 miles an hour in a black world with nothing to help you
but your memory of the road and a lot of flickering lights—
lights often almost obliterated by smoke and rain. And here's
another primitive thing: You can generally see nothing at all
through the glass windows of the cab at night because the reflections of the firelight make it impossible. To see the road, to see
the signals, you must put your head out at the side—weather or

no. The narrow glass screen prevents your eyes from being filled
with smoke and cinders, but, well, it seems a garden of Eden
sort of arrangement all the same.

ERIC GILL,
Letters (ed. Walter Shrewing)

NIGHT MAIL
(*Commentary for a G.P.O. Film*)

I

This is the Night Mail crossing the Border:
Bringing the cheque and the postal order.

Letters for the rich, letters for the poor.
The shop at the corner, the girl next door.

Pulling up Beattock, a steady climb:
The gradient's against her, but she's on time.

Past cotton-grass and moorland border,
Shovelling white steam over her shoulder.

Snorting noisily, she passes
Silent miles of wind-bent grasses.

Birds turn their heads as she approaches,
Stare from bushes at her blank-faced coaches.

Sheep-dogs cannot turn her course;
They slumber on with paws across.

In the farm she passes no one wakes,
But a jug in a bedroom gently shakes.

II

Dawn freshens. Her climb is done.
Down towards Glasgow she descends,
Towards the steam tugs yelping down a glade of cranes,

Towards the fields of apparatus, the furnaces
Set on the dark plain like gigantic chessmen.
All Scotland waits for her:
In dark glens, beside pale-green lochs,
Men long for news.

III
Letters of thanks, letters from banks,
Letters of joy from girl and boy,
Receipted bills and invitations
To inspect new stock or to visit relations,
And applications for situations,
And timid lovers' declarations,
And gossip, gossip from all the nations,
News circumstantial, news financial,
Letters with holiday snaps to enlarge in,
Letters with faces scrawled on the margin,
Letters from uncles, cousins and aunts,
Letters to Scotland from the South of France,
Letters of condolence to Highlands and Lowlands,
Written on paper of every hue,
The pink, the violet, the white and the blue,
The chatty, the catty, the boring, the adoring,
The cold and official and the heart's outpouring,
Clever, stupid, short and long,
The typed and the printed and the spelt all wrong.

IV
Thousands are still asleep,
Dreaming of terrifying monsters
Or a friendly tea beside the band in Cranston's or Craw-
    ford's:
Asleep in working Glasgow, asleep in well-set Edin-
    burgh,
Asleep in granite Aberdeen,
They continue their dreams,
But shall wake soon and hope for letters,
And none will hear the postman's knock
Without a quickening of the heart.
For who can bear to feel himself forgotten?

W. H. Auden

THE BOY IN THE TRAIN

Whit wey does the engine say *Toot-toot?*
   Is it feart to gang in the tunnel?
Whit wey is the furnace no pit oot
   When the rain gangs doon the funnel?
What'll I hae for my tea the nicht?
   A herrin', or maybe a haddie?
Has Gran'ma gotten electric licht?
   Is the next stop Kirkcaddy?

"And here is a mill and there a river,
Each a glimpse and gone forever"
(drawing by Kate Elizabeth Oliver)

There's a hoodie-craw on yon turnip-raw!
    An' sea-gulls!—sax or seeven.
I'll no fa' oot o' the windae, Maw,
    It's sneckit, as sure as I'm leevin'.
We're into the tunnel! we're a' in the dark!
    But dinna be frichtit, Daddy,
We'll sune be comin' to Beveridge Park,
    And the next stop's Kirkcaddy!

Is yon the mune I see in the sky?
    It's awfu' wee an' curly,
See! there's a coo and a cauf ootbye,
    An' a lassie pu'in' a hurly!
He's chackit the tickets and gien them back,
    Sae gie me my ain yin, Daddy.
Lift doon the bag frae the luggage rack,
    For the next stop's Kirkcaddy!

There's a gey wheen boats at the harbour mou',
    And eh! dae ye see the cruisers?
The cinnamon drop I was sookin' the noo
    Has tummelt an' stuck tae ma troosers. . . .
I'll sune be ringin' ma Gran'ma's bell,
    She'll cry, "Come ben, my laddie,"
For I ken mysel' by the queer-like smell
    That the next stop's Kirkcaddy!

M. C. SMITH

A journey to school

We reached Evesham station without misadventure. All the
porters from this small market town had long ago been called
up. Luckily the Member of Parliament for our division happened to be travelling to London with his wife and, I think, the
First Lord of the Admiralty, on the same train. Without the
slightest compunction my mother organized a relay of these
three august and correct personages to stagger with my domed
trunks, gladstone bags, play-, tuck- and hat-boxes across the

lines to the far platform. I can see now Lady Eyres-Monsell be-
jewelled, Ascoty and holding a pair of lorgnettes in one hand,
making a token gesture with very ill grace of dragging, with the
First Lord's assistance, the tuck-box across the railway sleepers,
while my mother on the far side shouted directions and warn-
ings that the through express to Worcester was due at any moment. When our "up" train drew in the problem of how to lift
the luggage into the van was far simpler. There were plenty of
passengers consisting of wounded soldiers and men too old to be
serving, who were more than anxious to oblige us. The Eyres-
Monsells and the First Lord had mysteriously disappeared to
the far end of the platform.

This was the first time I had ever been inside a train. Excursions to my grandmother's house in the north of the county,
which were the only journeys I had yet experienced, had been
made by road. I was thrilled but not a little alarmed. The prospect of arrival at Paddington, the bustle and noise of a terminus
and the awful probability of there again being no porters was
disturbing. Moreover I dreaded being told to button-hole the
Prime Minister or the Archbishop of Canterbury, and order
him to lift without argument my luggage into a taxi.

As it happened there was no need, for at Paddington the
train slowly drew up alongside a phalanx of female porters of
most formidable aspect. They were, I think, wearing trousers.
Certainly they wore short jackets very tightly buttoned across
the bust. This made them bulge in unexpected places and appear extremely unwomanly. They had fuzzy hair pulled over
shiny cheeks from under workmen's cloth caps. Even my
mother was shocked and hailed them with, for her, unwonted
asperity. They on their side were clearly shocked by her holiday
appearance, dressed as she was in her smartest clothes—an un-
fair judgment considering that this was probably her first day
off duty since August 1914, if taking me to school could exactly
be described as a treat. My mother need not have wasted her
breath, for the monstrous regiment paid no attention to her,
but precipitated themselves upon the soldiers. I was surprised
how indifferent the soldiers were to their attentions, and wondered why they preferred to shoulder their kit-bags when others
were offering to do it for them. It was only after waiting for the

Amazons' return to our platform that we managed to bribe one
of them reluctantly to fetch us a trolley.

The impression London made upon me as we drove across it
bolt upright in a high-roofed taxi with large windows is not
very distinct. It seemed incredibly large and incredibly ancient. I do not suppose that the squares and crescents on our way
to Euston station contained more than a dozen buildings of later
date than the Regency. There was hardly any traffic and our
taxi kept to the crown of the cambered, cobbled streets. I can
hear to this day the soothing purr of the metal studs in the tyres
as we sped along. It was however interrupted by the driver
ceaselessly pressing a fat, rubber horn like a ball-cock attached
to a brass serpent, which undulated over the right mudguard.
The noise emitted was disappointing—the thin chirrup of an
insolent sparrow. My other strong memory is of a deliciously
sweet smell of petrol fumes, mingled with that of horse drop-
pings and antirrhinums.

The unloading of our luggage from the taxi to the train
passed without incident. I rather think we obliged a postman to
stagger under the load, which must have taken him at least two
shifts. For my mother refused to discriminate between one uniform and another. Anyone under a peaked cap—and the more
gold braid the more peremptory it made her—was a railway
porter, if that is what she was wanting at the time. If she happened to be thinking of affairs of state she was apt to make a
similar mistake, in reverse as it were. A year or so later I recall
her addressing the hall porter at Brown's Hotel with the words:
"Well, Field Marshal, and how is the Peace Conference getting
on?"

We were soon comfortably ensconced in a first-class carriage
with twenty minutes to spare before the train was scheduled to
leave. By this time I had worked up a bit of an appetite. My
mother thereupon took the opportunity of preparing our picnic
luncheon. The contents of a basket which she had been carrying, were spread upon both seats, and a methylated spirit lamp
was balanced precariously upon the empty upturned basket. This
was lit and applied to a Cona coffee machine. On no account,
she explained, must the lamp be allowed to burn while the train
was running, or the whole apparatus might explode. Such a

thing had been known to happen even when a train was stationary. As I was a nervous child the warning slightly alarmed me. Then an unfortunate thing happened. My mother got bored.

This was by no means an unusual state of affairs with her. But I secretly wished she had not chosen this moment to leave the carriage in search of a newspaper. I was left alone with the methylated spirit lamp and a vast globe of glass, at the bottom of which a few drops of discoloured liquid began angrily to bubble, while up a tube gushed a fountain into a steaming cylinder of coffee grounds. While I watched, fascinated and impotent, the carriage gave a lurch, and the train drew out of Euston station. I dashed to the window, vainly scanning the crowded platform for my mother. There was not a vestige of her to be seen, and we plunged into a tunnel.

I was panic-stricken. Here I was alone for the first time in my life, on a train, bound for I knew not where. Like an idiot I had not had the curiosity or the gumption to enquire the name of the station we were booked for. As for the name of the school, that had escaped me. Going through a tunnel can at the best of times be an alarming experience. For the first time in a child's life it can be his idea of hell. A stifling, sulphurous smoke soon filled the compartment, while outside a roar of wheels was accompanied by sparks. The carriage however was not pitch dark, for on the picnic basket the blue flame from the methylated spirit lamp was wrapping itself round the empty bowl in a perfect frenzy of rage. Clearly the explosion and an end to existence were imminent. What was to be done? I adopted the only course available to me. I lost my head and, clutching my waist and tripping over my trouser legs, ran bellowing down the corridor.

The first thing that ought to be inculcated into children is that grown-ups of every age and every country are invariably nice to them when *in extremis*. They are seldom very nice to each other, and not always nice to children who have nothing the matter with them. But in order to melt the stoniest adult heart a child, howsoever unattractive and displeasing, has merely to appear slightly out of sorts. Thereupon the gruffest old maid and the most dyspeptic old colonel will instantly drop her knitting and his *Times* newspaper, and rush headlong to its support. I was unaware of this simple truth when I made a frightful hullabaloo in the first-class corridor of the 12:52 from Euston that day. Mercifully I soon found myself in the enormous hot bosom of a surprised lady passenger, who without hesitation administered succour and comfort. Through my tears I feebly pointed in the direction I had come from. It was as well that I did so. The lady's companion, hearing a deafening report, dashed into my compartment where the glass bulb, having indeed exploded in a thousand fragments, had not extinguished the spirit lamp which continued to blaze merrily. With great presence of mind the heroic companion hurled it out of the window.

Once I had recovered my composure I was bombarded with questions. What on earth was I doing by myself boiling water on a wicker basket in a railway train? Who was I? And where was I going? To the last question I was unable to give a satisfactory reply. To a school, I answered, to a large school of over 100 boys. Had anyone a notion where such a school was to be found? Or at what station I ought to get out? My new friends were at first nonplussed. They suggested at length that my wisest course would be to disembark at the next stop, which was Hemel Hempstead, and put my implicit trust in the station master. He would no doubt eventually establish my identity and possibly my ultimate destination. I fell in with this sensible proposition.

At Hemel Hempstead the train drew up. I got out, and my kind friends lowered the seven pieces of luggage, plus the picnic basket on to the platform. Before I had time to collect my wits and wave them goodbye, the train chugged off. I did not have long to look around. Suddenly a familiar voice screamed out my name, and there, running towards me was, of all people, my mother. To my surprise she was in a most extraordinary state of disorderliness and dirt. She had lost her hat, there were smuts on her face and hair, and her pretty dress was crumpled and covered with oil stains. My joy and relief were so great, however, that it never occurred to me to criticize her behaviour, which was at once explained in a breathless volley of excitement. On leaving the carriage at Euston she had failed to find a newspaper stall and, instead, had got into conversation with the engine driver, the most charming, the most sympathetic engine driver that ever was born. He had begged her to get into his cabin so that he might show her the most marvellous brass gadgets, all brightly polished and so clean you could see your reflection in them. Before she knew what was happening the whistle had blown and they were off. One of her life's ambitions was now fulfilled. She knew I would understand and not mind. Had the station master seen? And if so, would he arrest her? How clever I had been to get out at Hemel Hempstead and not get carried on to Crewe, or wherever the next stop was. She was ravenous. Had I eaten all the sandwiches and drunk all the coffee?

JAMES LEES-MILNE.
Another Self

———◆———

THE EVERLASTING PERCY

I used to be a fearful lad,
The things I did were downright bad;
And worst of all were what I done
From seventeen to twenty-one
On all the railways far and wide
From sinfulness and shameful pride.

For several years I was so wicked
I used to go without a ticket,
And travelled underneath the seat
Down in the dust of people's feet,
Or else I sat as bold as brass
And told them "Season," in first-class.
In 1921, at Harwich,
I smoked in a non-smoking carriage;
I never knew what Life nor Art meant,
I wrote "Reserved" on my compartment,
And once (I was a guilty man)
I swopped the labels in guard's van.

From 1922 to 4.
I leant against the carriage door
Without a-looking at the latch;
And once, a-leaving Colney Hatch,
I put a huge and heavy parcel
Which I were taking to Newcastle,
Entirely filled with lumps of lead,
Up on the rack above my head;
And when it tumbled down, oh Lord!
I pulled communication cord.
The guard came round and said, "You mule!
What have you done, you dirty fool?"
I simply sat and smiled, and said
"Is this train right for Holyhead?"
He said "You blinking blasted swine,
You'll have to pay the five-pound fine."
I gave a false name and address,
Puffed up with my vaingloriousness.
At Bickershaw and Strood and Staines
I've often got on moving trains,
And once alit at Norwood West
Before my coach had come to rest.
A window and a lamp I broke
At Chipping Sodbury and Stoke
And worse I did at Wissendine:
I threw out bottles on the line
And other articles as be
Likely to cause grave injury
To persons working on the line—
That's what I did at Wissendine.
I grew so careless what I'd do
Throwing things out, and dangerous too,
That, last and worst of all I'd done,
I threw a great sultana bun
Out of the train at Pontypridd—
It hit a platelayer, it did,
I thought that I should have to swing
And never hear the sweet birds sing.
The jury recommended mercy,
And that's how grace was given to Percy.

E. V. KNOX

Britain's changing landscape. An early steam train
approaches Bangor, North Wales.
Lithograph by T. Picken

THE WHITSUN WEDDINGS

That Whitsun, I was late getting away:
    Not till about
One-twenty on the sunlit Saturday
Did my three-quarters-empty train pull out,
All windows down, all cushions hot, all sense
Of being in a hurry gone. We ran
Behind the backs of houses, crossed a street
Of blinding windscreens, smelt the fish-dock; thence
The river's level drifting breadth began,
Where sky and Lincolnshire and water meet.

All afternoon, through the tall heat that slept
    For miles inland,
A slow and stopping curve southwards we kept.
Wide farms went by, short-shadowed cattle, and
Canals with floatings of industrial froth;
A hothouse flashed uniquely: hedges dipped
And rose: and now and then a smell of grass
Displaced the reek of buttoned carriage-cloth
Until the next town, new and nondescript,
Approached with acres of dismantled cars.

At first, I didn't notice what a noise
    The weddings made
Each station that we stopped at: sun destroys
The interest of what's happening in the shade,
And down the long cool platforms whoops and skirls
I took for porters larking with the mails,
And went on reading. Once we started, though,
We passed them, grinning and pomaded, girls
In parodies of fashion, heels and veils,
All posed irresolutely, watching us go,

As if out on the end of an event
    Waving goodbye
To something that survived it. Struck, I leant
More promptly out next time, more curiously,
And saw it all again in different terms:
The fathers with broad belts under their suits
And seamy foreheads; mothers loud and fat;
An uncle shouting smut; and then the perms,
The nylon gloves and jewellery-substitutes,
The lemons, mauves, and olive-ochres that

Marked off the girls unreally from the rest.
    Yes, from cafés
And banquet-halls up yards, and bunting-dressed
Coach-party annexes, the wedding-days
Were coming to an end. All down the line
Fresh couples climbed aboard: the rest stood round;
The last confetti and advice were thrown,
And, as we moved, each face seemed to define
Just what it saw departing: children frowned
At something dull; fathers had never known

Success so huge and wholly farcical;
   The women shared
The secret like a happy funeral;
While girls, gripping their handbags tighter, stared
At a religious wounding. Free at last,
And loaded with the sum of all they saw,
We hurried towards London, shuffling gouts of steam.
Now fields were building-plots, and poplars cast
Long shadows over major roads, and for
Some fifty minutes, that in time would seem

Just long enough to settle hats and say
   I nearly died,
A dozen marriages got under way.
They watched the landscape, sitting side by side
—An Odeon went past, a cooling tower,
And someone running up to bowl—and none
Thought of the others they would never meet
Or how their lives would all contain this hour.
I thought of London spread out in the sun,
Its postal districts packed like squares of wheat:

There we were aimed. And as we raced across
   Bright knots of rail
Past standing Pullmans, walls of blackened moss
Came close, and it was nearly done, this frail
Travelling coincidence; and what it held
Stood ready to be loosed with all the power
That being changed can give. We slowed again,
And as the tightened brakes took hold, there swelled
A sense of falling, like an arrow-shower
Sent out of sight, somewhere becoming rain.

PHILIP LARKIN

EUROPE

The Orient Express

1. Inaugural journey

On the evening of 4 October 1883 a group of frock-coated gentlemen with revolvers in their pockets assembled on a platform of the Gare de l'Est in Paris.

Attendants in buckled shoes, white stockings and dark-red velvet breeches and monkey-jackets took charge of their bags while they kissed their wives and children—"We did not part without a little nervousness," noted one of them in his diary. And they boarded the polished mahogany coaches that gleamed under the new electric chandeliers.

Relatives, friends and onlookers watched through the windows as the travellers installed themselves in their private salons, decorated in the style of Louis xiv, and gazed upon the tables in the restaurant car laid for dinner, with white damask cloths and intricately folded napkins, ornate silverware, hand-blown glasses, the ice buckets already containing champagne and the claret already decanted.

The doors slammed shut. The band stopped playing. The top-hatted stationmaster drew himself to attention. The guard blew his whistle, the crowd gave a cheer and, with a sudden lurch, the train drew out of the station.

As it steamed eastwards away from Paris, the passengers introduced themselves to one another—M. Boyer of *Le Figaro* to M. Opper de Blowitz of *The Times*, M. Olim, a member of the Belgian cabinet, to Missah Effendi, chief secretary of the Turkish Embassy to France, Dr. Harzé, the distinguished Parisian physician who was to care for the health of those on board, to General Falciano of Rumania, M. Edmund About, the Alsatian essayist, to M. Grimpel, a rising star of the French Ministry of Finance.

In all they numbered two dozen, including an impeccably mannered Dutchman named Jansson, whose position in life and purpose on board nobody established, Herr von Scala, an Austro-Hungarian official who had breached etiquette by bringing his wife and sister-in-law along, and a watchful clique of bankers who had financed the venture.

The leader of the group was M. Georges Nagelmackers, the young founder of the grandiosely named but still little-known Compagnie Internationale des Wagons-Lits et Grands Express Européens. The occasion was the first journey of the world's first great international train. Nagelmackers's Orient Express, which was to cross central Europe and the brigand-infested Balkans to Constantinople, the capital of the Ottoman Empire, in eighty-two hours.

"He is bent on revolutionizing Continental travelling," Opper de Blowitz, then the doyen not only of the journalists on board but of foreign correspondents everywhere, reported to *The Times*, "by introducing a comfort and facility hitherto unknown, and has had to struggle for ten years not only against internal difficulties and the conflicting interests of railway companies, but against the indifference of the very portion of the public which is destined to profit from the result." The ten years of "internal difficulties" to which Opper referred had included near-bankruptcy and an almost disastrous partnership with an American confidence-trickster. The "conflicting interests" that had opposed him had embroiled him in tortuous negotiations with ten different railway companies and as many governments.

Mortgaged to the hilt though it was before it had even set out, the Orient Express was the result of a thoroughly novel idea, and an unquestioned triumph for Nagelmackers—a supranational train operated by an individual entrepreneur, running along track and pulled by locomotives belonging to others.

However timorous his guests were at the prospect of being set down, eighty-two hours after their departure from Paris, in a strange and remote eastern city neither they nor many westerners had visited before, and of possibly being attacked on the way by bands of armed robbers (hence their revolvers), they were conscious of partaking in the history of travel. Indeed they were later to publish between them no less than six lengthy accounts of their journey.

Having effected the introductions, everyone set to inspecting the hitherto-unknown comforts of the train that was to take them far beyond the frontiers of western civilization. It was as brand new in its conception as it was in its construction.

There was a smoking room, a ladies' boudoir and a library. The compartments, or coupés, were miniature drawing rooms with Turkish carpets on the floors, inlaid tables and two red plush armchairs apiece. At night the silk-covered walls folded down to reveal two copiously upholstered beds, transforming each coupé into an equally luxurious sleeping compartment.

Christmas dinner on a European express, 1905

Between each coupé was a mosaic-floored *cabinet de toilette;* and in a special coach at the rear of the train, where there were ice-boxes crammed with exotic foods and a servants' dormitory, was a truly remarkable innovation—cubicles containing showers supplied with abundant hot and cold water.

But it was not until the cry of *"Messieurs les voyageurs, le diner est servi,"* that the travellers saw M. Nagelmackers's *pièce de résistance.* The Orient Express's dining room had a ceiling covered with embossed leather from Cordoue, walls lined with tapestries from the Atelier des Gobelins, founded by the Sun King, and drapes of finest Gênes velvet.

As for the five-course dinner cooked on board from entirely fresh materials by the vast, black-bearded Burgundian chef, Boyer wrote that he was "not merely of the first order but a man of genius—and my stomach protests such praise to be entirely inadequate." After the meal the travellers applauded the chef and retired to the smoking room for cigars, whisky and soda and some hands of whist before going to bed.

At speeds of forty miles an hour and more, the Orient Express raced across Europe, through Strasbourg, Vienna and Budapest, greeted at stations along the way by brass bands and local dignitaries. As they drew into Tsigany, in Hungary, a gypsy orchestra came on board, and serenaded them as far as the border. At the end of that dinner the chef emerged from his kitchen, his eyes, according to Opper, "ablaze with patriotic fervour," and led everyone in a stirring rendering of *La Marseillaise.* Early the next morning they steamed into Bucharest.

2. A royal engine driver

Probably the train's most famous and eccentric regular customer was King Boris of Bulgaria, who was a keen amateur engine driver and wore white overalls designed and made for him by his Parisian tailor. As long as he just stood in the cab, which he did for hours at a time, observing the professional driver at work, all was well, and Nagelmackers was pleased to indulge him—he was, after all, the most frequent hirer of the train's private carriage, which cost the equivalent of twenty first-class tickets. But then he began to pull monarchical rank, and to insist on taking over the controls himself. He was a devotee of speed and lacked a grasp of what signals meant. La Compagnie Internationale intervened, the King was firmly ordered to desist and drivers were told that the punishment for allowing him to enter the cab would be dismissal. Little daunted, Boris would sit in his private carriage until the train crossed the border into Bulgaria. Then he would alight, already garbed in his overalls, and defy anyone to stop him from driving a train across his own kingdom.

MARTIN PAGE,
Lost Pleasures of the Great Trains

3. Lack of catering

The Orient Express, once unique for its service, is now unique among trains for its lack of it. The Indian Rajdhani Express serves curries in its dining car, and so does the Pakistani Khyber Mail; the Meshed Express serves Iranian chicken kebab, and the train to Sapporo in Northern Japan smoked fish and glutinous rice. Box lunches are sold at the station in Rangoon, and Malaysian Railways always include a dining car that resembles a noodle stall, where you can buy *mee-hoon* soup; and Amtrak, which I had always thought to be the worst railway in the world, serves hamburgers on the James Whitcomb Riley (Washington–Chicago). Starvation takes the fun out of travel, and from this point of view the Orient Express is more inadequate than the poorest Madrasi train, where you exchange stained lunch coupons for a tin tray of vegetables and a quart of rice.

PAUL THEROUX,
The Great Railway Bazaar

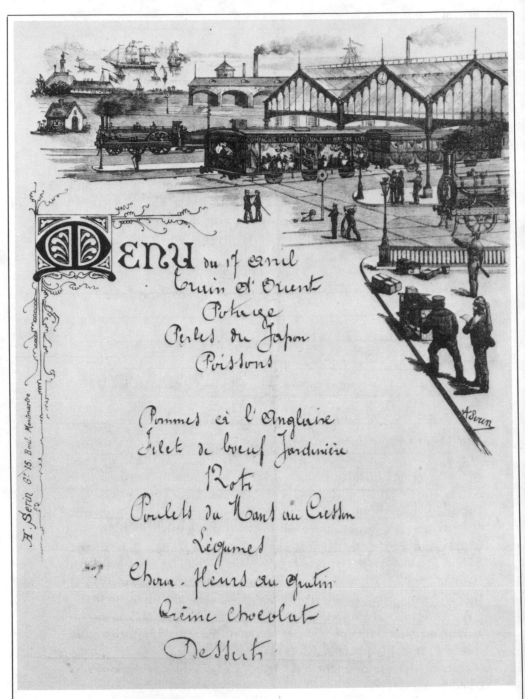

The former pleasures of railroad eating: menu
on the Orient Express, 6 December 1884

RESTAURANT CAR

Fondling only to throttle the nuzzling moment
Smuggled under the table, hungry or not
We roughride over the sleepers, finger the menu,
Avoid our neighbours' eyes and wonder what

Mad country moves beyond the steamed-up window
So fast into the past we could not keep
Our feet on it one instant. Soup or grapefruit?
We had better eat to pass the time, then sleep

To pass the time. The water in the carafe
Shakes its hips, both glass and soup plate spill,
The tomtom beats in the skull, the waiters totter
Along their invisible tightrope. For good or ill,

For fish or meat, with single tickets only,
Our journey still in the nature of a surprise,
Could we, before we stop where all must change,
Take one first risk and catch our neighbours' eyes?

Louis Macneice

4. A view from the window

There were women, but they were old, shawled against the
sun and yoked to green watering cans in trampled corn fields.
The landscape was low and uneven, barely supporting in its
dust a few farm animals, maybe five motionless cows, and a
herdsman leaning on a stick watching them starve in the same
way the scarecrows—two plastic bags on a bony cross-piece—
watched the devastated fields of cabbages and peppers. And beyond the rows of blue cabbage, a pink pig butted the splintery
fence of his small pen and a cow lay under a goal of saplings in
an unused football field. Red peppers, as crimson and pointed as
clusters of poinsettias, dried in the sun outside farm cottages in
districts where farming consisted of men stumbling after oxen
dragging wooden ploughs and harrows, or occasionally wob-
bling on bicycles loaded with hay bales. Herdsmen were not
simply herdsmen; they were sentries, guarding little flocks from
marauders: four cows watched by a woman, three grey pigs
driven by a man with a truncheon, scrawny chickens watched
by scrawny children. Freedom, women, and drinking was Ni-
kola's definition; and there was a woman in a field pausing to
tip a water bottle to her mouth; she swallowed and bent from
the waist to continue tying up cornstalks. Large ochre squashes
sat plumply in fields of withering vines; people priming pumps
and swinging buckets out of wells on long poles; tall narrow
haystacks, and pepper fields in so many stages of ripeness I first
took them for flower gardens. It is a feeling of utter quietness,
deep rural isolation the train briefly penetrates. It goes on without a change for hours, this afternoon in Yugoslavia, and then
all people disappear and the effect is eerie: roads without cars
or bicycles, cottages with empty windows at the fringes of
empty fields, trees heavy with apples and no one picking them.
Perhaps it's the wrong time—3.30; perhaps it's too hot. But
where are the people who stacked that hay and set those peppers
so carefully to dry? The train passes on—that's the beauty of a
train, this heedless movement—but it passes on to more of the
same. Six neat beehives, a derelict steam engine with wild
flowers garlanding its smokestack, a stalled ox at a level crossing.

In the heat haze of the afternoon my compartment grows dusty, and down at the front of the train Turks lie all over their seats, sleeping with their mouths open and children wakeful on their stomachs. At each river and bridge there were square brick emplacements, like Croatian copies of Martello towers, pocked by bombs. Then I saw a man, headless, bent over in a field, camouflaged by cornstalks that were taller than he; I wondered if I had missed all the others because they were made so tiny by their crops.

There was a drama outside Niš. At a road near the track a crowd of people fought to look at a horse, still in its traces and hitched to an overloaded wagon, lying dead on its side in a mud puddle in which the wagon was obviously stuck. I imagined its heart had burst when it tried to free the wagon. And it had just happened: children were calling to their friends, a man was dropping his bike and running back for a look, and farther along a man pissing against a fence was straining to see the horse. The scene was composed like a Flemish painting in which the pissing man was a vivid detail. The train, the window frame holding the scene for moments, made it a picture. The man at the fence flicks the last droplets from his penis and, tucking it in his baggy pants, begins to sprint; the picture is complete.

PAUL THEROUX,
The Great Railway Bazaar

———◆———

TO A FAT LADY SEEN FROM THE TRAIN

O why do you walk through the fields in gloves,
Missing so much and so much,
O fat white woman whom nobody loves.
Why do you walk through the fields in gloves,
When the grass is soft as the breasts of doves
And shivering sweet to the touch?
O why do you walk through the fields in gloves,
Missing so much and so much?

FRANCIS CORNFORD

THE FAT WHITE WOMAN SPEAKS

Why do you rush through the field in trains,
Guessing so much and so much.
Why do you flash through the flowery meads,
Fat-head poet that nobody reads;
And why do you know such a frightful lot
About people in gloves as such?

And how the devil can you be sure,
Guessing so much and so much,
How do you know but what someone who loves
Always to see me in nice white gloves
At the end of the field you are rushing by,
Is waiting for his Old Dutch?

G. K. CHESTERTON

With Zola to visit Flaubert
and Maupassant at Rouen

Easter Sunday, 28 March 1880

Today we set off, Daudet, Zola, Charpentier, and I, to dine and
stay the night at Flaubert's house at Croisset.

Zola was as gay as an auctioneer's clerk going to make an
inventory, Daudet as excited as a henpecked husband out on a
spree, and Charpentier as merry as a student who can see a succession of beers coming his way. As for myself, I was happy at
the prospect of embracing Flaubert once more.

Zola's happiness was marred by a great preoccupation, the
question whether, taking an express train, he would be able to
piddle in Paris, at Mantes, and at Vernon. The number of times
the author of *Nana* piddles or at least tries to piddle is quite incredible.

Daudet, a little tipsy from the porter he had drunk with his
lunch, started talking about *Chien Vert* and his affair with that
mad, crazy, demented female, whom he had inherited from
Nadar: a mad affair, drenched in absinthe and given a dramatic

touch every now and then by a few knife-thrusts, the marks of which he showed us on one of his hands. He gave us a humorous account of his wretched life with that woman, whom he lacked the courage to leave and to whom he remained attached to some extent by the pity he felt for her vanished beauty and the front tooth she had broken on a stick of barley-sugar. When he decided to get married and had to break with her, he was afraid of the scene she would create in a house where other people were living, and took her into the heart of the Meudon woods under the pretext of treating her to a dinner in the country. There, among the bare trees, when he told her that it was all over, the woman rolled at his feet in the mud and snow, bellowing like a young heifer and crying: "I shan't be nasty to you any more, I'll be your slave. . . ." Then they had supper together, with the woman eating like a workman, in a sort of stupid bewilderment. This story was followed by the account of his liaison with a charming young thing called Rosa, and the description of a night of passion they spent in a room at Orsay shared with seven or eight companions who in the morning cast a slight chill over the poetry and frenzy of their love by piddling at length into their chamberpots and farting noisily. . . . A love that was rather frightening in its unhealthiness and vulgarity.

"Here we are, look, just past the bridge." It was Zola's voice telling us to look out for his house at Médan. I caught a glimpse of a feudal-looking building which seemed to be standing in a cabbage-patch.

Maupassant came to meet us with a carriage at Rouen station, and soon we were being greeted by Flaubert in a Calabrian hat and a bulky jacket, with his big bottom in a pair of well-creased trousers and his kindly face beaming affectionately.

Sunday, 23 November 1890

Did not sleep all night, for fear of not being awake at the early hour fixed for our departure. At three o'clock, looked at my watch by the light of a match. At five o'clock, out of bed.

Finally, in the filthiest weather imaginable, there I was in the train for Rouen, with Zola, Maupassant, etc.

I was struck this morning by Maupassant's unhealthy appearance, by the thinness of his face, by his brick-coloured complexion, by the *marked* character, as they say in the theatre, which he had taken on, and even by his sickly stare. It seemed to me that he was not destined to make old bones. As we were crossing the Seine just before Rouen, he pointed to the river shrouded in fog and exclaimed: "It's rowing in that every morning that I have to thank for what I've got today!"

E. AND J. GONCOURT,
Journals (trans. R. Baldrick)

The line to Rouen. Barentin Viaduct, between Rouen
and Le Havre on the main line to Paris,
in the 1850's.

Another visitor to Rouen

After we had looked at the Church for a little time we mounted
the omnibus to go to the railway station where we were to take
train to Rouen—it was about 5 miles I should think from Louviers to the station. What a glorious ride that was, with the sun,
which was getting low by that time, striking all across the valley that Louviers lies in; I think that valley was the most glorious of all we saw that day, there was not much grain there, it
was nearly all grass land and the trees, O! the trees! it was all
like the country in a beautiful poem, in a beautiful Romance
such as might make a background to Chaucer's Palamon and
Arcite; how we could see the valley winding away along the
side of the Eure a long way, under the hills: but we had to leave
it and go to Rouen by a nasty, brimstone, noisy, shrieking railway train that cares not twopence for hill or valley, poplar tree
or lime tree, corn poppy, or blue cornflower, or purple thistle
and purple vetch, white convolvulus, white clematis, or golden
S. John's wort; that cares not twopence either for tower, or
spire, or apse, or dome, till it will be as noisy and obtrusive
under the spires of Chartres or the towers of Rouen, as it is
under Versailles or the Dome of the Invalides, verily railways
are ABOMINATIONS; and I think I have never fairly realised this
fact till this our tour: fancy, Crom, all the roads (or nearly all)
that come into Rouen dip down into the valley where it lies,
from gorgeous hills which command the most splendid views of
Rouen, but we, coming into Rouen by railway, crept into it in
the most seedy way, seeing actually nothing at all of it till we
were driving through the town in an omnibus.

WILLIAM MORRIS,
from S. LEGG (ed.),
The Railway Book (1952)

A Trip to Paris and Belgium

LONDON TO FOLKESTONE

A constant keeping-past of shaken trees,
And a bewildered glitter of loose road;
Banks of bright growth, with single blades atop
Against white sky: and wires—a constant chain—
That seem to draw the clouds along with them
(Things which one stoops against the light to see
Through the low window; shaking by at rest,
Or fierce like water as the swiftness grows);
And, seen through fences or a bridge far off,
Trees that in moving keep their intervals
Still one 'twixt bar and bar; and then at times
Long reaches of green level, where one cow,
Feeding among her fellows that feed on,
Lifts her slow neck, and gazes for the sound.

Fields mown in ridges; and close garden-crops
Of the earth's increase; and a constant sky
Still with clear trees that let you see the wind;
And snatches of the engine-smoke, by fits
Tossed to the wind against the landscape, where
Rooks stooping heave their wings upon the day.

Brick walls we pass between, passed so at once
That for the suddenness I cannot know
Or what, or where begun, or where at end.
Sometimes a station in grey quiet; whence,
With a short gathered champing of pent sound,
We are let out upon the air again.
Pauses of water soon, at intervals,
That has the sky in it;—the reflexes

O' the trees move towards the bank as we go by,
Leaving the water's surface plain. I now
Lie back and close my eyes a space; for they
Smart from the open forwardness of thought
Fronting the wind.

*   *   *
                    I did not scribble more,
Be certain, after this; but yawned, and read,
And nearly dozed a little, I believe;
Till, stretching up against the carriage-back,
I was roused altogether, and looked out
To where the pale sea brooded murmuring.

Le train des maris. The husbands arrive at Deauville
on the train from Paris during summer vacation.

REACHING BRUSSELS

There is small change of country; but the sun
Is out, and it seems shame this were not said.
For upon all the grass the warmth has caught;
And betwixt distant whitened poplar-stems
Makes greener darkness; and in dells of trees
Shows spaces of a verdure that was hid;

And the sky has its blue floated with white,
And crossed with falls of the sun's glory aslant
To lay upon the waters of the world;
And from the road men stand with shaded eyes
To look; and flowers in gardens have grown strong;
And our own shadows here within the coach
Are brighter; and all colour has more bloom.

So, after the sore torments of the route;—
Toothache, and headache, and the ache of wind,
And huddled sleep, and smarting wakefulness,
And night, and day, and hunger sick at food,
And twenty-fold relays, and packages
To be unlocked, and passports to be found,
And heavy well-kept landscape;—we were glad
Because we entered Brussels in the sun.

DANTE GABRIEL ROSSETTI

Dickens at Calais

Calais up and doing at the railway station, and Calais down and
dreaming in its bed; Calais with something of "an ancient and
fish-like smell" about it, and Calais blown and sea-washed pure;
Calais represented at the Buffet by savoury roast fowls, hot coffee, cognac, and Bordeaux; and Calais represented everywhere

by flitting persons with a monomania for changing money—
though I never shall be able to understand in my present state
of existence how they live by it, but I suppose I should, if I
understood the currency question—Calais *en gros*, and Calais
en détail, forgive one who has deeply wronged you.—I was not
fully aware of it on the other side, but I meant Dover.

Ding, ding! To the carriages, gentlemen the travellers.
Ascend then, gentlemen the travellers, for Hazebroucke, Lille,
Douai, Bruxelles, Arras, Amiens, and Paris! I, humble representative of the uncommercial interest, ascend with the rest. The
train is light to-night, and I share my compartment with but two
fellow-travellers; one, a compatriot in an obsolete cravat, who
thinks it a quite unaccountable thing that they don't keep "London time" on a French railway, and who is made angry by my
modestly suggesting the possibility of Paris time being more in
their way; the other, a young priest, with a very small bird in a
very small cage, who feeds the small bird with a quill, and then
puts him up in the network above his head, where he advances
twittering, to his front wires, and seems to address me in an elec-
tioneering manner. The compatriot (who crossed in the boat,
and whom I judge to be some person of distinction, as he was
shut up, like a stately species of rabbit, in a private hutch on
deck) and the young priest (who joined us at Calais) are soon
asleep, and then the bird and I have it all to ourselves.

A stormy night still; a night that sweeps the wires of the
electric telegraph with a wild and fitful hand; a night so very
stormy, with the added storm of the train-progress through it,
that when the Guard comes clambering round to mark the
tickets while we are at full speed (a really horrible performance
in an express train, though he holds on to the open window by
his elbows in the most deliberate manner), he stands in such a
whirlwind that I grip him fast by the collar, and feel it next to
manslaughter to let him go. Still, when he is gone, the small
small bird remains at his front wires feebly twittering to me—
twittering and twittering, until, leaning back in my place and
looking at him in drowsy fascination, I find that he seems to jog
my memory as we rush along.

Uncommercial travels (thus the small small bird) have lain
in their idle thriftless way through all this range of swamp and

dyke, as through many other odd places; and about here, as you very well know, are the queer old stone farmhouses, approached by drawbridges, and the windmills that you get at by boats. Here are the lands where the women hoe and dig, paddling canoe-wise from field to field, and here are the cabarets and other peasant-houses where the stone dove-cotes in the littered yards are as strong as warders' towers in old castles. Here, are the long monotonous miles of canal, with the great Dutch-built barges garishly painted, and the towing girls, sometimes harnessed by the forehead, sometimes by the girdle and shoulders, not a pleasant sight to see. Scattered through this country are mighty works of Vauban, whom you know about, and regiments of such corporals as you heard of once upon a time, and many a blue-eyed Bebelle. Through these flat districts, in the shining summer days, walk those long grotesque files of young novices in enormous shovel-hats, whom you remember blackening the ground checkered by the avenues of leafy trees. And now that Hazebroucke slumbers certain kilometers ahead, recall the summer evening when your dusty feet strolling up from the station tended hap-hazard to a Fair there, where the oldest inhabitants were circling round and round a barrel-organ on hobby-horses, with the greatest gravity, and where the principal show in the Fair was a Religious Richardson's—literally, on its own announcement in great letters, THEATRE RELIGIEUX. In which improving Temple, the dramatic representation was of "all the interesting events in the life of our Lord, from the Manger to the Tomb"; the principal female character, without any reservation or exception, being at the moment of your arrival, engaged in trimming the external Moderators (as it was growing dusk), while the next principal female character took the money, and the Young Saint John disported himself upside down on the platform.

Looking up at this point to confirm the small small bird in every particular he has mentioned, I find he has ceased to twitter, and has put his head under his wing. Therefore, in my different way I follow the good example.

CHARLES DICKENS,
The Uncommercial Traveller

Lenin goes home

In the train that left the morning of 8th April there were thirty Russian exiles, including not a single Menshevik. They were accompanied by the Swiss socialist Platten, who made himself responsible for the trip, and the Polish socialist Radek. Some of the best of the comrades had been horrified by the indiscretion of Lenin in resorting to the aid of the Germans and making the trip through an enemy country. They came to the station and besieged the travellers, begging them not to go. Lenin got into the train without replying a word. In the carriage he found a comrade, who had been suspected of being a stool-pigeon. "The man had made a little too sure of his seat. Suddenly we saw Lenin seize him by the collar and in an incomparably matter-of-fact manner pitch him out on to the platform."

The Germans overpowered them with meals of a size to which they were far from accustomed, in order to demonstrate to the Russians the abundance of food in Germany. Lenin and Krúpskaya, who had never up to now been in any of the belligerent countries during this later period of the War, were surprised, as they passed through Germany, at the absence of adult men: at the stations, in the fields and the city streets, there were only a few women and children, and boys and girls in their teens. Lenin believed they would be arrested as soon as they arrived in Russia, and he discussed with his comrades a speech of defence which he was preparing on the way. But on the whole he kept much to himself. At Stuttgart, the trade union man got on with a cavalry captain and sat down in a special compartment. He sent his compliments to the Russians through Platten in the name of the liberation of peoples, and requested an interview. Platten answered that they did not want to talk to him and could not return his greeting. The only person who spoke to the Germans was the four-year-old son of one of the Russians, who stuck his head into the compartment and said in French: "What does the conductor do?"

On the way to Stockholm, Lenin declared that the Central Committee of the Party must positively have an office in Swe-

den. When they got in, they were met and feted by the Swedish
socialist deputies. There was a red flag hung up in the waiting-
room and a gigantic Swedish repast. Radek took Lenin to a shop
and bought him a new pair of shoes, insisting that he was now
a public man and must give some thought to the decency of his
appearance; but Lenin drew the line at a new overcoat or extra
underwear, declaring that he was not going to Russia to open a
tailor's shop.

They crossed from Sweden to Finland in little Finnish
sleighs. Platten and Radek were stopped at the Russian frontier.
Lenin sent a telegram to his sisters, announcing that he was
arriving Monday night at eleven. In Russianised Finland,
Krúpskaya says, "everything was already familiar and dear to
us: the wretched third-class cars, the Russian soldiers. It was
terribly good." Here the soldiers were back in the streets again.
The station platforms were crowded with soldiers. An elderly

Lenin arrives at the Finland station, Petrograd,
April 1917 (M. Sokolov)

man picked the little boy up and fed him some Easter cheese. A
comrade leaned out the window and shouted, "Long live the
world revolution"; but the soldiers looked around at him puzzled. Lenin got hold of some copies of *Právda*, which Kámenev
and Stalin were editing, and discovered that they were talking
mildly of bringing pressure on the Provisional Government to
make it open negotiations for peace, and loyally proclaiming
that so long as the German army obeyed the Emperor, so long
must the Russian soldier "firmly stand at his post, and answer
bullet with bullet and shell with shell."

He was just expressing himself on the subject when the
train whistle blew and some soldiers came in. A lieutenant with
a pale face walked back and forth past Lenin and Krúpskaya,
and when they had gone to sit in a car that was almost empty,
he came and sat down beside them. It turned out that, he, too,
believed in a war for defence. Lenin told him that they should
stop the war altogether, and he, too, grew very pale. Other soldiers came into the car and they crowded around Lenin, some
standing up on the benches. They were jammed so tight you
could hardly move. "And as the minutes passed," says Krúpskaya, "they became more attentive, and their faces became
more tense." He cross-examined them about their lives and
about the general state of mind in the army: "How? what?
why? what proportion?" reports a non-commissioned officer
who was there.—Who were their commanders?—Mostly officers
with revolutionary views.—Didn't they have a junior staff?
Didn't these take any part in the command? . . . Why was
there so little promotion?—They didn't have the knowledge of
operations, so they stuck to their old staff.—It would be better
to promote the non-commissioned officers. The rank and file
can trust its own people more than it can the white-handed
ones.—He suggested that they ask the conductor to let them into
a car with more space so that they could hold something in the
nature of a meeting, and he talked to them about his "theses"
all night.

Early in the morning, at Beloóstrov, a delegation of Bolsheviks got in, Kámenev and Stalin among them. The moment
Lenin laid eyes on Kámenev, whom he had not seen in several
years, he burst out: "What's this you're writing in *Právda?*

We've just seen some numbers, and we gave it to you good and proper!" Lenin's younger sister María was also there, and a delegation of women workers. The women wanted Krúpskaya to say something, but she found that words had left her. There was a demand for Lenin to speak, and the train-crew, who knew nothing about their passenger except that he was somebody special, picked him up and carried him into the buffet and stood him on a table. A crowd slowly gathered around; then the conductor came up and told the train men that it was time to start on. Lenin cut short his speech. The train pulled out of the station. Lenin asked the comrades whether they thought that the group would be arrested as soon as they arrived in Petrograd. The Bolsheviks only smiled.

EDMUND WILSON,
To the Finland Station

The Englishman abroad

Foreigners in your compartment could also be a blight. One report told of an English gentleman who mounted a second-class carriage in Prussia and attempted to engage the two ladies there in amicable conversation. After a while, one of them broke their stony silence with the remark: "Sir, it would seem that you have never travelled second class before, and do not know how to behave."

"I must confess, madame, I have not," replied the Englishman, for once getting the upper hand. "I have previously travelled only by first and third class. I have observed that in first class, the passengers insult the railway staff, whereas in the third class the railway staff insult the passengers. Now I learn that in second class, the passengers insult each other."

Another Englishman travelling on the continent, Lord Russell, was acclaimed for putting a native with whom he was sharing a compartment in his place. As the train drew out of the station the foreigner proceeded to open his carpet-bag, take out a pair of slippers and untie the laces of his shoes.

"If you do that, sir," proclaimed the great Victorian jurist, "I shall throw your shoes out of the window."

The foreigner remarked that he had a right to do as he wished in his own country, so long as he did not inconvenience others. Lord Russell demurred. The man took off his shoes, and Lord Russell threw them out of the window.

Yet another article told of the phoney Belgian baggage inspector who allegedly haunted Nagelmackers's trains departing from Ostend. Equipped with a cheap season ticket and a steel measure one metre long he would enter a compartment, engage the passengers in cordial conversation and then whip out his rule, measure a suitcase, "assume his official bearing and address the owner with becoming severity as follows: 'Sir, your portmanteau is five centimetres over the prescribed length. I am one of the company's inspectors and charge you at once five francs tax on unauthorised luggage.'" And the timorous English paid up to the scoundrel.

MARTIN PAGE,
Lost Pleasures of the Great Trains

DAWN

Opposite me two Germans snore and sweat.
    Through sullen swirling gloom we jolt and roar.
We have been here for ever: even yet
    A dim watch tells two hours, two aeons, more.
The windows are tight-shut and slimy-wet
    With a night's foetor. There are two hours more;
Two hours to dawn and Milan; two hours yet.
    Opposite me two Germans sweat and snore. . . .

One of them wakes, and spits, and sleeps again.
The darkness shivers. A wan light through the rain
Strikes on our faces, drawn and white. Somewhere
A new day sprawls; and, inside, the foul air
Is chill, and damp, and fouler than before. . . .
Opposite me two Germans sweat and snore.

RUPERT BROOKE

First and Third Class, 1891

Lord Curzon's valet

The train was waiting at Victoria Station and there remained but three minutes to the time when it was scheduled to leave. In front of the Pullman reserved for Lord Curzon clustered the photographers, holding their hooded cameras ungainly. The station-master gazed towards the barrier. Already the two typists were ensconced in the saloon: Sir William Tyrrell in the next compartment had disappeared behind a newspaper: the red despatch boxes were piled upon the rack, and on the linoleum of the gangway Lord Curzon's armorial dressing-case lay cheek by jowl with the fibre of Miss Petticue's portmanteau. I waited with Allen Leeper on the platform. We were joined by Mr. Emmott of Reuter's. "Is the Marquis often as late as this?" he inquired. "Lord Curzon," I answered, "is never late," and as I said the words a slight stir was observable at the barrier. Majestically, and as if he were carrying his own howdah, Lord Curzon proceeded up the platform accompanied by the police, paused for a moment while the cameras clicked, smiled graciously upon the station-master, and entered the Pullman. A whistle shrieked, a flag fluttered, the crowd stood back from the train and began to wave expectantly. It was then that I first saw Arketall. He was running with haste but dignity along the platform: in his left hand he held his bowler, and in his right a green baize foot-rest. He jumped on to the step as the train was already moving. "Crakey," said Arketall, as he entered the saloon.

Leeper and I sat opposite each other, going through the telegrams which had been sent down to the station from the Foreign Office. We sat there in the green morocco chairs of the Southern Railway: the marquetry on the panels behind us squeaked softly: the metal reading lamp chinked ever so slightly against the glass top of the table: to our right the houses of Purley, to our left the houses of Lewisham, passed rapidly below us in the autumn sunshine: someone came and told Leeper that he was wanted by Lord Curzon. I pushed the telegrams aside and leant back in my chair. Miss Petticue was read-

ing the *Royal* magazine: Miss Bridges was reading her own
passport: I had ample time to study Arketall.

He sat opposite to me at the end of the saloon. A man, I
should have said, of about fifty-five; a tall man, at first impression, with a large naked face and large white bony hands. The
fine Victorian modelling of his brow and chin was marred by a
puffy weakness around the eyes and mouth: at certain angles
the thoughtful refinement of his features suggested a drawing of
Mr. Galsworthy by George Richmond: he would then shift his
position, the illusion would pass, there would be a touch of red
ink around the eyelids, a touch of violet ink about the lips: the
pallor of his cheeks, the little bleached ridges around his mouth,
would lose all suggestion of asceticism: when he leant forward
in the full light of the window he had the appearance of an aged
and dissolute pro-consul. His face, if he will forgive my saying
so, seemed at such moments, self-indulgent. "That man," I reflected, "drinks."

*   *   *

Our arrival at Dover somewhat disconcerted Arketall. It was
evident that he was proud of his competence as a travelling
valet and anxious to win confidence by a brisk display of merit.
Before the train had come to a standstill he was out on the platform, his face assuming the expression of "Leave everything to
me." He was at once brushed aside by an inspector of police and
two Foreign Office messengers. A phalanx of porters stood behind the inspector and leapt upon our baggage. The Foreign
Office messengers seized the despatch boxes. Before Arketall had
realised what had happened, Lord Curzon was walking slowly
towards the boat chatting to the inspector with not unconscious
affability. We strolled behind. Arketall came up to me and murmured something about passports. I waved him aside. There
was a man beside the gangway with a cinematograph, the handle of which he began to turn gently as we approached. I
glanced behind me at Arketall. His attitude had stiffened suddenly into the processional. "Arketall," I said to him, "you have
forgotten the foot-rest." "Crakey!" he exclaimed as he turned to
run towards the train. The other passengers were by then begin-

ning to dribble through the pens in which they had been herded: I leant over the taffrail, watching the single agitation meeting the multiple agitation: widows hurrying along searching frantically in their reticules for those yellow tickets which would take them to Bordighera: Arketall, in acute anxiety, breasting this fumbling torrent with his bowler in his hand. A policeman touched me on the shoulder: he was holding the footrest. "His lordship generally requires this with him on the voyage." But by then Arketall was but a distant dome-shaped head bobbing against a panic stream. The little cords that tied the awning above me were pattering against the stays in an offshore wind: in the gap between the pierheads a swell tumbled into foam, the inner harbour was wrinkled with scudding frowns: clearly we were in for a rough crossing. I took the footrest to Lord Curzon. He was sitting at his cabin table writing on loose sheets of foolscap in a huge flowing hand: his pencil dashed over the paper with incredible velocity: his lips moved: from time to time he would impatiently throw a finished sheet upon the chintz settee beside him. I adjusted the foot-rest. He groaned slightly as he moved his leg. He was much too occupied to notice my ministrations. I returned to the deck outside. A voice wailed to me from the shore: "It's gone; it's gone." Arketall flung into the words that forlorn intensity which throbs in the earlier poems of Lord Tennyson. I replied by reassuring gestures indicative that he should come on board. He was mopping his forehead with a large linen handkerchief: little white drops were still forming on it as he stood panting beside me. "Crakey," he gasped. "You had better go downstairs," I answered, "it is going to be rough." He closed one eye at me. "A little peg ay don't think." His words, at the moment, had little apparent meaning.

I did not see Arketall again until we were approaching Calais. I found him talking to Sir William Tyrrell outside the cabin. "Now Ostend," he was saying, "that's another question. Nane francs a day and no questions asked." "And no questions asked," he repeated looking wistfully at the sand dunes. The inspector came up to me with a packet of passports: he said he would hand them over to the *commissaire de police* on arrival. I took them from him, desiring to solve a problem which had often assailed me, namely, whether Lord Curzon made out a passport for himself. It was there all right—"We George Nathaniel," and then his name written again in the blank spaces. That amused me, and I was still considering the curious associations evoked by such official Narcissism when we sidled up to the Calais landing-stage. The gangway was immediately opposite Lord Curzon's cabin: on the pier below stood the Consul in a top-hat, and some French officials: I went in to Lord Curzon and told him we were arriving: he was still writing hard, and paid no attention: on the settee beside him was a pile of foolscap and at least twenty envelopes stamped and addressed. A muffled jerk showed that we were already alongside. Sighing deeply Lord Curzon addressed and stamped the last envelope. "Send me that valet man," he said. I fetched Arketall, telling him to hurry as the other passengers were being kept waiting: there they were on my left secured by a cord across the deck, a serried wedge of passengers looking their part. Lord Curzon emerged genially from his cabin at the exact moment the gangway was fixed: Arketall followed with the foot-rest: he stumbled as he stepped on to the gangway and clasped the rail. "Yes, I thought he was drunk," said Sir W. Tyrrell as we followed in our correct order. Lord Curzon was being greeted by the Representative of the French Republic. He moved slowly towards the train, leaning on his ebony cane; behind him zigzagged Arketall, clasping the green baize foot-rest. "Hadn't we better warn the Marquis . . . ?" I asked. "Oh, he'll notice it soon enough." Lord Curzon had paused by the train to say a few chosen words to the Consul. Behind him stood Arketall, very rigid as to the feet, but swaying slightly with the upper part of the body, bending slowly forwards and then straightening himself with a jerk. We left for Paris.

Following their arrival in Paris, Lord Curzon and his party endured a hectic round of diplomatic activity, dined at nine that evening, and enjoyed what rest they could before boarding the train for Lausanne early next morning.

We gathered sleepily at 7.5 a.m. in the hall of the Ritz: the revolving glass door was clamped open and a man in a striped apron was shaking an india-rubber mat out on to the Place Vendôme: the luggage had already preceded us, the typists were sitting in the third motor rather pinched and blue: we waited for Lord Curzon. At 7.16 a.m. he appeared from the lift escorted by Mr. Ellis. He climbed slowly into the motor, falling back on to the cushions with a sigh of pain: he beckoned to me: "I shall want my foot-rest." I dashed back into the hotel to search for Arketall. Mr. Ellis was standing by the staircase, and as I approached him I could hear someone pattering above me down

The British Foreign Secretary, Lord Curzon, leaves London for Paris, November 1922. Lord Curzon in the train, Arketall in the centre of the picture, Harold Nicolson third from the left and Lady Curzon beside him.

the stairs: at the last turning there was a bump and a sudden exclamation, and Arketall shot round and down the staircase like a bob-sleigh, landing beside me with his feet in the air and the foot-rest raised above him. "Crakey," he remarked. We had by then only eleven minutes in which to reach the Gare de Lyon. The three motors swayed and dashed along the boulevards like fire-escapes to an incessant noise of Claxons. Then very slowly, processionally, sleepily we walked up through the station towards the platform. M. Poincaré in a black silk cap with a peak was waiting, a little irritably I thought, beside the train. There was a saloon for the French Delegation, a saloon for the British Delegation, and separating them a satin-wood drawing-room carriage and a dining-car. The large white clocks marked 7.29 as we entered the train. At 7.30 we slid out into the grey morning past a stiff line of saluting police and railway officials. Arketall was standing beside me: "Ay left me 'at behind," he remarked in sudden dismay. I had a picture of that disgraceful bowler lying upwards on the stair carpet of the Ritz: "Tiens," they would exclaim, "le chapeau de Lord Curzon." "You can get another," I answered, "at Lausanne." Miss Petticue came up to me holding a bowler. "They threw this into our motor as we were leaving the Ritz." I handed it in silence to Arketall.

For the greater part of that twelve-hour journey we sat in the drawing-room carriage discussing with our French colleagues the procedure of the impending conference: from time to time a Frenchman would rise and retire to the back of the train to consult M. Poincaré: from time to time Allen Leeper or I would make our way to the front of the train to consult Lord Curzon: outside his door Arketall sat on a spring bracket-seat which let down on to the corridor: he would stand up when we came, and the seat would fly up smack against the wood-work: Arketall looked shaken and unwell. Lord Curzon in his *coupé* carriage reclined in a dove-coloured armchair with his leg stretched out on the foot-rest. On the table beside him were at least thirty envelopes stamped and addressed: he did not appear to relish our interruptions.

Towards evening the lights were lit in that satin-wood saloon. We sat there, M. Barrère, General Weygand, Admiral
Lacaze, Sir William Tyrrell, Laroche, Massigli, Allen Leeper
and myself. The discussion had by then become desultory: from
time to time a station would leap up at us from the gathering
dusk, flick past the train in a sudden rectangle of illuminated
but unfocussed shapes, be lost again in the brooding glimmer
of the Côtes d'Or. We stopped at Pontarlier and telephoned to
M. Mussolini. He answered from Locarno. He wanted us to dine
with him that night at Vevey. We pattered up and down the
platform conveying messages from M. Poincaré to Lord Curzon,
from Lord Curzon to M. Poincaré. It was agreed that they
would both proceed to Vevey, and then the train slid onwards
down upon Lausanne. Lord Curzon in his dove-coloured armchair was slightly petulant. He was all for dining with M. Mussolini but would have preferred another night. "And why
Vevey?" he said. "Why indeed?" I echoed. Lord Curzon sighed
deeply and went on writing, writing. I left him and stood in the
corridor. Arketall had pulled up the blind, and as the train
jigged off to the left over some points a row of distant lights
swung round to us, low lying, coruscating, white and hard.
"Evian," I said to Arketall. "Ho indeed," he answered. Ten
minutes later, the train came to rest in the station of Lausanne:
there was a pause and silence: the arc-lamps on the platform
threw white shapes across the corridor, dimming our own
lights, which but a few minutes before had seemed so garish
against the darkness. I returned to Lord Curzon's compartment.
"I think," he said, "that you and Leeper had better get out
here. It is quite unnecessary for you to come on to Vevey." "Oh,
but, sir . . ." I protested. "Quite unnecessary," he repeated. I
usually enjoyed an argument with Lord Curzon, but there was
something in his voice which indicated that any argument at
that moment would be misplaced. I went and told Leeper: we
both seized our despatch boxes and climbed down on to the
platform. Bill Bentinck, who had been sent on two days before to
complete arrangements, came up to us, immaculate, adolescent
and so reliable. "There are four motors," he said, "and a lorry
for the luggage." "The Marquis isn't coming," I informed him,
"he and M. Poincaré are going on to Vevey to dine with Musso-

lini. They won't get back here till midnight." "Oh Lud," he
exclaimed, "and there's a vast crowd outside and the Mayor of
Lausanne." "Lud," I echoed, and at that the slim presidential
train began to slide past us towards the night and Mussolini. It
was only then that I noticed that the platform was empty from
excess rather than from lack of public interest: behind the barrier, behind a double row of police, stretched the expectant citizens of the Swiss Confederation. On the wide bare desert of the
platform stood Leeper in a little brown hat, myself in a little
black hat, and Arketall in his recovered bowler: Miss Petticue:
Miss Bridges: pitilessly the glare of forty arc-lamps beat down
upon our isolation and inadequacy. We walked (with dignity I
feel) towards the barrier: at our approach the magnesium wire
flashed up into its own smoke and there was a stir of excitement
in the crowd: somebody cheered: Arketall raised his bowler in
acknowledgment: the cheers were repeated: he held his bowler
raised at exactly the correct angle above his head: the Mayor
advanced towards him. I intervened at that moment and explained the situation. The Mayor turned from me, a little
curtly perhaps, and said something to the police inspector. The
wide lane which had been kept open for us ceased suddenly to
be a lane and became a crowd leaving a station: we left with it.
In a few minutes we were hooting our way under the railway
bridge and down to Ouchy. . . .

HAROLD NICOLSON,
Some People

Night train to Spain

I am in Spain at last. For years I have promised myself this
adventure—for in spite of the railway it is an adventure still, in
a way that a journey through Italy, where almost every other
person one sees is a foreigner, has ceased to be for ever—and at
last I am here in the land of Spain. The journey from Paris was
a nightmare hideous and full of horrors: the continual noise of
the train, the groans and attitudes of the sleepers, the shrieking

as of lost souls that came now and again out of the darkness, the
heat of the long night spent with seven strangers, the inevitable
contact with that grotesque, weary, fetid humanity, in so small
a space, for so long a time—the brutality of all that. For to me
sleepless, in all the reticence of consciousness, the gesture, the
rhetoric of that animal in humanity set free by sleep, its inarticulate noises and struggles, its indifference to human dignity, its
brutal obliteration of everything in man but the flesh, were a
kind of vision, in which I saw all the achievements of the years
swept away in a moment, and primitive man, filthy and covered with sweat, unconscious of anything but weariness, seeking
his lair at nightfall with the beasts with whom he shared the
world. Gradually the carriage came to be a prison; for there was
no corridor in which I might have found an escape from the
rancid stench of life that had long since loaded the air with
débris which now seemed to be falling upon me, crushing me
beneath its foulness where I lay surrounded by darkness, astonished and aghast at the terms on which we must accept life.

Before me, in the sickly light of the partly covered lamp, a
man of some fifty years, fat and disgusting, crouched in the attitude of a wild beast, his mouth open, snoring, while the saliva
dripped over the sensual, pathetic lips. Every now and then as
the train swayed a grotesque shadow leaped upon his face,
flabby and swollen with all the excesses that sleep had recalled
and made so visible, dragging it into the horrible contortions of a
madman. There were three women in the compartment; one in
the farthest corner with colourless, thin hair, still young, her face
in the deepest shadow, was asleep, I make no doubt, since her
body seemed to have collapsed within itself, so that she seemed
a sort of cripple or dwarf misshapen and hideous. Another, her
arms dropped over her knees, seemed as though she were in
despair; while the third from time to time suckled her child. Of
the rest of my companions I took no notice—in every sort of
attitude they lay at the mercy of the train, subject to the grotesque dances of the lamplight, unconscious of the frightful brutality that we suffered, slaves as we are to our own inventions.
Three times I opened the window; but each time some one
stirred, rushed back from the delights of oblivion, and half
awake, half asleep, thrust himself in front of me and shut out

the sweetness of the night. And once, as I stood up to open it a little way just for a moment, she who held her child so tightly under her bowed shoulders looked up at me quickly, piteously I thought, and covered her shapeless treasure with the cape of her cloak. And I, not to add to my torture, fell back into my seat, helpless to deliver myself from the body of that death. So night passed slowly, slowly, and at last the summer stars, so large, so few, began to pale, and I saw the faint grey lines of dawn far, far away across the world.

EDWARD HUTTON,
The Cities of Spain (1906)

Courier's train

Once I worked as a clerk in an office and I grew thinner and my suits fell to bits and I watched the seagulls out of the window. The months passed and I knew I had taken the wrong road. "You're not paid to watch seagulls," said the manager. In my spare time I went to Victoria station and bought cups of tea and watched the trains. The ceiling of the station shook with the thunder of wheels, and men with fur collars and attaché cases disappeared in clouds of steam. There was a faint imported smell of sea, a catch in the throat, a volley of shouts, and an explosion of children like fireworks. The Golden Arrow drew in. Out came the eternal over-wrapped exiles from operas and roulette, pampered ghosts from Anglo-French hotels, lovers, swindlers, actresses, impostors, believers, bores and magicians. But all that mattered to me was the gold and blue of the places they had been to, the singing names, like Leman, Maggiore, Garda, Ischia, Ibiza.

Eventually I joined a travel agency. I almost lived in trains, pushing hordes of people round monuments, cramming them into cathedrals, and winkling them out of gondolas. Once, on the Paris–Vallorbe run, my train split in two. Half my clients disappeared down a gradient. The runaway carriages reappeared half an hour later at Vallorbe station and were greeted by hysterical shouts, as though they had come back from Siberia. But the train didn't pull up. It puffed off busily in the general direction of Italy, and I found it quite impossible to control the pandemonium on the station platform. Even I, the courier, wasn't aware that this divided train was returning to another platform.

I lived in a world of smoke, station buffets, Customs offices and rattling corridors; the antiseptic rush through the Simplon tunnel; the gleaming run beside the lake of Geneva; carriages of priests, soldiers, Chianti and garlic between Pisa and Rome; and the eternal stolid caravanserai of British clients getting constipated from pasta and ruins. I was still a prisoner entangled in a web of questions, complaints and prejudices. But

Returning from market: a local train in France
(*Third Class* by Honoré Daumier, 1862)

through the carriage window, past the vacuum flask and the knitting needles, I could see the running rainbow feet of beauty.

After a time I began to weary of trains and to long for London. But I could not escape. The demon which had haunted me in the office and dragged me to Victoria Station to gape at the expresses would not release me. It was my living. Sleeping past Lyons, breakfast at the frontier, loving past Stresa, eating past the Apennines. Eventually I broke up a highly organized tour of Italy by running off with one of the clients, was sacked by the agency and took up writing.

A summer and a winter passed and London lay on my stomach like a lobster supper. I was making no money. The current was turned off, and I dreamed of the Continental railroads like swallows whose wings flutter in their sleep. Somewhere, someone was waving to me. "You should be here!" Again I haunted Victoria Station. Then I paid a visit to another travel agency. "I am a railway expert," I said. "Can you speak Spanish?" asked the manager. "Certainly," I replied. "We are experimenting with a place called Sitges in the north of Spain. We would like you to take about fifty clients there from London. Would you be prepared to do that?" "Yes," I said. "Be careful with them," said the manager. "Some of them are old ladies and not used to travel. You start in a fortnight, and if you call in tomorrow I will give you the list."

We went on the Newhaven–Dieppe–Paris route, and left for Port Bou from the Gare de'Austerlitz. So far it was an uneventful journey, except that four of the old ladies recognized me from my last Italian tour, and I could see them rustling up and down the corridors with scandal. The next morning we steamed into Cerbère, and I was smoked out of my carriage with questions. Do we change here? Is this Spain? Is Franco here? Shall we change our money? Can we use the lavatories in this station or would they arrest us? Can we get coffee? Tea? Aspirins?

Before I need answer all the questions the train slid through a tunnel and we arrived in Port Bou, Spain. Directly we got down on to the platform it was obvious that all the officials hated us on sight. Many of them were armed to the teeth. We were driven into a gloomy barrack-like Customs shed, our suitcases were wrenched open and the contents scattered right and left.

One of my old ladies burst into tears. Have you any drugs, fire-arms, or pornographic literature? an official was asking her.

There were six ticket-windows operated by six dour, sadistic railway employees. When you presented a form to be stamped each one said "Wrong window." Finally, at the risk of being shot, I got out on to the Port Bou–Barcelona platform and made inquiries about my agency reservations. A very old man in a peaked cap with RAILWAY SERVICES written on it pointed at a carriage. "They are there," he said. The carriage was bursting with people. "But I have fifty clients," I shouted. The old man looked at me with terrible patient sadness. "That which has to be . . ." he said and crept away.

Finally we arranged ourselves on the train. I stood next a plump Spaniard in the corridor who was looking out of the window at the embittered tourists flapping about the platform like intolerably harassed poultry. "In an odd way it pays," he said, offering me a cigarette. "All of you foreigners, after this ghastly experience at the frontier, are expecting the worst from us. But when you find how friendly we are, and how much we hate our railways, it will seem all the better. Where are you going to?" "I am taking fifty English people to Sitges." "Be prepared for the worst," said the Spaniard, "and beware of the tunnels." He gave me details of the journey.

We reached Barcelona in the afternoon. Three of my old ladies had fainted, and there were ten cases of diarrhoea. ("You should have told us about the water.") There were two trains to Sitges. One said "Very Fast" and the other "Highly Rapid." I chose the Highly Rapid and chased my party into two or three amazingly empty carriages. There was another train which I had not noticed. It was called "Supremely Quick." This left almost immediately. We waited in our train, starving, for about an hour, while it gradually filled up. When it was obviously crammed it left for the next Barcelona station, Paseo de Gracia.

Here was a waiting cargo of fresh passengers. Women lay on the floor like threshed wheat, suckling babies. Aerated-water sellers climbed through a trellis of arms and legs and half the station got on to the train to say goodbye. At the next station the beggars were waiting, followed by the lottery sellers carrying dolls and bags of sweets.

An hour later, remembering what the Spaniard at Port Bou had advised me, I squeezed my way through the train and warned all my party to take down their luggage and put it on to the outside platform. "The train only stops for a minute at Sitges," I told them. In the middle of this operation we entered the first tunnel. The carriages filled with smoke and the lottery sellers, coughing with rage, stumbled over their dolls, aerated water rolled over the floor and pickpockets got to work. In all, there were nine tunnels and they were very long and the train was slow. Finally we came into the light, and the town of Sitges, white as ice-cream, glimmered into view.

We poured out of the carriages, the fists of the lottery sellers pistoning through the windows, grappling with a cascade of luggage. Suddenly, with horror, I remembered I had placed some old ladies on the front carriage. I could see no sign of them. I ran forward to the platform behind the engine.

They were there. Five of them. Their faces were quite black. From one desperate feathered hat I could distinctly see a little spiral of smoke ascend, like the aftermath of Red Indian massacre. "This is Sitges," I said in a small voice. But they just looked at me.

And the train, with no warning, as much as to show it *was* a train, made off towards Valencia.

I am back at Victoria Station again. Meet me at Platform Eight.

ANTHONY CARSON,
from PUNCH 2 *June 1954*

A mystery in Lapland

It was 10 P.M. and, in the drowsy warmth of the train from Stockholm, 44-year-old Mrs Karin Edholm sleepily opened her eyes as the train began to slow down.

She must be nearing home at last. The 700-mile journey to Murjek, in Lapland near the Arctic Circle, had taken hours. Then the train suddenly jolted to a stop. "Is this Murjek?" she asked a fellow passenger. He nodded and, grabbing her hand-bag, Mrs Edholm hastily opened the compartment door, stepped out and found herself falling.

Thick snow broke her fall. As she got to her feet, she looked around in alarm. There was no platform, no station, no lights and not a sign of anybody in sight.

She was in the middle of nowhere, her teeth already chatter-ing in the bitter temperature of 27 degrees below freezing. As she turned to try to climb back on board the train started to move off.

She stumbled alongside for a few feet screaming: "Stop, stop. For God's sake stop." But nobody answered and nothing happened. She stood there shivering as she watched the lights of the train disappear in the distance.

And she was still in summer clothes. For she and her hus-band had arrived back from a six-week holiday in the heat of Sri Lanka. At Stockholm she had decided to return home by train rather than face the tiring journey by car. Her husband would still be on the road somewhere miles away to the south.

Now there was only one thing for her to do . . . walk and follow the rail tracks to Murjek. She began to stumble along, jumping up and down, flapping her arms and holding her breath in a bid to beat the bitter cold.

The country was in the grip of the fiercest winter for 100 years and, as she slipped and fell, losing her shoes at one point, she became convinced she would just freeze to death.

But she was still alive after half-an-hour and she leapt with joy when she heard another train rumbling towards her. She waved and shouted. But nobody saw her and, with sinking heart, she watched the train thunder past.

An hour later she was almost unconscious on her feet. But she still managed to drag one foot after the other even though her clothes were now stiff with ice.

Then a breakdown trolley came clattering along the line on the way to thaw out a frozen set of points. This time she was spotted and the railway workers wrapped her in coats and took her to Murjek where she was immediately taken to hospital.

Doctors there said: "She would not have lasted another thirty minutes."

Now reunited with her husband, who arrived home to find the house empty and then went to the police, Mrs Edholm is wondering why her fellow passenger told her that the train had stopped at Murjek?

Was it an honest mistake? Or had she been the victim of a callous sense of humour?

"I find it hard to believe that anybody could play a joke as grim as that," she said. "But I had been sleeping and he was wide awake.

"And we were 20 miles from Murjek when I got out of the train. I don't suppose I will ever see him again so I will never know. But I'll never forget his face for the rest of my life."

Terry Greenwood in Stockholm,
The Sunday Express (London),
18 February, 1979

U.S.A.

The *DeWitt Clinton*

From the same West Point Foundry which built *The Best Friend*, the Mohawk and Hudson had ordered a locomotive. This was the now-famous *DeWitt Clinton*, twelve feet in length, with four forty-eight-inch wooden, iron-capped driving wheels, and weighing 6,758 pounds. After some test runs, this twelve-foot, fire-eating iron horse was pronounced ready to go into service. Everyone in Albany was on hand that hot August morning in 1831—members of the legislature, leading citizens, drummers. Stretching out from Albany all the way to Schenectady, lining the right of way, were farmers with their families decked out in their Sunday best, sitting in wagons and carriages. The horses hitched to these vehicles calmly munched grass, grateful for a day off from heavier work. Their calmness was to be of short duration.

The *DeWitt Clinton* was backed up and hooked onto its train. Right behind it was a small flat car with two barrels of water and a pile of wood. The water was hooked up to the engine's boiler by a leather hose. Behind this forerunner of the coal car were hooked three passenger cars, looking exactly like what they were, stagecoach bodies on flanged wheels. Each coach had seating room for six, but so mad was the scramble to take a ride on this first steam train that additional passengers clambered aboard the roofs of the coaches. Behind the passenger cars were six more flat cars with wooden benches for seating. Every seat was taken within minutes after the cry went up for all to get aboard.

John T. Clark, probably the first conductor in America, went up and down the train, with the call which has come down through railroad history, "Tickets, please." Retracing his steps,

Clark climbed aboard the "coal car," took out a long tin horn, and gave a mighty blast. Engineer Dave Matthews, who had built the engine, gave a yank on the throttle, and the *DeWitt Clinton* leaped forward to its task. Each car behind the engine gave a similar leap, but not at the same time. Three-foot iron chains connected each car with the one behind it. The slack snapped taut by the lurch of the engine. Conductor Clark would have gone sprawling overside had he not quickly grasped a roof support and held on for dear life. In turn, each car behind sprang forth with a similar jerk. Passengers inside the coaches fared far better than those on top, several of whom were tossed to the ground. But those on the wooden benches on the six rear flat cars fared the worst. As each car snapped into action, the benches went over backward, depositing the passengers on the floor and in each other's laps. Once the train stretched out, the going was smooth, and shouts of approval went up. But not for long.

As the *DeWitt Clinton* gathered speed, the smoke and blazing sparks from the engine's pine-pitch fuel flattened out, forming a long black cloud of smoke and hurling embers directly on the ten-car train. Again, the passengers in the coaches had the better of it. Although blinded by smoke, not as many burning embers settled inside the coaches as came to rest among those on the open flat cars. Back at the rear of the train, passengers were soon flailing away at their own and other's bodies in an attempt to put out the fire of their burning clothes. Those who had umbrellas raised them to fend off the falling sparks, but soon the umbrellas caught fire and were hastily jettisoned. After only a few miles the whole train was composed of volunteer firemen, fighting a moving conflagration. Along the route sightseers were thrown into confusion: their horses reared and ran away, and the spectators screamed.

Fortunately, the *DeWitt Clinton* was nearing its first watering stop. Engineer Davis applied his brakes—only the engine had them—and they worked. The *DeWitt* came to a plunging halt, and a reverse replica of the train's start took place. Passengers were plunged forward this time, as each car jounced to a stop, blockaded by the car in front of it.

The first thing the passengers did when they tumbled from the cars was rush to the water and finally extinguish their burning clothes. Next they tore down the rails of a farmer's wooden fence, cut them into correct lengths, and wedged them between each car comprising the train. When the *DeWitt Clinton* started up for the remainder of its run, the fence rails held firm, and the train moved off with only gentle lurching. The rest of the trip brought no new adventures. True, smoke and blazing embers continued to rain down on the unprotected heads of the passengers, but by this time their clothes had become so badly damaged that they didn't care. Not a single passenger abandoned the ride—pioneer bravery indeed.

ROBERT N. WEBB,
The Illustrated True Book of American Railroads

The first train in America

LIMITED

I am riding on a limited express, one of the crack trains
    of the nation.
Hurtling across the prairie into blue haze and dark air
    go fifteen all-steel coaches holding a thousand people.
(All the coaches shall be scrap and rust and all the men
    and women laughing in the diners and sleepers shall
    pass to ashes.)
I ask a man in the smoker where he is going and he
    answers: "Omaha."

CARL SANDBURG

Across the plains

Late in the evening we were landed in a waiting-room at Pitts-
burg. I had now under my charge a young and sprightly Dutch
widow with her children; these I was to watch over providen-
tially for a certain distance farther on the way; but as I found
she was furnished with a basket of eatables, I left her in the
waiting-room to seek a dinner for myself.

I mention this meal, not only because it was the first of
which I had partaken for about thirty hours, but because it was
the means of my first introduction to a coloured gentleman. He
did me the honour to wait upon me after a fashion, while I was
eating; and with every word, look, and gesture marched me
farther into the country of surprise. He was indeed strikingly
unlike the negroes of Mrs. Beecher Stowe, or the Christy Min-
strels of my youth. Imagine a gentleman, certainly somewhat
dark, but of a pleasant warm hue, speaking English with a slight
and rather odd foreign accent, every inch a man of the world,
and armed with manners so patronisingly superior that I am at
a loss to name their parallel in England. A butler perhaps rides
as high over the unbutlered, but then he sets you right with a

reserve and a sort of sighing patience which one is often moved to admire. And again, the abstract butler never stoops to familiarity. But the coloured gentleman will pass you a wink at a time; he is familiar like an upper form boy to a fag; he unbends to you like Prince Hal with Poins and Falstaff. He makes himself at home and welcome. Indeed, I may say, this waiter behaved himself to me throughout that supper much as, with us, a young, free, and not very self-respecting master might behave to a good-looking chambermaid. I had come prepared to pity the poor negro, to put him at his ease, to prove in a thousand condescensions that I was no sharer in the prejudice of race; but I assure you I put my patronage away for another occasion, and had the grace to be pleased with that result.

Lightning Express trains leaving a junction,
by Currier & Ives

Seeing he was a very honest fellow, I consulted him upon a
point of etiquette: if one should offer to tip the American
waiter? Certainly not, he told me. Never. It would not do. They
considered themselves too highly to accept. They would even resent the offer. As for him and me, we had enjoyed a very pleasant conversation; he, in particular, had found much pleasure in
my society; I was a stranger; this was exactly one of those rare
conjunctures. . . . Without being very clear seeing, I can still
perceive the sun at noonday; and the coloured gentleman deftly
pocketed a quarter.

*   *   *

At Ogden we changed cars from the Union Pacific to the
Central Pacific line of railroad. The change was doubly welcome; for, first, we had better cars on the new line; and, second,
those in which we had been cooped for more than ninety hours
had begun to stink abominably. Several yards away, as we returned, let us say from dinner, our nostrils were assailed by rancid air. I have stood on a platform while the whole train was
shunting; and as the dwelling-cars drew near, there would come
a whiff of pure menagerie, only a little sourer, as from men instead of monkeys. I think we are human only in virtue of open
windows. Without fresh air, you only require a bad heart, and
a remarkable command of the Queen's English, to become such
another as Dean Swift; a kind of leering, human goat, leaping
and wagging your scut on mountains of offence. I do my best to
keep my head the other way, and look for the human rather
than the bestial in this Yahoo-like business of the emigrant
train. But one thing I must say, the car of the Chinese was no-
tably the least offensive.

The cars on the Central Pacific were nearly twice as
high, and so proportionally airier; they were freshly varnished,
which gave us all a sense of cleanliness as though we had
bathed; the seats drew out and joined in the centre, so that there
was no more need for bed boards; and there was an upper tier
of berths which could be closed by day and opened at night.

I had by this time some opportunity of seeing the people
whom I was among. They were in rather marked contrast to the

emigrants I had met on board ship while crossing the Atlantic. They were mostly lumpish fellows, silent and noisy, a common combination; somewhat sad, I should say, with an extraordinary poor taste in humour, and little interest in their fellow-creatures beyond that of a cheap and merely external curiosity. If they heard a man's name and business, they seemed to think they had the heart of that mystery; but they were as eager to know that much as they were indifferent to the rest. Some of them were on nettles till they learned your name was Dickson and you a journeyman baker; but beyond that, whether you were Catholic or Mormon, dull or clever, fierce or friendly, was all one to them. Others who were not so stupid, gossiped a little, and, I am bound to say, unkindly. A favourite witticism was for some lout to raise the alarm of "All aboard!" while the rest of us were dining, thus contributing his mite to the general discomfort. Such a one was always much applauded for his high spirits. When I was ill coming through Wyoming, I was astonished—fresh from the eager humanity on board ship—to meet with little but laughter. One of the young men even amused himself by incommoding me, as was then very easy; and that not from ill-nature, but mere clod-like incapacity to think, for he expected me to join the laugh. I did so, but it was phantom merriment. Later on, a man from Kansas had three violent epileptic fits, and though, of course, there were not wanting some to help him, it was rather superstitious terror than sympathy that his case evoked among his fellow-passengers. "Oh, I hope he's not going to die!" cried a woman, "it would be terrible to have a dead body!" And there was a very general movement to leave the man behind at the next station. This, by good fortune, the conductor negatived.

There was a good deal of story-telling in some quarters; in others, little but silence. In this society, more than any other that ever I was in, it was the narrator alone who seemed to enjoy the narrative. It was rarely that any one listened for the listening. If he lent an ear to another man's story, it was because he was in immediate want of a hearer for one of his own. Food and the progress of the train were the subjects most generally treated; many joined to discuss these who otherwise would hold their tongues. One small knot had no better occupation than to worm out of me my name; and the more they tried, the more

obstinately fixed I grew to baffle them. They assailed me with
artful questions and insidious offers of correspondence in the future; but I was perpetually on my guard, and parried their as-
saults with inward laughter. I am sure Dubuque would have
given me ten dollars for the secret. He owed me far more, had
he understood life, for thus preserving him a lively interest
throughout the journey. I met one of my fellow-passengers
months after, driving a street tramway car in San Francisco;
and, as the joke was now out of season, told him my name without subterfuge. You never saw a man more chapfallen. But had
my name been Demogorgon, after so prolonged a mystery he
had still been disappointed.

ROBERT LOUIS STEVENSON,
Across the Plains (1892)

"The Modern Ship of the Plains" by Rufus Zogbaum
Immigrants crossing the Great Plains by railroad,
from *Harper's Magazine*, 1886.

THE CITY OF NEW ORLEANS

Ridin' on the City of New Orleans,
Illinois Central Monday morning rail,
15 cars and 15 restless riders,
three conductors, 25 sacks of mail.
All on the southbound odyssey
the train pulls out of Kankakee
and rolls past houses, farms and fields;
passing towns that have no name and
freight yards full of old black men and
the graveyards of rusted automobiles.

Singin': "Good morning America! How are you?
Say, don't you know me? I'm your native son.
I'm the train they call the City of New Orleans.
I'll be gone 500 miles when day is done."

Dealin' card games with the old men in the club
    car.
Penny a point and no one's keeping score.
Pass the paper bag that holds the bottle
and feel the wheels a-rumblin' 'neath the floor.
And the sons of Pullman porters and the sons of
    engineers
ride their fathers' magic carpet made of steel.
And mothers with their babes asleep
are rocking to the gentle beat,
the rhythm of the rail is all they dream.

"Good morning America! How are you?
Say, don't you know me? I'm your native son.
I'm the train they call the City of New Orleans
I'll be gone 500 miles when day is done."

Nighttime on the City of New Orleans,
changing cars in Memphis, Tennessee.
Halfway home and we'll be there by morning,
through the Mississippi darkness rollin' to the
    sea.

But all the towns and people seem to fade into a
     bad dream.
Well, the steel rail hasn't heard the news:
The conductor sings his song again
it's "passengers will please refrain,
this train has the disappearin' railroad blues."

"Goodnight America! How are you?
Say, don't you know me? I'm your native son.
I'm the train they call the City of New Orleans
I'll be gone 500 miles when day is done."

STEVE GOODMAN

Dickens in America

Before leaving Boston, I devoted one day to an excursion to
Lowell. I assign a separate chapter to this visit; not because I am
about to describe it at any great length, but because I remember
it as a thing by itself, and am desirous that my readers should do
the same.

I made acquaintance with an American railroad, on this occasion, for the first time. As these works are pretty much alike
all through the States, their general characteristics are easily
described.

There are no first and second class carriages as with us; but
there is a gentlemen's car and a ladies' car: the main distinction
between which is that in the first, everybody smokes; and in the
second, nobody does. As a black man never travels with a white
one, there is also a negro car; which is a great blundering
clumsy chest, such as Gulliver put to sea in, from the kingdom
of Brobdingnag. There is a great deal of jolting, a great deal of
noise, a great deal of wall, not much window, a locomotive engine, a shriek, and a bell.

The cars are like shabby omnibuses, but larger: holding
thirty, forty, fifty, people. The seats, instead of stretching from
end to end, are placed crosswise. Each seat holds two persons.
There is a long row of them on each side of the caravan, a nar-

row passage up the middle, and a door at both ends. In the centre of the carriage there is usually a stove, fed with charcoal or anthracite coal; which is for the most part red-hot. It is insufferably close; and you see the hot air fluttering between yourself and any other object you may happen to look at, like the ghost of smoke.

In the ladies' car, there are a great many gentlemen who have ladies with them. There are also a great many ladies who have nobody with them: for any lady may travel alone, from one end of the United States to the other, and be certain of the most courteous and considerate treatment everywhere. The conductor or check-taker, or guard, or whatever he may be, wears no uniform. He walks up and down the car, and in and out of it, as his fancy dictates; leans against the door with his hands in his pockets and stares at you, if you chance to be a stranger; or enters into conversation with the passengers about him. A great many newspapers are pulled out, and a few of them are read.

Arrival of the first train of the Atlantic and
Great Western Railroad at Jamestown from New York

Everybody talks to you, or to anybody else who hits his fancy. If you are an Englishman, he expects that that railroad is pretty much like an English railroad. If you say "No," he says "Yes?" (interrogatively), and asks in what respect they differ. You enumerate the heads of difference, one by one, and he says "Yes?" (still interrogatively) to each. Then he guesses that you don't travel faster in England; and on your replying that you do, says, "Yes?" again (still interrogatively), and it is quite evident, don't believe it. After a long pause he remarks partly to you, and partly to the knob on the top of his stick, that "Yankees are reckoned to be considerable of a go-ahead people too"; upon which *you* say "Yes," and then *he* says "Yes" again (affirmatively this time); and upon your looking out of the window, tells you that behind that hill, and some three miles from the next station, there is a clever town in a smart lo-ca-tion, where he expects you have concluded to stop. Your answer in the negative naturally leads to more questions in reference to your intended route (always pronounced rout); and wherever you are going you invariably learn that you can't get there without immense difficulty and danger, and that all the great sights are somewhere else.

If a lady takes a fancy to any male passenger's seat, the gentleman who accompanies her gives him notice of the fact, and he immediately vacates it with great politeness. Politics are much discussed, so are banks, so is cotton. Quiet people avoid the question of the Presidency, for there will be a new election in three years and a half, and party feeling runs very high: the great constitutional feature of this institution being, that directly the acrimony of the last election is over, the acrimony of the next one begins; which is an unspeakable comfort to all strong politicians and true lovers of their country; that is to say, to ninety-nine men and boys out of every ninety-nine and a quarter.

Except where a branch road joins the main one, there is seldom more than one track of rails; so that the road is very narrow, and the view, where there is a deep cutting, by no means extensive. When there is not, the character of the scenery is always the same. Mile after mile of stunted trees: some hewn down by the axe, some blown down by the wind, some half fallen and resting on their neighbours, many more logs half hidden in the swamp, others mouldered away to spongy chips. The very soil of the earth is made up of minute fragments such as these; each pool of stagnant water has its crust of vegetable rottenness; on every side there are the boughs, and trunks, and stumps of trees, in every possible stage of decay, decomposition, and neglect. Now you emerge for a few brief minutes on an open country, glittering with some bright lake or pool, broad as many an English river, but so small here that it scarcely has a name; now catch hasty glimpses of a distant town, with its clean white houses and their cool piazzas, its prim New England church and schoolhouse; when whir-r r-r! almost before you have seen them, comes the same dark screen: the stunted trees, the stumps, the logs, the stagnant water—all so like the last that you seem to have been transported back again by magic.

The train calls at stations in the woods, where the wild im-possibility of anybody having the smallest reason to get out, is only to be equalled by the apparently desperate hopelessness of there being anybody to get in. It rushes across the turnpike road, where there is no gate, no policeman, no signal, nothing but a rough wooden arch, on which is painted "WHEN THE BELL RINGS, LOOK OUT FOR THE LOCOMOTIVE." On it whirls headlong, dives through the woods again, emerges in the light, clatters over frail arches, rumbles upon the heavy ground, shoots be-neath a wooden bridge which intercepts the light for a second like a wink, suddenly awakens all the slumbering echoes in the main street of a large town, and dashes on haphazard, pell-mell, neck-or-nothing, down the middle of the road. There—with mechanics working at their trades, and people leaning from their doors and windows, and boys flying kites and playing mar-bles, and men smoking, and women talking, and children crawl-ing, and pigs burrowing, and unaccustomed horses plunging and rearing, close to the very rails—there—on, on, on—tears the mad dragon of an engine with its train of cars; scattering in all directions a shower of burning sparks from its wood fire; screeching, hissing, yelling, panting; until at last the thirsty monster stops beneath a covered way to drink, the people clus-ter round, and you have time to breathe again.

*   *   *

The Lackawanna Valley by George Innes

The journey from New York to Philadelphia is made by railroad, and two ferries; and usually occupies between five and six hours. It was a fine evening when we were passengers in the train: and watching a bright sunset from a little window near the door by which we sat, my attention was attracted to a remarkable appearance issuing from the windows of the gentlemen's car immediately in front of us, which I supposed for some time was occasioned by a number of industrious persons inside, ripping open featherbeds, and giving the feathers to the wind. At length it occurred to me that they were only spitting, which was indeed the case; though how any number of passengers which it was possible for that car to contain, could have maintained such a playful and incessant shower of expectoration, I am still at a loss to understand: notwithstanding the experience in all salivatory phenomena which I afterwards acquired.

I made acquaintance, on this journey, with a mild and modest young quaker, who opened the discourse by informing me in a grave whisper, that his grandfather was the inventor of cold-drawn castor oil. I mention the circumstance here, thinking it probable that this is the first occasion on which the valuable medicine in question was ever used as a conversational aperient.

CHARLES DICKENS,
American Notes (1842)

THE LACKAWANNA RAILROAD

The Lackawanna Railroad where does it go?
It goes from Jersey City to Buffalo.
Some of the trains stop at Maysville but they are few
Most of them go right through
Except the 8.22
Going west but the 10.12 bound for Jersey City
That is the train we like the best
As it takes you to Jersey City
Where you can take a ferry or tube for New York City.
The Lackawanna runs many freights
Sometimes they run late
But that does not make so much difference with a freight
Except the people who have to wait for their freight
Maysville people patronise the Interurban aspecialty the
          farmers
So the Interurban cuts into the business of the Lacka-
          wanna,
But if you are going to New York City or Buffalo
The Lackawanna is the way to go.
Will say in conclusion that we consider it an honor
That the City of Maysville is on the Lackawanna.

STEPHEN GALE

How they started

1. Thomas Edison

While I was a newsboy on the Grand Trunk I had a chance to learn that money can be made out of a little careful thought, and, being poor, I already knew that money is a valuable thing. Boys who don't know that are under a disadvantage greater than deafness. That was a long time ago. The Civil War was on and the Battle of Pittsburgh Landing, sometimes called the Battle of Shiloh, was in progress—and I was already very deaf. In my isolation (insulation would be a better term) I had time to think things out. I decided that if I could send ahead to outlying stations a hint of the big war news which I, there in Detroit, had learned was coming, I could do a better than normal business when I reached them.

I therefore ran to the office of the *Detroit Free Press* and asked Mr. Seitz, the man in charge, if he would trust me for a thousand newspapers. He regarded me as if perhaps I might be crazy, but referred me to Mr. Story. Mr. Story carefully considered me. I was poorly dressed. He hesitated, but finally told Mr. Seitz to let me have the papers.

I got them to the station and into the baggage car as best I could and then attended to my scheme. All along the line I had made friends of the station-agents, who also were the telegraphers, by giving them candy and other things which a train-boy dealt in in those days. They were a good-natured lot of men, too, and had been kind to me. I wired ahead to them, through the courtesy of the Detroit agent, who also was my friend, asking them to post notices that when the train arrived I would have newspapers with details of the great battle.

When I got to the first station on the run I found that the device had worked beyond my expectations. The platform literally was crowded with men and women anxious to buy newspapers. After one look at that crowd I raised the price from five cents to ten and sold as many papers as the crowd could absorb. At Mount Clemons, the next station, I raised the price from ten cents to fifteen. The advertising worked as well at all the other stations. By the time the train reached Port Huron I had advanced the price of the *Detroit Free Press* for that day to thirty-five cents per copy and everybody took one.

Out of this one idea I made enough money to give me a chance to learn telegraphy. This was something I long had wished to do, for thus early I had found that my deafness did not prevent me from hearing the clicking of a telegraph instrument when I was as near to it as an operator always must be. From the start I found that deafness was an advantage to a telegrapher. While I could hear unerringly the loud ticking of the instrument, I could not hear other and perhaps distracting sounds. I could not even hear the instrument of the man next to me in a big office. I became rather well-known as a fast operator, especially at receiving.

THOMAS ALVA EDISON,
Diary and Sundry Observations

2. George Pullman

One cold night in 1853, George Mortimer Pullman, twenty-two-year-old woodworker, living in Albion, New York, was traveling in a sleeping car between Buffalo and Westfield, a distance of some fifty-eight miles. It was an uncomfortable experience. The car had neither sheets, blankets, nor pillows. Lying in his clothes and shoes, and trying to sleep on the rough mattress, the young Pullman—who, according to one observer, grew up "conveying the impression that the world rested on his shoulders"—was thinking to himself how such a car might be improved.

It was one of the earliest sleeping cars. Stanley Buder, a Pullman historian, describes them as "ordinary coaches with a few crude extras added. Three wooden shelves were permanently fixed to the sides in a tier arrangement so that the sleeper could not be used for day travel. Lacking privacy and adequate bedding, the passenger would climb fully dressed onto a shelf. . . . Everyone knew that the problem was to build a sleeping car that could be used comfortably day and night. What was lacking, however, was the know-how."

George Mortimer Pullman provided that know-how. His
first chance at doing so came in 1858, when he went to Bloom-
ington, Illinois, and converted two old passenger coaches into
sleeping cars, for the Chicago and Alton Railroad. Though they
were not much of an improvement upon the existing sleepers,
he converted several more, and persuaded a few railroads to use
them. When passenger travel fell off, during the Civil War,
Pullman left for the gold fields of Colorado, where he ran a trad-
ing post from 1862 to 1863, and saved his money. With his sav-

George Pullman explaining his compressed paper wheels
(from Frank Leslie's *Illustrated Newspaper* of 1877)

ings, he returned to Chicago toward the end of the war, determined to build "the biggest and best car ever."

This turned out to be the *Pioneer*. It was built at a cost of $20,000, five times more than any previous sleeping car had cost. Many who had seen it under construction had laughed it away as "Pullman's Folly." But when Pullman unveiled the *Pioneer*, it was hailed as "the wonder of the age." "Never before," writes Joseph Husband, one of Pullman's biographers, "had such a car been seen; never had the wildest flights of fancy imagined such magnificence." The floor was covered with a rich red carpet, the seats upholstered with brocaded fabrics, the doorframes made of polished woods, the berths paneled with ornamented wood, and the entire car lit with silver-trimmed oil lamps and hung with gilt-edged mirrors. Arthur Dubin, of Chicago, a collector of Pullman memorabilia, says, "There was a sense of order about this man which must have been in his personal life. He was a very religious man. He built seminaries and left money to churches. George Pullman was a lover of beautiful things. That's an interesting facet to a man considered by so many to be ruthless."

For a time, the *Pioneer* seemed to be the wonder of the age in more ways than one. Because it was too large to fit between any of the existing station platforms, the railroad companies displayed little interest in it, and people started wondering what on earth Pullman was going to do with his sleeper. It was the assassination of President Lincoln that provided an answer, and opened up a future for the *Pioneer*. When the body of the slain President arrived in Chicago, on its way to Springfield, Illinois, state officials looked around for the most splendid conveyance to bear Lincoln on the final leg of his journey. And, of course, there was nothing more splendid in Chicago at the time than the *Pioneer*. Platforms along the way were hurriedly widened. The dead President was placed aboard the *Pioneer*, and the magnificent sleeper received everywhere an outpouring of publicity and acclaim that exceeded even George Pullman's most optimistic dreams.

JERVIS ANDERSON,
*A. Philip Randolph: A
Biographical Portrait*

Adventures of a hobo

Brum informed me of a freight train that was to leave the yards at midnight, on which we could beat our way to a small town on the borders of the hop country. Not knowing what to do with ourselves until that time arrived, we continued to drink until we were not in a fit condition for this hazardous undertaking—except we were fortunate to get an empty car, so as to lie down and sleep upon the journey. At last we made our way towards the yards, where we saw the men making up the train. We kept out of sight until that was done and then in the darkness Brum inspected one side of the train and I the other, in quest of an empty car. In vain we sought for that comfort. There was nothing to do but to ride the bumpers or the top of the car, exposed to the cold night air. We jumped the bumpers, the engine whistled twice, toot! toot! and we felt ourselves slowly moving out of the yards. Brum was on one car and I was on the next facing him. Never shall I forget the horrors of that ride. He had taken fast hold on the handle bar of his car, and I had done likewise with mine. We had been riding some fifteen minutes, and the train was going at its full speed when, to my horror, I saw Brum lurch forward, and then quickly pull himself straight and erect. Several times he did this, and I shouted to him. It was no use, for the man was drunk and fighting against the over-powering effects, and it was a mystery to me how he kept his hold. At last he became motionless for so long that I knew the next time he lurched forward his weight of body must break his hold, and he would fall under the wheels and be cut to pieces. I worked myself carefully towards him and woke him. Although I had great difficulty in waking him, he swore that he was not asleep. I had scarcely done this when a lantern was shown from the top of the car, and a brakesman's voice hailed us. "Hallo, where are you two going?" "To the hop fields," I answered. "Well," he sneered, "I guess you won't get to them on this train, so jump off, at once. Jump! d'ye hear?" he cried, using a great oath, as he saw we were little inclined to obey. Brum was now wide awake. "If you don't jump at once," shouted this irate brakesman, "you will be thrown off." "To jump," said Brum quietly,

"will be sure death, and to be thrown off will mean no more."
"Wait until I come back," cried the brakesman, "and we will
see whether you ride this train or not," on which he left us, making his way towards the caboose. "Now," said Brum, "when he
returns we must be on the top of the car, for he will probably
bring with him a coupling pin to strike us off the bumpers, making us fall under the wheels." We quickly clambered on top and
in a few minutes could see a light approaching us, moving along
the top of the cars. We were now lying flat, so that he might not
see us until he stood on the same car. He was very near to us,
when we sprang to our feet, and unexpectedly gripped him, one
on each side, and before he could recover from his first astonishment. In all my life I have never seen so much fear on a human
face. He must have seen our half drunken condition and at once
gave up all hopes of mercy from such men, for he stood helpless,
not knowing what to do. If he struggled it would mean the fall
and death of the three, and did he remain helpless in our hands,
it might mean being thrown from that height from a car going
at the rate of thirty miles an hour. "Now," said Brum to him,
"what is it to be? Shall we ride this train without interference,
or shall we have a wrestling bout up here, when the first fall
must be our last? Speak!" "Boys," said he, affecting a short
laugh, "you have the drop on me; you can ride." We watched
him making his way back to the caboose, which he entered, but
every moment I expected to see him reappear assisted by others.
It might have been that there was some friction among them,
and that they would not ask assistance from one another. For
instance, an engineer has to take orders from the conductor, but
the former is as well paid, if not better, than the latter, and the
most responsibility is on his shoulders, and this often makes ill
blood between them. At any rate, American tramps know well
that neither the engineer nor the fireman, his faithful attendant,
will inform the conductor or brakesman of their presence on a
train. Perhaps the man was ashamed of his ill-success, and did
not care to own his defeat to the conductor and his fellow brakesmen; but whatever was the matter, we rode that train to its destination and without any more interference.

W. H. DAVIES,
The Autobiography
of a Super-Tramp (1908)

Private varnish

For approximately five decades, or roughly the period between 1890 and the second world war, no status symbol in the lexicon of wealth glittered more refulgently than the private railroad car. No property was more explicit evidence of having arrived both socially and financially, since its occupancy breathed of privilege and aloofness and its resources of luxury were almost limitless. When all else had been achieved—a château on Fifth Avenue, English butlers, fleets of Rolls-Royce town cars, powdered footmen, a box in the Diamond Horseshoe, gold plate at table and old masters on the walls, there remained a crowning cachet of elegance, the capstone of material success. It was a sleek, dark-green private hotel car outshopped to one's own specification by Pullman and attached to the rear of the great name trains of the period when its owner wished to travel. It was absolute tops.

The first private cars were built for railroaders of presidential rank and their immediate subordinates, general managers, division superintendents and operating vice-presidents, but by the late eighties their vogue had spread to men of means who were merely directors or large stockholders in railroads, and soon they were a necessary property for men of exalted financial status who had no railroad connections at all.

Men of means everywhere began commissioning splendid hotel cars from Pullman or one of the several competing carbuilders in existence until Pullman achieved an absolute monopoly in the field in the late nineties. In California, Darius Ogden Mills, silver-whiskered old moneybags of the Mother Lode and Montgomery Street, ordered the first private car in the region from Harlan & Hollingsworth of Wilmington, Delaware. The tab was a modest $25,000. A few years later, in the Middle West, Adolphus Busch commissioned the first *Adolphus* from Pullman with chilled beer piped under pressure into its every apartment and stateroom. Silver senator William Sharon of Nevada owned a beauty; so did copper senator William Andrews Clark of Montana. For $50,000 Pullman in the late eighties outshopped *Katharyne* to the order of coal baron R. C. Kerens. E. H. Talbot, editor of *Railway Age*, had Pullman build him *Railway Age*, and mining millionaire James Ben Ali Haggin of San Francisco and Kentucky became owner of *Salvator*, which had a gold dinner service and a chef ravished from Foyot's in Paris. Newspaper publisher John McLean of Cincinnati came by the car *Ohio*, and Harry Oliver, pioneer ironmaster in the Mesabi region, rode comfortably in *Tyrone*, named by the sentimental Irishman for the county of his birth in the old country. Charles M. Schwab was at various times owner of two *Lorettos*, the second even more magnificent than the first.

For five full decades the order books at Pullman and to an only slightly lesser degree at American Car & Foundry were a roster of the great names and powerful personalities of American industry, society, and politics.

Interior of Pullman smoking car, c. 1900,
Southern Pacific Railroad

The cost of private cars rose with the passing years. In the early seventies $25,000 was considered ample and all California was gratified, vicariously, when Mrs. Leland Stanford paid that amount for *Stanford* as a birthday present for her husband. By the turn of the century the going price had about doubled, although Charles M. Schwab paid a reported $100,000 for the first *Loretto*, the most elaborate and ornate ever seen at that time. By 1915, the general run of private cars from Pullman was $75,000 and in the late twenties Joseph Widener, William R. Reynolds, and Thomas Fortune Ryan were signing checks for $300,000. Perhaps the top price of the era, which incidentally was the final flowering of the private railway car, was $350,000, reportedly paid by Mrs. James P. Donahue to American Car & Foundry for *Japauldon*, named for her late husband.

For these substantial sums private car owners could point to a considerable variety of conveniences and luxurious appointments, all of them contained of necessity within the clearances and dimensions decreed by the specifications of the Association of American Railroads. Beyond these basic functional properties, the imagination and financial resources of the owner took over. English butlers and French chefs were often supplemented by valets and personal maids and secretaries. The mother-of-pearl call buttons in Mrs. Schwab's stateroom on *Loretto II* suggested the availability of seven servants. Gold dinner services were often indicated, and as mentioned elsewhere, Mrs. E. T. Stotesbury pointed to her gold-plated plumbing fixtures as a genuine economy: "Save so much polishing, you know." The first air conditioning on any railroad car was an innovation on Major Max Fleischmann's *Edgewood*. Jewel safes, wine bins, and other capacious repositories for food and valuables came in all dimensions. Aboard *Lalee*, Lily Langtry was happy to announce there was a food locker capable of holding an entire stag. Adelina Patti aboard her appropriately named *Adelina Patti* had a sunken marble bathtub which, when the car was finally dismantled, turned out to be painted metal. Fritzi Scheff, another thrush, had a bathtub neither sunken nor allegedly marble, but the water splashed so that she could only take a bath when her train paused for twenty minutes or more. Sometimes this was at three in the morning, an incovenient hour.

Jay Gould had ulcers of the stomach and when he traveled on *Atalanta* with a private physician in attendance and a chef specially trained in the preparation of the ladyfingers which were one of his staples of diet, the Gould cow whose butterfat content was just suited to the financier's requirements rode in a private baggage car up ahead. When J. P. Morgan, who never owned a car of his own, voyaged afar, he rented as many private cars as his party might need and had a baggage car fitted with racks for carrying his own stock of champagnes, Rhine wines, and Madeiras. When the Goulds traveled as a family there might be as many as four Gould cars with a special engine traveling as an extra; Jay aboard *Atalanta*, Helen Gould on her own car, *Stranrear*, George Gould on his *Dixie*, and guests and miscellaneous retainers on still another Gould car, *Convoy*.

When Cissy Patterson, publisher of the *Washington Times-Herald*, had *Ranger* in commission, her butler carried with him seven complete and different sets of slip covers for every piece of furniture in the car. Mrs. Patterson liked variety and they were changed every day in the week. She was also devoted to flowers, and florists along the right-of-way were alerted in advance by telegraph and had wagonloads of fresh blooms at strategic stopping places. The flower bill on occasion came to $300 a week.

The private car on the Great Northern Railroad of Louis Hill, son of the Empire Builder and an ardent motorist in the early days of gasoline, contained a garage at one end available by a ramp, and sleeping space for a chaffeur and a mechanic. The staff on August Belmont's *Mineola* was uniformed by Wetzel, at the time the most expensive men's tailor in the United States, and a number of private cars including George M. Pullman's own *Monitor* and Arthur E. Stillwell's No. 100 on the Kansas City, Pittsburgh & Gulf, boasted parlor organs for music either sacred or profane.

The Stillwell car later came into the possession of Bet-a-Million Gates, and it was aboard this car and as a result of a wager on a raindrop's progress down a window pane with James R. Keene that, according to one school of thought, he derived his nickname.

Henry Ford distrusted the safety of Pullman Standard construction and *Fair Lane* was so heavily trussed and reinforced with steel that it had to be routed to avoid all but the most massive trestles on carrier railroads.

Perhaps the most sybaritic devising of all was designed and built by Pullman as part of the architectural economy of *Errant*, the 100-ton car of Charlie Clark, son of Senator William A. Clark. At the touch of a lever a partition beside the master stateroom's double bed dissolved to reveal it in convenient juxtaposition with the equally capacious bed in the adjacent guest stateroom.

LUCIUS BEEBE,
The Big Spenders

LaGrande, Oregon, Union Pacific Depot
with locomotive No. 63

Sunday on board the Union Pacific

A Pullman dining car of the 1870's.

A crowded coach

(*left*) Railway Interiors. Railway conductor going the round
of the cars at night.

THIS TRAIN

This train is bound for glory, this train,
This train is bound for glory, this train,
This train is bound for glory,
If you ride in it, you must be holy, this train.

This train don' pull no extras, this train,
Don' pull nothin' but de Midnight Special.

This train don' pull no sleepers, this train,
Don' pull nothin' but the righteous people, this train.

This train don' pull no jokers, this train,
Neither don' pull no cigar smokers, this train.

This train is bound for glory, this train.
If you ride in it, you mus' be holy, this train.

ANON

The making of the President, 1968

1. Bobby Kennedy returns to Washington

We crowd-counted, as political people always do, as the cortège wound away from the Cathedral through New York City. So many of us who followed could not quickly adjust from the manners of last week's political cavalcades to the procession of death. And the crowd was better than good—at least half a million; all of them, somberly, with him. It was only, however, when the funeral train that was to bear him to Washington emerged from the tunnel under the Hudson that one could grasp what kind of man he was and what he meant to Americans. Kenneth O'Donnell said, as he glanced from the windows of the train, "Now you can see what the Hell it was all about—he could really turn them on."

For 225 miles from the Hudson to Washington, he had turned them on. There were the family groups: husband holding sobbing wife, arm about her shoulders, trying to comfort her. Five nuns in a yellow pick-up truck, tiptoeing high to see. A very fat father with three fat boys, he with his hand over his heart, each of the boys giving a different variant of the Boy Scout or school salute. And the people: the men from the great factories that line the tracks, standing at ease as they were taught as infantrymen, their arms folded over chests. Women on the back porches of the slum neighborhoods that line the tracks, in their housedresses, with ever-present rollers in their hair, crying. People in buildings, leaning from office windows, on the flat roofs of industrial plants, on the bluffs of the rivers, on the embankments of the railway cuts, a crust on every ridge and height. Pleasure boats in the rivers lined up in flotillas; automobiles parked on all the viaducts that crossed the line of the train. Brass bands—police bands, school bands, Catholic bands. Flags: individual flags dropped in salute by middle-aged men as the train passed, flags at half-staff from every public building on the way, entire classes of schoolchildren holding the little eight-by-ten flags, in that peppermint-striped flutter that marks every campaign trip. He turned them on, black and white, rich and poor. And they cried.

There, as one passed through New Jersey, Pennsylvania, Maryland and Delaware, to Washington, was the panorama of American industrial might. There were the famous brand names of all America's skills from steel and chemicals to pickles and mustards. There were the old red-brick factories of the last century and the new industrial architecture of glistening turquoise, orange, blue, red-tiled electronic plants, their workers no longer uniformed in blue overalls but in sterile white smocks. There, for example, was the Ford plant, and a delivery yard of almost a quarter of a mile of gleaming new Mustangs, shining on racks in their glossy colors, promising pleasure for the pleasure society; and the medicinal plants, with all their secret wonders, too. It was a nation of unlimited skills and crafts but plagued by the madness of violence.

It should have been a four-hour trip by train; accidents, crowds, and fatalities in the crowds delayed the trip, stretching it to eight and a half hours. Thus, slowly, almost grotesquely, then with relief and acceptance, the atmosphere in the funeral train changed. It could not have changed without the bravery and grace of behavior of Ethel Kennedy, her black veil turned back, proceeding through the cars of the cortege to speak friendship and comfort to his grieving friends. One finally understood aboard the train the purpose of an Irish wake: to make a man come alive again in the affection and memory of his friends. The memory of Robert Kennedy came back and the range of his friendships slowly transformed the mood from stark tragedy to an abashed yet real joy in this companionship brought together by one man's personality.

2. Nixon at Deshler

The campaign moved smoothly, as always. The techniques of the advance men improved—from airport greetings at arrival, to the multiplicity of balloons, to internal communications, to the phalanxes of pretty Nixon girls with their slim legs and blond hair who were seated in rectangles, front-center, before the cameras to screen the few hecklers from national view. It was all smooth, pre-programmed, efficient. And yet, occasionally there would still come a day to remind that a Presidential contest remained a personal matter between a leader and his people.

Such a day was the one that closed at dusk in Deshler, Ohio, in late October. We had been traveling all day by train north from Cincinnati, through industrial Ohio toward Toledo. Whistle-stop campaigning in America has been obsolete since Harry Truman's campaign of 1948, but candidates still toss a salute to the past by a railway excursion now and then; and the rail journey through Ohio is classic. I had accompanied Nixon in 1960 over exactly the same route, and was following him now both for comparison with the past and to see what effect the Key Biscayne strategy might have on his behavior.

The trip was obviously planned for TV coverage; by now the TV cameras had become tired of Mr. Nixon's normal procedure and required new happenings to enliven the audiences ("One thing we decided in Key Biscayne," said William Safire, "is that the campaign needed some excitement"). The trip would also, in accord with the Key Biscayne plan, step up the stress on the theme of law-and-order.

Yet there was more to it than that. All day we drummed along the railway tracks fringed by paradox. The factories spewed smoke, their parking lots were crowded, trucks carrying away cargo and product in unending stream. But wherever the train pulled to a halt in the old downtown centers, one could observe the boarding up of the railway stations, the decay of the central business districts which had grown up on the rails because they were arteries of life. The old downtown centers of community were husks that had been gutted by change. The people who gathered at the rallies were prosperous, well-dressed, sober, in robust health. But they were afraid, and whenever Nixon spoke of crime, they cheered ("When Richard Nixon got finished," wrote Jimmy Breslin, "there was a strangler's hand coming out of every cornfield in Ohio"). All day we journeyed through peaceful countryside spotted with the sycamores, wild oaks and hardwoods of the great valley. But all day the view

from Mr. Nixon's rear observation car as it rattled north could
be seen only through the silhouette of the three Secret Service
agents standing shoulder to shoulder on the observation platform, searching the receding tracks and the beautiful land for
snipers who might kill.

We came to Deshler, Ohio, a town of about 2,000, after dark,
and Mr. Nixon emerged on the platform in a tan topcoat, shivering in the chill. Deshler is famous for its feed grains, its to-
mato-production and its seed corn. A huge grain elevator to
which farmers bring shelled corn is its outstanding monument,
and along the tracks, nubbles of red-gold-yellow-white kernels
lay thick as pebbles, where trucks had spilled them; an Ohio reporter told me that the best pheasant-shooting in the neighbor-
hood lay along the tracks because the pheasants grew fat here
on spilled kernels. Deshler much more than Los Angeles, Key
Biscayne or Manhattan is Nixon's spiritual country, and so in
this, his eighth speech of the day (with two more to come), he
could talk plain language. He did his crime passage, the media
theme for the day ("I was looking at some figures that my staff
had prepared for me on the forty-five-minute train ride from
Lima up here to [Deshler]. . . . In forty-five minutes, just
forty-five minutes . . . here is what happened in America.
There was one murder, there were two rapes, there were forty-
one forcible crimes . . .", etc). Then, in a brief burst at the
close, he tried to sum up his campaign: "I want you to remember, my friends, that at the moment when you vote, you are
going to determine your future, your peace, peace at home, you
are going to determine whether or not you are going to have
real income or imaginary income. You are going to determine
whether America again is respected in the world or whether it's
not. You are going to determine whether America is to go forward with new leadership or whether we are going to be satisfied with leadership that has failed us, that has struck out on
every count."

THEODORE WHITE,
*The Making of the President
1968*

Mr. and Mrs. Pitman

When it was time to leave for Washington, it was snowing hard, and the airport had closed down. So I took the train. Penn Station was rebuilding, and the redcap who took my bags along with those of a lady from Buffalo said that we would have quite a walk. We had a half-mile marathon; up ramps, down ramps, into elevators, out of elevators, round pillars (sometimes *into* pillars), through tunnels, out of tunnels, all over. Sometimes the redcap told us to go one way while he went another; he said we would meet up, and we did, though *how* we did was a mystery. When we reached the train, the lady from Buffalo asked how much she should give the redcap. My feeling, in view of all the exercise we'd had, was that he ought to give us something; but I said, how about a dollar? The redcap said, "Five pieces at a quarter a piece is one dollar and twenty-five cents. Thank you, ma'am." I had three cases and gave him a dollar; he didn't give me any change.

The train to Washington was pretty crowded. I went along to the club car and found myself next to a delightfully tight man of about fifty with sandy hair and a Hitler mustache. "My name's Pitman," he said, "and I'm in adult education. I arrange workshops and seminars and things all over the country. Christ, how I hate it. This is Mother." Mrs. Pitman was a large spreading blonde. She was holding a newspaper and pencil, and she said, "Barnyard fowl. Eight letters." Mr. Pitman said, "Mother's produced three daughters. They're all married and have children. Christ, are they prolific!" He sipped at his drink. "Mother and I are on our way home. We went to New York last night to see *Hello Dolly*. Isn't that a great show? Isn't that something?" I said I had found it so boring I had come out halfway through. "Oh, we didn't find it boring at *all*," said Mr. Pitman, "did we, Mother?" Mrs. Pitman said, without looking up, "It was lovely, just perfectly lovely." Mr. Pitman said, "Oh, we both thought it was just *great*."

Mr. Pitman looked around and noticed a man in a blue suit who had sat down beside us. "This man looks like Faulkner," said Mr. Pitman. The man looked embarrassed. "My *God*," said Mr. Pitman, "he *is* Faulkner."

Mrs. Pitman said, "Honey, Mr. Faulkner's dead; you know that"; and to me, "What's 'Alcoholic refreshment' in five letters?" I said, "Scotch?" and Mrs. Pitman said, "No, that's six."

Mr. Pitman said, "Do you know where this man's going? He's going to Hickory, North Carolina, to get better. Do you know how many people there are in Hickory? Forty-eight. That's right, forty-eight. Christ, there's nothing else to *do* in Hickory but get better. He can't miss." His mind went off at a tangent, and he said, "Our eldest girl married a young Jewish boy. He hasn't got a thing. But he's a real doll."

Mrs. Pitman said, "*E, F*, blank. Salamander."

"What do you mean, *E, F*, blank, salamander?" said Mr. Pitman, and the man who looked like Faulkner said, "I think it's *eft*, which is a kind of newt."

"Well, my, aren't you clever?" said Mrs. Pitman. Mr. Pitman said. "Noot? Who said anything about a noot? You're crazy. I'm going to wee-wee."

He got up and lumbered off down the corridor. Mrs. Pitman put down her pencil and said, "I love Gordon, though his mother was a nut. We have three beautiful children. My second daughter's blind—did he tell you? She's just the loveliest creature in the world. Both her sisters are pregnant right now, and boy, are they jealous of her figure! My youngest is a joy, too. She's been borrowing the car Tuesday nights. She wouldn't say where she was going for a long time, and then last week we finally got it out of her. She's been going to give extra coaching to some of the backward colored kids. Now that the schools are integrated, the backward ones can't keep up unless they have extra coaching. Isn't that just wonderful?"

Mr. Pitman came back, and Mrs. Pitman said, "Honey, that was a real good idea you had there"; and she got up and teetered down the train. Mr. Pitman yawned and said, "Oh, boy!" He looked as though he had sobered up a bit. He said to me, "You know, you were right about that *Hello Dolly* thing. I thought it was a load of horseshit." I said, "Why didn't you say so?" He said, "Well you can't, can you? Not in public. Not about a big hit like that. Besides, it would have upset Mother."

LUDOVIC KENNEDY,
Very Lovely People

The trains in Maine

I made my first rail journey into Maine in the summer of 1905, and have been riding to and fro on the cars ever since. On that first trip, when I was led by the hand into the green sanctuary of a Pullman drawing room and saw spread out for my pleasure its undreamed-of facilities and its opulence and the porter holding the pillow in his mouth while he drew the clean white pillowcase up around it and the ladder to the upper and the three-speed electric fan awaiting my caprice at the control switch and the little hammock slung so cunningly to receive my clothes and the adjoining splendor of the toilet room with its silvery appointments and gushing privacy, I was fairly bowled over with childish admiration and glee, and I fell in love with railroading then and there and have not been the same boy since that night.

American express train on the banks of
the Hudson River, by Currier & Ives

We were a family of eight, and I was the youngest member. My father was a thrifty man, and come the first of August every summer, he felt that he was in a position to take his large family on a month's vacation. His design, conceived in 1905 and carried out joyously for many summers, was a simple one: for a small sum he rented a rough camp on one of the Belgrade lakes, then turned over the rest of his savings to the railroad and the Pullman Company in return for eight first-class round-trip tickets and plenty of space on the sleeper—a magnificent sum, a magnificent gesture. When it came to travel, there was not a second-class bone in my father's body, and although he spent thousands of hours of his life sitting bolt upright in dusty day coaches, commuting between Mount Vernon and Grand Central, once a year he put all dusty things aside and lay down, with his entire family, in Pullman perfection, his wife fully dressed against the possibility of derailment, to awake next morning in the winy air of a spruce-clad land and to debouch, surrounded by his eager children and full of the solemnity of trunk checks, onto the platform of the Belgrade depot, just across the tracks from Messalonskee's wild, alluring swamp. As the express train pulled away from us in Belgrade on that August morning of 1905, I got my first glimpse of this benign bog, which did not seem dismal to me at all. It was an inseparable part of the first intoxication of railroading, and, of all natural habitats, a swamp has ever since been to me the most beautiful and most seductive.

Today, as my thoughts wander affectionately back over fifty-five years of railroading, the thing that strikes me as most revealing about that first rail trip in 1905 is the running time of the train. We left New York at eight o'clock in the evening and arrived at Belgrade next morning at half past nine—a thirteen-and-a-half-hour run, a distance of four hundred and fifteen miles, a speed of thirty-one miles an hour. And what is the speed of our modern Iron Horse in this decade as he gallops through the nights? I timed him from New York to Bangor not long ago, divided the mileage by the number of hours, and came up with the answer: thirty-four miles an hour. Thus, in fifty-five years, while the motorcar was lifting its road speed to the dazzling rate of seventy miles an hour on the thruways, and the airplane

was becoming a jet in the sky, the railroad steadfastly maintained its accustomed gait, between thirty and thirty-five miles
an hour. This is an impressive record. It's not every institution
that can hold to an ideal through fifty-five years of our fastest-
moving century. It's not every traveller who is content to go
thirty-four, either. I am not sure that even I, who love the rails,
am content. A few of us visionaries would like to see the railroad step up the pace from thirty-four to forty, so we could leave
New York after dinner at night and get home in time for lunch
next day. (I've just learned that the Maine Central has a new
schedule, effective early next month. Soon I can leave New
York after dinner and be home the following *afternoon* in time
for dinner. There's to be a four-hour layover in Portland, an
eighteen-hour trip all told. Thus the speed of my Horse has just
dropped from thirty-four miles an hour to twenty-eight. He's a
very sick horse.)

Railroads are immensely complex, and they seem to love
complexity, just as they love ritual and love the past. Not all
sick roads die, as I have pointed out, but a road can sometimes
put on a pretty good show of dying, and then its ritual seems to
be part of the scheme of dying. During 1959, because of some
sickness of my own, and of my wife's, and of other members of
our two families, she and I patronized the railroad more often
than usual, observing its agony while using what remained of
its facilities. There was one memorable night last fall, when,
sitting forlorn in the deserted waiting room of the Portland
depot, waiting to take the sleeper for New York, we seemed
actually to be the principal actors in the deathbed scene of railroading in America; no Hollywood director could have improved on the thing. For reasons too dull to go into, we were
taking our departure from Portland instead of Bangor. The old
station hung tomblike above and around our still forms, drear
and drafty. (No social crowd was gathered here.) The only
other persons in the place were the ticket agent, at ease behind
his counter, and a redcap in slow conversation with two friends.
Now and then the front door would open and a stray would
enter, some fellow to whom all railroad stations are home.
Shortly before train time, a porter appeared, dragging a large

wooden table and two chairs, and set the stage for the rites of ticket-taking. The table looked to be the same age as the depot and to have been chewed incessantly by porcupines. Two conductors in faded blue now walked stiffly onto the set and seated themselves at the table. My wife and I, catching the cue, rose and approached the oracle, and I laid our tickets down in front of one of the men. He grasped them, studied them closely, as though he had never seen anything quite like them in all his life, then turned to his companion and shouted, for all to hear in the room where no one was, "B in the Twenty-three!" To which the other replied, in a tremendous voice, "B in the Twenty-three!" (and seemed to add, *"for the last two passengers on earth"*). Then he tore off the stub and handed it to me.

The words of the ceremony, spoken so loudly, although familiar to us seemed unnaturally solemn and impressive, and we felt more as though we were taking marriage vows than taking a train. After the ceremony was over, we followed the redcap with our luggage, walking slowly out, the last two passengers, into the cold train shed, and picked our way across the tracks toward our waiting sleeper. Halfway there, we passed an ancient trainman, his arms full of kerosene lanterns, on his way to harness the Horse with the honored trappings of the past. There was something ineffably sad about the departure of this train; death seemed in the air.

When I came to live in Maine, the depot was twenty-three miles away, in Ellsworth. Then the depot got to be fifty miles away, in Bangor. After tomorrow night, it will be a hundred and forty miles away (for a sleeping car), in Portland. A year from now, there may be no depot in the whole state—none with a light burning, that is. I cannot conceive of my world without a rail connection, and perhaps I shall have to pull up stakes and move to some busier part of the swamp, where the rails have not been abandoned. Whether I move away or stay put, if the trains of Maine come to a standstill I will miss them greatly. I will miss cracking the shade at dawn—and the first shafts of light in the tinted woods, and the old excitement. I'll miss the Canada geese in the Kennebec in the seasons of migration, and the breakfast in bed, drinking from the punctured can of grapefruit juice as we proceed gravely up the river, and the solid old

houses of Gardiner, and Augusta's little trackside glade with
the wooden staircase and the vines of the embankment and the
cedar waxwing tippling on berries as I tipple on juice. I'll miss
the peaceful stretches of the river above Augusta, with the
stranded sticks of pulpwood along the banks; the fall overcast,
the winter brightness; the tiny blockhouse of Fort Halifax, at
Winslow, mighty bastion of defense; and at Waterville the
shiny black flanks of Old No. 470, the Iron Horse that has been
enshrined right next to what used to be the Colby campus—the
steam locomotive that pulled the cars on the last prediesel run
from Portland to Bangor.

Early last spring, as my train waited on a siding for another
train to go through, I looked out of the window and saw our conductor walking in the ditch, a pocketknife in his hand. He
passed out of sight and was gone ten minutes, then reappeared.

Carrying the United States Mail
across the Sierra Nevada, 1870

In his arms was a fine bunch of pussy willows, a gift for his wife, I don't doubt. It was a pleasing sight, a common episode, but I recall feeling at the time that the scene was being over-played, and that it belonged to another century. The railroads will have to get on with the action if they are to boost that running speed from twenty-eight to forty and lure customers.

Perhaps the trains will disappear from Maine forever, and the conductor will then have the rest of his life to cut pussies along the right of way, with the sand a-blowing and the blackberries a-growing. I hope it doesn't happen in my lifetime, for I think one well-conducted institution may still regulate a whole country.

E. B. WHITE,
The Points of My Compass

I LIKE TO SEE IT LAP THE MILES

I like to see it lap the miles,
And lick the valleys up,
And stop to feed itself at tanks;
And then, prodigious, step

Around a pile of mountains,
And, supercilious, peer
In shanties by the sides of roads;
And then a quarry pare

To fit its sides, and crawl between,
Complaining all the while
In horrid, hooting stanza;
Then chase itself down hill

And neigh like Boanerges;
Then, punctual as a star,
Stop—docile and omnipotent—
At its own stable door.

EMILY DICKINSON

Wendy in Zen

There would be no food until Albany, when the New York section, with its diner, was hooked to this train. So I went into the lounge car and had a beer. I packed my pipe and set it on fire and savored the trancelike state of lazy reflection that pipe smoke induces in me. I blew myself a cocoon of it, and it hung in clouds around me, so comforting and thick that the girl who entered the car and sat down opposite seemed wraithlike, a child lost in fog. She put three bulging plastic bags on her table, then tucked her legs under her. She folded her hands in her lap and stared stonily down the car. Her intensity made me alert. At the next table a man was engrossed in a Matt Helm story, and near him, two linesmen—they wore their tools—were playing poker. There was a boy with a short-wave radio, but his racket was drowned by the greater racket of the train. A man in a uniform —a train man—was stirring coffee; there was an old greasy lantern at his feet. At the train man's table, but not speaking, a fat woman sneaked bites at a candy bar. She did it guiltily, as if she feared that at any moment someone would shout, *Put that thing away!*

"You mind not smoking?"

It was the girl with the bags and the stony gaze.

I looked for a NO SMOKING sign. There was none. I said, "Is it bothering you?"

She said, "It kills my eyes."

I put my pipe down and took a swig of beer.

She said, "That stuff is poison."

Instead of looking at her I looked at her bags. I said, "They say peanuts cause cancer."

She grinned vengefully at me and said, "Pumpkin seeds."

I turned away.

"And these are almonds."

I considered relighting my pipe.

"And this is cashews."

Her name was Wendy. Her face was an oval of innocence, devoid of any expression of inquiry. Her prettiness was as remote from my idea of beauty as homeliness and consequently was not at all interesting. But I could not blame her for that: it is hard for anyone to be interesting at twenty. She was a student, she said, and on her way to Ohio. She wore an Indian skirt, and lumberjack boots, and the weight of her leather jacket made her appear round shouldered.

"What do you study, Wendy?"

"Eastern philosophy? I'm into Zen."

Oh, Christ, I thought. But she was still talking. She had been learning about the Hole, or perhaps the Whole—it still made no sense to me. She hadn't read all that much, she said, and her teachers were lousy. But she thought that once she got to Japan or Burma she would find out a lot more. She would be in Ohio for a few more years. The thing about Buddhism, she said, was that it involved your whole life. Like everything you did—it was Buddhism. And everything that happened in the world—that was Buddhism, too.

"Not politics," I said. "That's not Buddhism. It's just crooked."

"That's what everyone says, but they're wrong. I've been reading Marx. Marx is a kind of Buddhist."

Was she pulling my leg? I said, "Marx was about as Buddhist as this beer can. But anyway, I thought we were talking about politics. It's the opposite of thought—it's selfish, it's narrow, it's dishonest. It's all half truths and short cuts. Maybe a few Buddhist politicians would change things, but in Burma, where . . ."

"Take this," she said, and motioned to her bags of nuts. "I'm a raw-foodist–nondairy vegetarian. You're probably right about politics being all wrong. I think people are doing things all wrong—I mean, completely. They eat junk. They *consume junk.* Look at them!" The fat lady was still eating her candy bar, or possibly another candy bar. "They're just destroying themselves and they don't even know it. They're smoking themselves to death. Look at the smoke in this car."

I said, "Some of that is my smoke."

"It kills my eyes."

" 'Nondairy,' " I said. "That means you don't drink milk."

"Right."

"What about cheese? Cheese is nice. And you've got to have calcium."

"I get my calcium in cashews," she said. Was this true? "Anyway, milk gives me mucus. Milk is the biggest mucus-producer there is."

"I didn't know that."

"I used to go through a box of Kleenex a day."

"A box. That's quite a lot."

"It was the milk. It made mucus," she said. "My nose used to run like you wouldn't believe."

"Is that why people's noses run? Because of the milk?"

"Yes!" she cried.

* * *

At the time, I did not think Wendy was crazy in any important sense. But afterward, when I remembered our conversation, she seemed to me profoundly loony. And profoundly incurious. I had casually mentioned to her that I had been to Upper Burma and Africa. I had described Leopold Bloom's love of "the faint tang of urine" in the kidneys he had for breakfast. I had shown a knowledge of Buddhism and the eating habits of Bushmen in the Kalahari and Gandhi's early married life. I was a fairly interesting person, was I not? But not once in the entire conversation had she asked me a single question. She never asked what I did, where I had come from, or where I was going. When it was not interrogation on my part, it was monologue on hers. Uttering rosy generalities in her sweetly tremulous voice, and tugging her legs back into the lotus position when they slipped free, she was an example of total self-absorption and desperate self-advertisement. She had mistaken egotism for Buddhism. I still have a great affection for the candor of American college students, but she reminded me of how many I have known who were unteachable.

PAUL THEROUX,
The Old Patagonian Express

The heart of the matter

Paint me a small railroad station then, ten minutes before dark. Beyond the platform are the waters of the Wekonsett River, reflecting a somber afterglow. The architecture of the station is oddly informal, gloomy but unserious, and mostly resembles a pergola, cottage or summer house although this is a climate of harsh winters. The lamps along the platform burn with a nearly palpable plaintiveness. The setting seems in some way to be at the heart of the matter. We travel by plane, oftener than not, and yet the spirit of our country seems to have remained a country of railroads. You wake in a pullman bedroom at three a.m. in a city the name of which you do not know and may never discover. A man stands on the platform with a child on his shoulders. They are waving goodbye to some traveler, but what is the child doing up so late and why is the man crying? On a siding beyond the platform there is a lighted dining car where a waiter sits alone at a table, adding up his accounts. Beyond this is a water tower and beyond this a well-lighted and empty street. Then you think happily that this is your country— unique, mysterious and vast. One has no such feelings in airplanes, airports and the trains of other nations.

JOHN CHEEVER,
Bullet Park

U.S.S.R.

The Trans-Siberian Express

1. Tsar Alexander gives the go-ahead

To the Grand Duke Czarevich . . .

YOUR IMPERIAL HIGHNESS!

Having given the order to build a continuous line of railway across Siberia, which is to unite the rich Siberian provinces with the railway system of the Interior, I entrust to you to declare My will, upon your entering the Russian dominions after your inspection of the foreign countries of the East. At the same time, I desire you to lay the first stone at Vladivostok for the construction of the Siberian Railway, which is to be carried out at the cost of the State and under direction of the Government.

I remain your sincerely loving

ALEXANDER
from S. LEGG (ed.),
The Railway Book (1952)

2. The first train

The great sensation of the Paris Universal Exhibition of 1900 was Nagelmackers's Trans-Siberian International Express. He placed it on show in the Tuileries before putting it into service across Russia, to provide the first overland link between Western Europe and the Far East. It drew huge crowds and was awarded the gold medal; and no wonder. Nagelmackers's career as creator and pioneer of the *train de luxe* was one of repeatedly surpassing himself in his achievements. Now came his announcement that he was to provide not only the means of travelling to Peking, Shanghai, Seoul and even Tokyo in a fortnight by rail, but the possibility of doing so in conditions "equal to the special trains reserved in Western Europe for the sole use of Royalty."

The Odessa–Kiev Express, 1864. The kitchen (*top left*) is one of the earliest pictures of cooking facilities in any train. The second-class carriage and washroom (*lower left*) look comfortable enough, but pale beside the luxury of the white upholstery, pile carpets, and ornate ceilings of the first class (*above*).

Each of the coaches accommodated but eight people. Each two-berth coupé had a connecting *cabinet de toilette* and was decorated with the opulence of the *salon privé* of a St Petersburg merchant. Every carriage had its own drawing room and smoking room. One was decorated with white-lacquered limewood, mirrored walls, a ceiling frescoed with figures from Greek mythology and embroidered curtains. Another was in the style of Louis xvi, with bulging furniture of gold-embellished oak; a third was French Empire, and a fourth imperial Chinese.

The train had a library stocked with books in English, French, German and Russian, a glass-walled observation car and music room equipped with a full-sized grand piano, a hairdressing salon in white sycamore, a bathroom in green sycamore with a novel bath specially designed so that water could not spill out while the train was in motion, a gymnasium equipped with dumb-bells, exercise bicycle and rowing machine, and—although Nagelmackers had built both Catholic and Protestant churches along the route so that passengers might worship according to their custom during breaks in their journey—a chapel car. There was also a fully equipped darkroom for amateur photographers—though it is to be doubted whether this was provided for their convenience so much as for the tsarist censors, to whom undeveloped, exposed film in the possession of foreigners was as much anathema as it is to their Soviet successors.

MARTIN PAGE,
Lost Pleasures of the Great Trains

3. The beginnings of Gulag— an early passenger remembers

At Missovaia we found another *train de luxe* awaiting us, and it was here, from the warmth of a saloon car, that I first saw a batch of Siberian exiles, although I had previously seen the cars with caged windows wherein they are now transported, instead of having to undergo that weary tramp of 4000 miles.

It was already dark and the train had not yet started, when I saw a band of armed soldiers surrounding some thirty people carrying bundles, coming along the dimly-lighted platform, and then form up at one end of it, the people always being surrounded by the soldiers. What had especially attracted my attention, or I might not have noticed in the uncertain light of what the band consisted, was a little boy of about ten or twelve years of age, who was carrying a large bundle of what looked like clothing, trying to pass on the wrong side of some palings, when he was roughly seized by the ear by one of the Cossack guards and quickly brought back.

Russian Orthodox Church car
at a wayside stop

Wishing to post some letters, I tried to pass along that end
of the platform in search of the pillar-box, but was at once
stopped by the guard. The steam from our engine, congealed by
the sharp frost, fell in a fine snow about this luckless band, and
glistened white on their clothes in the station lights, and it almost seemed to add an uncalled-for insult to the misery of their
lot. I could not help wondering as to what their thoughts might
be as they watched our waiting train replete with every comfort
and blazing with electric light. I have never before seen the extremes of misery and captivity on the one hand, the extremes of
freedom and luxury on the other, brought into such close and
striking contrast, and I hope never to see it again. Subsequently,
the dejected-looking throng, in which I fancied I saw women,
were marched through a doorway into a darkened passage in the
station, and so disappeared from sight.

Probably they were all criminals who deserved their fate.
Possibly not. Preconceived ideas and old tradition, however,
stirred one's sympathies and left an unpleasant feeling in the
mind for some time. I was constrained to compare our lots, and
be thankful for mine. I, free to go my way in comfort.
They . . . ?

ANON
Quoted in *Lost Pleasures of
the Great Trains*

4. An exchange of gifts

Compartments in Russian sleeping cars are come-as-you-are,
and mingling of the sexes is common. My four charges have a
compartment to themselves; I am the odd man out. On three
other Russian trains, I was assigned lady commissars as room-
mates—whether it was accident or whether it was hoped I would
talk in my sleep and give away some dread secret, I do not know.
Once I even accidentally got *locked* in a compartment with a
lady commissar, but that is another story. On the *Russia Express*
I drew two young Russian Army officers and the wife of one of
them. The berths are permanent, and on a journey of this length

many people don't bother to dress, spending the day in pajamas, sandals, and a dressing gown. The routine when there are ladies present, of course, is *toujours politesse*—gestures meaning "I am going to bed," "I am getting up," "Please turn your back," "Please leave the room." I had no topics of conversation with the Army officers, but my Intourist girl, realizing this was a bit of a fix for me, came in and told them I was an American who had been a railroad transport officer in the last war. Well, it turned out one of the Russians was a railway transport officer, and he kindly lent me a technical Russian magazine, of which I could not understand a word.

The Russian etiquette toward strangers goes like this: the afternoon we leave Moscow, my Intourist guide introduces me to the Army officers. All right. I go off to dinner, go to bed, and in the morning, when I come back from my very early shaving, I see two cucumbers and a tomato sitting on my pillow. Large smiles from the Army officers, and waving, indicating that this is a present from them and the one wife to me. I twig to this, so at the next long stop—there is one several times every day; the engine takes on water and fuel and there is a general embarking and disembarking—I discover on the station platform a long line of women with all sorts of things to sell (this is more like Mexico or Peru or Bolivia, where people seem to make their living by selling things to eat at railway stations, than it is like Europe). I see an old lady selling huge boxes of cookies (I had noticed that my Army-officer companions didn't use the dining car—perhaps it was too expensive for them?), and I buy a box, and then when my companions are out of the compartment, I put the box on one of their pillows. When I come back after lunch—ah! Great greetings, smiles, bowings, and so forth, and so forth. The next morning, other vegetables on my pillow—and some black bread and a bit of cheese. At the next stop I spot some likely looking vegetables and buy a sack of cucumbers (Russians are extremely fond of cucumbers), and when my companions are out of the way, I lay six cukes, in little oval patterns, on each pillow. Great delight!

ROGERS E. M. WHITAKER and
ANTHONY HISS,
All Aboard with E. M. Frimbo

5. The dining-car

The dining-car was certainly unchanged. On each table there still ceremoniously stood two opulent black bottles of some unthinkable wine, false pledges of conviviality. They were never opened, and rarely dusted. They may contain ink, they may contain the elixir of life. I do not know. I doubt if anyone does.

Lavish but faded paper frills still clustered coyly round the pots of paper flowers, from whose sad petals the dust of two continents perpetually threatened the specific gravity of the soup. The lengthy and trilingual menu had not been revised; 75 per cent of the dishes were still apocryphal, all the prices were exorbitant. The cruet, as before, was of interest rather to the geologist than to the gourmet. Coal dust from the Donetz Basin, tiny flakes of granite from the Urals, sand whipped by the wind all the way from the Gobi Desert—what a fascinating story that salt-cellar could have told under the microscope! Nor was there anything different about the attendants. They still sat in huddled cabal at the far end of the car, conversing in low and disillusioned tones, while the *chef du train*, a potent gnome-like man, played on his abacus a slow significant tattoo. Their surliness went no deeper than the grime upon their faces; they were always ready to be amused by one's struggles with the language or the cooking. Sign-language they interpreted with more eagerness than apprehension: as when my desire for a hard-boiled egg—no easy request, when you come to think of it, to make in pantomime—was fulfilled, three-quarters of an hour after it had been expressed, by the appearance of a whole roast fowl.

PETER FLEMING,
One's Company

Next there is the matter of food, the other great event of the day. You can with success visit the restaurant of Rossiya—if you have a telepathic sense of timing—and the journey will take you across a devil's leap: the barely insulated connecting platform between the cars where you cling to frosty rails at the point of the

Food-sellers at a Siberian country station

train's greatest mechanical turbulence; the cold wind shouts, and the blast reminds you of the real scale of what is being done here. The rapidshooter's reward is a Czarist salon in dark polished wood and cream of the kind presumed to be left behind on the Nakhodka sleeper, operated by motherly *mujiks* swathed from head to foot in what look like single great sweatrags. They tot on an abacus governed by an impenetrable system, and work from a twelve-page menu printed in four languages which boasts every conceivable national delicacy from *blinis* to redcurrant vodka; a point which should by no means distract you from the fact that the choice is always limited to beefsteak and cheese. However, you are not allowed to order until you have studied the menu attentively. Actually to be fair, this is to ignore the excellent black bread, robust and tangy, the rich jam and the excellent tea. Chekov, implacable in these matters, found Siberian tea to have the flavour of sage and beetles, but I find it sweet and light. Delicious. Also, there is suspicious milk and gallons of bottled plums and sherry-type wine; and comfortable meat and vegetable soups crop up more often now that the whole new consignment of provisions taken on at Irkutsk is seen to repair the ravages on the system of not only feeding the travellers for some days but also of acting as local grocery store to forty-odd towns on the way. There is also the occasional blast of canned peas that arrives on the plate frozen as the landscape of Siberia, reminding you of how much worse it could be.

MICHAEL PENNINGTON,
Rossiya

Afterwards, whenever I thought of the Trans-Siberian Express, I saw stainless steel bowls of *borscht* spilling in the dining car of the Rossiya as it rounded a bend on its way to Moscow, and at the curve a clear sight from the window of our green and black steam locomotive—from Skovorodino onwards its eruptions of steamy smoke diffused the sunlight and drifted into the forest so that the birches smouldered and the magpies made for the sky. I saw the gold-tipped pines at sunset and the snow lying softly around clumps of brown grass like cream poured over the

ground; the yachtlike snowploughs at Zima; the ochreous flare
of the floodlit factory chimneys at Irkutsk; the sight of Marinsk
in early morning, black cranes and black buildings and escaping figures casting long shadows on the tracks as they ran towards the lighted station—something terrible in that combination of cold, dark, and little people tripping over Siberian tracks;
the ice-chest of frost between the cars; the protrusion of Lenin's
white forehead at every stop; and the passengers imprisoned in
Hard Class: fur hats, fur leggings, blue gym suits, crying children, and such a powerful smell of sardines, body odour, cabbage, and stale tobacco that even at the five-minute stops the
Russians jumped on to the snowy platform to risk pneumonia for
a breath of fresh air; the bad food; the stupid economies; and
the men and women ("No distinction is made with regard to
sex in assigning compartments"—Intourist brochure), strangers
to each other, who shared the same compartment and sat on opposite bunks, moustached male mirroring moustached female from
their grubby nightcaps and the blankets they wore as shawls,
down to their hefty ankles stuck in crushed slippers. Most of
all, I thought of it as an experience in which time had the trick
distortions of a dream: the Rossiya ran on Moscow time, and
after a lunch of cold yellow potatoes, a soup of fat lumps called
solyanka, and a carafe of port that tasted like cough syrup, I
would ask the time and be told it was four o'clock in the morning.

PAUL THEROUX,
The Great Railway Bazaar

6. Some secret bridges

"What I want to know," I said to Mischa (never one to let
sleeping dogs lie), "is why your government gets so steamed up
about bridges. This book I've got describes every bridge on the
Trans-Siberian Railway in detail, and there are photographs of
all the really big ones. I know we're not in Siberia yet; but I bet
there's another book with pictures of all the bridges on the way
to the Urals. Anyway, what difference does it make? They all
get photographed from satellites."

"I have never seen such a book," he said.

"Well, would you like to look at it? Here!"

"I do not want to look at it."

"Well, just listen to this then: 'At the 1328 verst the line crosses the river . . .' "

"Which river?"

"The Ob. Would you mind if I get on with it, as it's rather long?

The line crosses the river by a bridge 372.50 sahzens long having seven spans. The I and VI openings are 46.325 sahzens, the II, IV, 53.65 sahzens, and III and V, 53.15 sahzens. The upper girders of the bridge are on the Herber's system.

"I'm going to cut it short:

The stone abutments of the bridge are laid on granite rocks, the right pier, No. 1, near the bank is not supported on a caisson, the other piers, Nos. 2, 3, 4, 5, and 6 are laid on caissons sunk to a depth of 1.81 to 3.40 sahzens below the lowest water level. The minimum elevation of the trusses above the low water mark is 8.23 sahzens and 4.42 above its highest level . . .

Look, there's an awful lot more: you don't want me to go on do you? It's terribly boring."

"You should not be in possession of such a book," said Mischa, severely. "Such a book is a confidential publication."

ERIC NEWBY,
The Big Red Train Ride

7. Some assorted drunks

I went to my own compartment to drink my vodka and saw in my solitary activity something of the Russians' sense of desolation. In fact they did nothing else but drink. They drank all the time and they drank everything—cognac that tasted like hair tonic, sour watery beer, the red wine that was indistinguishable from cough syrup, the nine-dollar bottles of champagne, and the smooth vodka. Every day it was something new: first the vodka ran out, then the beer, then the cognac, and after Irkutsk one saw loutish men who had pooled their money for champagne, passing the bottle like bums in a doorway. Between drinking they slept, and I grew to recognize the confirmed alcoholics from the way they were dressed—they wore fur hats and fur leggings because their circulation was so poor; their hands and lips were always blue. Most of the arguments and all the fights I saw were the result of drunkenness. There was generally a fist fight in Hard Class after lunch, and Vassily provoked quarrels at every meal. If the man he quarrelled with happened to be sober, the man would call for the complaints' book and scribble angrily in it.

"*Tovarich!*" the customer would shout, requesting the complaints' book. I only heard the word used in sarcasm.

There was a nasty fight at Zima. Two boys—one in an army uniform—snarled at a conductor on the platform. The conductor was a rough-looking man dressed in black. He did not react immediately, but when the boys boarded he ran up the stairs behind them and leaped on them from behind, punching them both. A crowd gathered to watch. One of the boys yelled, "I'm a soldier! I'm a soldier!" and the men in the crowd muttered, "A fine soldier *he* is." The conductor went on beating them up in the vestibule of the Hard-Class car. The interesting thing was not that the boys were drunk and the conductor sober, but that all three were drunk.

Paul Theroux,
The Great Railway Bazaar

8. The Red Army with its trousers down

The car opposite our own on the other train was occupied by soldiers, and from our compartment we had an unprecedented view of its lavatory accommodation through its window which, unlike the lavatory windows on any other Russian train I had ever seen, or on any other train anywhere else in the world I had ever seen, was made of clear glass.

Both trains left a little late and in the course of the next few minutes we were treated to the extraordinary spectacle of a succession of Russian soldiers each one of whom, on entering the lavatory, stood astride the pan and, as if he was performing a drill movement, lowered his trousers, in doing so revealing one of the most closely guarded military secrets of the Soviet Union —that its soldiers, like those of kilted, Highland regiments in the British Army, are not issued with underpants. If this is a calumny and they are issued with underpants, then they had forgotten to put them on.

ERIC NEWBY,
The Big Red Train Ride

9. A storm in Siberia

We were emerging from the permafrost now and the *Rossiya* was running through birch forests full of little lakes, on some of which men were fishing from rowing boats, and when the train stopped you could hear hundreds of birds chattering away. Then, while we breakfasted off more of the *omul*, of which we were beginning to tire, the country began to open out. In the fields the wheat was already 18 inches high, which showed that we were really out of the permafrost zone, and there were lush meadows full of buttercups and bog cotton, and grassy banks covered with yellow lilies and lupins. Even the forest was changing. The everlasting larches and birches were thinning out and being replaced by oaks. Around one o'clock we crossed a big river, the Zeya, a tributary of the Amur (as were all the rivers we were crossing now). There were gold mines on its upper waters and in the ranges away to the north of the line. By now we were ravenous and we all trooped off to the restaurant car to find that it had been miraculously replenished with food, although the drink situation was the same; and there, with the temperature up to 86°F, we ate fish soup and minced steak, washed down with lemonade. All the time now the big, brilliantly painted containers from Japan and the United States were rushing past on their flat cars on their way to Europe. All that day the *Rossiya* travelled eastwards under a cloudless sky. Then, towards evening, away to the north, an enormous swirling cloud as black as night appeared over what was a practically limitless horizon and came racing towards the railway. In order to get a better view of this phenomenon I rushed to the back of

the train and looked out of the window of the last car. By now it
was nearing the line and not more than 100 feet above it. An
apocalyptical wind began to blow, bending the trees and tearing the leaves from them, and forked lightning began to shoot
earthwards from it while at the same time the sun continued to
shine, bathing the whole landscape in a ghastly, yellowish
light. Then, when the cloud was over the *Rossiya*, it released a
deluge of rain, which was accompanied by prolonged and deafening peals of thunder. It was at this moment, just as we
reached the 8020th kilometre mark from Moscow, that *Rossiya*
No. 1 roared past in the opposite direction, inward bound from
Vladivostok, streaming water and illuminated by the lightning
which was now continuous, a magnificent sight. I shared this
grandstand view of a Siberian storm with a very drunk Russian
who was armed with a half-full bottle of vodka, and he was so
overcome by the spectacle that in the course of those few minutes he finished it off. Soon this great cloud was gone beyond the
Amur where it would presumably give the Chinese the same
treatment as it had given us, once more leaving the sky overhead clear and blue as if nothing had happened.

Eric Newby,
The Big Red Train Ride

10. The *Vostok*

The eastern terminus of the *Rossiya* is Vladivostock, which
is now a restricted city. So at Khabarovsk, some 500 miles
from Vladivostock (and 5,400 from Moscow), passengers for
Japan and Hong-Kong disembark and enter another train
called the *Vostok*.

The *Vostok* was made up of a half-dozen green passenger cars,
drawn by an electric engine, and from the outside looked no
different to any normal Russian passenger train. On the inside it was fantastic, a train-that-never-was, something that
might have been designed by Beaton for Garbo, using for
money the three-year box office take from *My Fair Lady:* the

perfect train, kept forever behind the wall in Plato's Cave, of which only distorted shadows are seen in the outer world, all shining mahogany, brass and scintillating glass.

Each of the two-berth compartments was loaded with mahogany, some of it gilded. The mahogany armchair was covered in red plush (and so was the brass door chain) and the coved roof was also banded with mahogany. The finely chased door furniture was solid brass, and the screws in the brass door hinges had been aligned by some artisan so that each of the cuts in the heads of the screws was parallel with the ones below it and next to it. The mahogany table had a brass rim around it; there were brass rails around the luggage compartment overhead to stop the cabin trunks crashing between one's ears, the ashtrays were solid brass, and the cut-glass ceiling light had a brass finial on it.

On the floor there was a thick red and green Turkey carpet. On the beds of snow-white pillows had been arranged in a manner that suggested that this work had been performed by a parlourmaid who had majored in household management around 1903. The sheets were freshly ironed and so were the white voile curtains which were also supported on a brass rail.

In the bathroom, with which the compartment was connected by way of a mahogany door, there was a full-length looking glass, a stainless steel washbasin as big as a font, furnished with nickel-plated taps (the sort that stay on once you have turned them on), and the stainless steel lavatory basin had a polished mahogany seat. The shower head was attached to a flexible tube. The towels were thick and sumptuous and the heavy water carafe held two litres. Illumination in the bathroom was provided by a frosted glass window which gave on to the corridor. On the outside this window was embellished with an art-nouveau motif, also in solid brass, and in the corridor this motif was echoed in the decoration of the ceiling lights. The corridor, in which golden curtains oscillated with the movement of the train (which, admittedly was far more bumpy than that of the *Rossiya*), was provided with a number of tip-up seats, also upholstered in red plush, for those who had grown weary while on the way to and from the restaurant car, and the carpet was the same as those in the compartments.

And everything worked. If this was not enough, our particular car was equipped with the most beautiful conductress I had seen on the Russian or any other railway system. She was reputed to be of Czech origin. Perhaps the whole thing came from Czechoslovakia, for it was newly built, and she with it. If it was built in Russia, where had the Russians found the artisans to build it? From the same source that produced the men and women who refurbished the Summer Palace at Tsarskoye Selo?

ERIC NEWBY,
The Big Red Train Ride

TO A LOCOMOTIVE IN WINTER

Thee for my recitative,
Thee in the driving storm even as now, the snow, the
    winter-day declining,
Thee in thy panoply, thy measur'd dual throbbing and
    thy beat convulsive,
Thy black cylindric body, golden brass and silvery steel,
Thy ponderous side-bars, parallel and connecting rods,
    gyrating, shuttling at thy sides,
Thy metrical, now swelling pant and roar, now tapering
    in the distance,
Thy great protruding head-light fix'd in front,
Thy long, pale, floating vapor-pennants, tinged with
    delicate purple,
The dense and murky clouds out-belching from thy
    smoke-stack,
Thy knitted frame, thy springs and valves, the trem-
    ulous twinkle of thy wheels,

Thy train of care behind, obedient, merrily following,
Through gale or calm, now swift, now slack, yet steadily
    careering;
Type of the modern—emblem of motion and power—
    pulse of the continent,
For once come serve the Muse and merge in verse, even
    as here I see thee,

With storm and buffeting gusts of wind and falling snow,
By day thy warning ringing bell to sound its notes,
By night thy silent signal lamps to swing.

Fierce-throated beauty!
Roll through my chant with all thy lawless music, thy
    swinging lamps at night,
Thy madly-whistled laughter, echoing, rumbling like an
    earthquake, rousing all,
Law of thyself complete, thine own track firmly holding,
(No sweetness debonair of tearful harp or glib piano
    thine,)
Thy trills of shrieks by rocks and hills return'd,
Launch'd o'er the prairies wide, across the lakes,
To the free skies unpent and glad and strong.

WALT WHITMAN

The ordeal of Gladys
Aylward, missionary

Expedition "Gladys Aylward" assembled on the platform at
Liverpool Street Station on Saturday, 18th October, 1930. It
must be numbered amongst the most ill-equipped expeditions
ever to leave the shores of England, possessing in currency exactly ninepence in coin and one two-pound Cook's travellers'
cheque. The cheque was sewn carefully into an old corset, which
also contained her Bible, fountain pen, tickets and her passport.

    She kissed her mother, father, and sister good-bye, and set-
tled herself into the corner seat of her third-class compartment.
The whistle blew, the train hissed and puffed; she waved
through the window until her family were out of sight. She
dried her eyes, sat back and spread out on the seat beside her
the old fur coat which a friend had given her and which her
mother had cut up and made into a rug. Her two suitcases were
on the rack. One contained her clothes, the other an odd assort-
ment of tins of corned beef, fish and baked beans, biscuits, soda
cakes, meat cubes, coffee essence, tea and hard-boiled eggs. She

also had a saucepan, a kettle and a spirit stove. The kettle and the saucepan were tied to the handle of the suitcase with a piece of string.

Soon they were out of the city, past the suburbs. In the country she pressed her face against the cold, misted window and whispered, "God bless you, England." She did not know—she would not have wished to know—that it would be twenty long years before she saw that landscape again.

She disembarked at The Hague, tipped the porter who carried her bags the ninepence in coppers and secured a corner seat. From Holland the train rattled across Germany, Poland and into the great steppes of Russia. She sat "facing the engine," cocooned in her fur rug and watched the Continent slide past. In Russia she was shocked by what she saw: the crowds of apathetic people waiting on the bare, cheerless stations, surrounded by their bundles; women working in gangs; poverty and peasantry on a scale she had never imagined.

Ten days after leaving England the train crossed into Siberia, and she was at once enchanted by the grandeur of the scenery: the towering mountains, the great belts of dark pines, the endlessly stretching snow, the bright sunshine and the immense loneliness. At one halt a man came into her compartment who could speak a little English, and through him the other people, who had long ago tired of trying to ask her questions in sign language, now began to satiate their curiosity. He was a kindly man, and he conveyed to Gladys that the conductor of the train who had examined her tickets wished to tell her that no trains were running to Harbin, and that she would probably be held up at the Siberian-Manchurian border. If this were true—and she concentrated on trying hard not to believe it—then her chances were remote of proceeding onwards through Harbin to Dairen, and so by steamer to Tientsin.

To increase her fears, at each station halt more and more soldiers crowded on to the train. Two officers shared her compartment now, and although they could not talk to her except by gesticulation, they were quite pleasant. At Chita the train emptied of all civilians, except Gladys. The conductor came along and with fantastic signs tried to entice her out on to the platform. Gladys, however, now firmly rooted in the compartment, was having none of it; she believed that every mile forward was a mile towards China. She stayed put.

The train filled up with soldiers and rumbled onwards. A few hours later in the darkness it halted again at a tiny station and the soldiers got out, formed up on the platform and marched off up the line into the darkness. The train lights went out. She took a short walk up the corridor and satisfied herself that she was the only person left aboard. Then, borne on the thin, freezing wind, came a noise which, even although she had never heard it before, she recognised immediately. The sound of gunfire! Rumbling, ominous, terrifying! She poked her head out of the carriage window and saw the distant flashes light the sky. She scrambled her belongings together, wandered along the platform and, in a small hut by the track, found four men clustered round a stove: the engine-driver, stoker, the station-master and the conductor who had unsuccessfully urged her to get off the train at Chita. They made her a cup of strong coffee and with a running commentary amplified by gymnastic gesticulations reiterated the fact that she had, indeed, reached the end of the line. Beyond was the battlefield. The train, they said, would remain at this halt for days, perhaps weeks, until such time as it was needed, then it would take wounded back to hospitals behind the line. They pointed down the track the way they had come. "Go back," they said.

The line wound drearily through snow-covered pines. It ducked through dark tunnels; it was hemmed in by high mountains; the snow in between the sleepers was thick and soft; icicles hung from the pine-cones. But to walk back to Chita, they said, was her only hope.

She set off. Not many miles from the Manchurian border, the Siberian wind gusting the powdered snow around her heels, a suitcase in either hand, one still decorated ludicrously with kettle and saucepan, fur rug over her shoulders, she crunched off into the night. God obviously did not mean her to be eaten by the wolves, for there were plenty about.

Four hours later, when the cold and exhaustion became too much for her, she sat down on the icy rail, lit her spirit stove and boiled some water for her coffee essence. She ate two soda cakes, and felt miserable. She decided she must sleep, at least for an hour or two. She arranged her suitcases into a windbreak, scooped up snow to fill the cracks, wrapped herself firmly into her old fur rug and lay down. Drowsily, she listened to the noise of far-off howling, and with childlike innocence said to herself, "Now I wonder who let all those big dogs out at this time of night? Noisy lot!" Not until a couple of years later in China did she realise that she had heard a hunting wolf-pack.

A pale dawn was lighting the mountains when she woke up, stiff but refreshed. She made herself more coffee, ate another soda cake, gathered up her luggage and set off again along the interminable railway track. Late that night, staggering along, almost unconscious with cold and weariness, she saw the lights of Chita gleaming far down the track. It gave her new strength. She struggled onwards, lifted herself wearily on to the platform, dropped her suitcases into a heap and draped herself on top of them.

ALAN BURGESS,
The Small Woman

Travelling to Samarkand

1. Lord Curzon

Installed in a broad-gauge railway carriage, Curzon settled down to enjoy the three days of effortless travel that were to transport him from Uzun Ada to Samarkand. Around him were stowed his bedding and his portable rubber bath, his tinned meat and chocolate, his notebooks and his flea powder. His journalistic conscience was disturbed by the difficulty of gathering facts and figures about the rolling stock—"it is, indeed, as hard to extract accurate statistics or calculations from a Russian as to squeeze juice from a peachstone." Nor was there much else to engage his attention as for more than twenty-four hours the train rolled slowly through Kara Kum, the desert of black sand.

On the afternoon of the second day, the train halted at Geok Tepe, where, seven years before, General Skobeleff's army had

stormed the fortress in one of the most bloody encounters of the
Russian drive into Central Asia. As at Tel-el-Kebir in 1883,
Curzon paced the battlefield, reconstructed the action, gloomily
noted the debris of war and a carpet of bleached bones. Then on
through fertile country to Askabad, the capital of Transcaspia
and seat of the Russian Governor-General. Here Curzon's suspicions were aroused by the construction of a broad road leading to the Persian frontier. "Already," he wrote, "the north of
Persia and Khorasan are pretty well at Russian mercy from a
military point of view."

Merv, once called Queen of the World and believed to be the
cradle of civilization, resolved itself into "a nascent and as yet
very embryonic Russian town, with some station buildings, two
or three streets of irregular wooden houses. . . . No ancient
city, no ruins, no signs of former greatness or reviving prosper-
ity." What he did see, however, was enough to remind him how
impotent Great Britain had been in attempting to check the
Russian annexation of Merv in 1884. "The flame of diplomatic
protest blazed fiercely forth in England," he recalled with bitterness, "but, after a momentary combustion, was as usual extinguished by a flood of excuses from the inexhaustible reser-
voirs of the Neva." It would have been a very different matter,
he implied, had George Nathaniel Curzon sat penning des-
patches at the desk of the Foreign Secretary.

Once more the train drew away to the East across a land
wiped almost clean of history and Curzon composed its epitaph:

In these solitudes, the traveller may realise in all its sweep the
mingled gloom and grandeur of Central Asian scenery. Throughout
the still night the fire-horse, as the natives have sometimes christened
it, races onward, panting audibly, gutturally, and shaking a mane of
sparks and smoke. Itself and its riders are all alone. No token or sound
of life greets eye or ear; no outline redeems the level sameness of the
dim horizon; no shadows fall upon the staring plain. The moon shines
with dreary coldness from the hollow dome, and a profound and tearful solitude seems to brood over the desert. The returning sunlight
scarcely dissipates the impression of sadness, of desolate and hopeless
decay, of a continent and life sunk in a mortal swoon. The traveller
feels like a wanderer at night in some desecrated graveyard, amid
crumbling tombstones and half-obliterated mounds. A cemetery, not
of hundreds of years but of thousands, not of families or tribes but of

nations and empires, lies outspread around him: and ever and anon, in falling tower or shattered arch, he stumbles upon some poor un-earthed skeleton of the past.

Meanwhile the line ran through green, well-timbered coun-try that paved the approach to Bokhara, capital of a quasi-inde-pendent State already succumbing to Russian influence. At first Curzon could see no more than a distant outline of minaret and dome: for the train, having skirted the city walls, perversely drew away into the shelter of a modern Russian-built station nearly ten miles from Bokhara itself. Although some of the local merchants had wished the station to be sited nearer the city, the general attitude of the Bokhariots towards the railway was one of suspicion. It was regarded as foreign, subversive, anti-national and even Satanic: they called it Shaitan's Arba, or the Devil's Wagon. Even in Russia such an attitude was not uncommon. Readers of Dostoyevsky's *The Idiot*, published in 1866, will recall how Lebedyev was taunted with believing that "railways are a curse, that they are the ruin of mankind, that they are a plague that has fallen upon the earth to pollute the 'springs of life.' " To which he replied: "The railways alone won't pollute the 'springs of life,' but the whole thing is ac-cursed; the whole tendency of the last few centuries in its gen-eral, scientific and materialistic entirety is perhaps really ac-cursed."

The Russian railway authorities readily adopted the sugges-tion of the Bokhariots that the line should not approach the city. It gave them an excuse for building a rival town and a canton-ment of troops for its protection: an unobtrusive yet effective safeguard against possible unruliness on the part of a recently occupied and still semi-independent state. But already the mer-chants of Bokhara were regretting their early hostility to the line, much as English land-owners had come to lament the wealth lost by their having opposed the advance of the railway across their estates. Everywhere, Curzon noted, apprehension had given way to ecstasy: "I found the third-class carriages re-served for Mussulman passengers crammed to suffocation, just as they are in India; the infantile mind of the Oriental deriving an endless delight from an excitement which he makes not the slightest effort to analyse or to solve." Sometimes, it must be confessed, he did live up to the reputation of a Superior Person.

KENNETH ROSE,
Superior Person: A Portrait
of Curzon and His Circle in
Late Victorian England

2. Peter Fleming

It was a three or four day journey to Samarkand. Night fell soon after we had started on this journey and it was discouraging to find that the electric light on the train was not working. My fellow-passengers in the soft-class coach all turned out to be fairly senior railway officials bound for a conference in Tashkent. It was to be what the Russians call a Self-Criticism Conference at which the delegates, theoretically, take it in turns to explain the appalling blunders for which each of them has been responsible and to suggest how these blunders can be avoided in the future. One of the possible remedies is so obvious that I cannot believe that these conferences are much fun, and if I had been going to one I know that I should not have felt at my best; but I cannot say that I was much impressed by the reaction of the twenty or thirty railway officials to the complete failure of the electric lighting system on a train in which they had to spend three long nights. All this happened, you must remember, in the nineteen-thirties, and in those distant days to be deprived without warning and in one's own country of some essential service or amenity was looked on by the British, not as another thorn in an outsize martyr's crown which it is their duty to wear with as good a grace as possible, but as a cue for action, or at least for vigorous protest. If nothing came of the protest, one improvised. The Russians neither protested nor improvised.

As the deserts turned from gold to dove-grey and the dusk closed in across them on the thin black line of the Trans-Caspian Railway, my fellow-passengers put their soup-stained memoranda back into their portfolios of imitation leather and let the darkness flow over them till it obscured everything in the compartment except the glowing tips of their cigarettes, eternally agitated in debate. Nobody tried to mend the dynamo, nobody tried to buy candles when we stopped at the occasional villages and the still more occasional towns. "Oriental fatalism" is perhaps the explanation that suggests itself to those of you who know the Russians; and I agree that there is nothing more fatalistic than the Chinese, and I remember thinking that if the other passengers in that coach had been senior Chinese railway officials, or even ordinary Chinese, some poor stationmaster would have been intimidated or bribed into providing us with lamps and we should have travelled in a blaze of light.

Still, we travelled, which was the main thing. I think I have said that there was no dining-car on the train; nor was any other source of food or drink provided. This added greatly to the interest of a slow and rather tedious journey. It meant that one depended entirely for victuals on the stations at which the train stopped; and although I say "one depended," I really mean that about three hundred depended, for of course everybody on the train was equally anxious to avoid starvation. Imagine for a moment that you are a passenger on a slow train without a dining car, travelling through Russian Central Asia twenty-five years ago. Tomorrow morning you wake up as soon as it gets light. You have an upper berth. The other men in the compartment are inert, untidy molehills of humanity. Soon they will wake up too, and make themselves once more into mountains, full of self-importance and statistics and perhaps also of an abstruse charm. But now they are huddled with their knees up to their chins. They are clenched like a fist against the cold, and although the cold is not all that severe they are not as well equipped to meet it as the peasants in the hard-class carriages. Those three molehills are important people, senior officials of a nationalized service in a Socialist state. Being important people, they are entitled to certain privileges and priorities. As a result, instead of wearing sheepskins and felt boots like most of the hard-class passengers, they are dressed in European-style suits and shoes, and although these clothes make them feel *ochin kulturni* or very cultured, they also make them feel the cold much more than their social inferiors. Which only goes to show that you can't have everything.

As you peer down from your upper berth the first thing that strikes you is what a terrible mess the compartment is in. The whole floor is carpeted, like the floor of a parrot's cage, with the husks of sunflower seeds. The spittoon has become a sort of cornucopia, overflowing with melon-rind and bread-crusts and grape-skins and egg-shells and cigarette-ends. You climb down from your berth and pick your way through this debris into the corridor. The sun is rising over the desert and on the southward horizon you can see a line of blue mountains beyond which lies Persia. The express train is tearing along at a steady twenty-five miles an hour. Presently it begins to slow down, whistling in that rather hysterical way to which so many foreign trains are addicted, and at length comes convulsively to a stop in a small wayside station, where with any luck you can buy something to eat for breakfast—melons, sour milk, grapes, bread, perhaps the dusty carcass of a chicken sold by wild-looking Turkomen or Uzbeks.

At last the train, by now in an indescribably filthy state, reached Samarkand, only about twelve hours late. However

"Death to the Bourgeoisie."
A propaganda train showing peasants and
workmen attacking "capitalists."

blasé you may be, it is no good pretending that there is not something romantic about the sound of Samarkand; and I got out of the train in a state of pleasurable curiosity. The road had not been exactly golden, but here at any rate, I thought, was Samarkand. It turned out that I was mistaken, for the railway station is some five miles from the city. Night had fallen and it was very cold. I chartered a droshky and we set off clip-clopping through the dust under poplar trees that rustled in the chill night wind.

PETER FLEMING,
With the Guards to Mexico

In the Gulag Archipelago

1. Marie Avinov

In 1938 Marie Avinov, the wife of a former Russian landowner, was sent east in one of Stalin's mass deportations.

Early one cold, snowbound December morning, I and some two hundred other women were packed into a few ill-smelling motor-vans known as "Black Ravens." I could not tell which railway station we were driving to, since there was no opening in the walls of the van. Finally the doors opened on the Kazan station—the same station from which my family used to embark each spring for our beloved Kotchemirovo. I couldn't help smiling at the contrast between then and now.

Rifle-carrying NKVD men lined us up on the slippery station platform. We certainly were a motley throng of deportees with only our gender in common: former noblewomen shifted their weight from foot to foot along with thieves, intellectuals, and prostitutes. More than half our number were wives, legitimate or otherwise, of Party members fallen victim to Stalin's purges. This Communist "élite" stood apart, with a defiant air.

We stood there for an hour or more until our legs felt weak and our knees wobbly. One woman fell. A guard gave her a hard blow with his rifle, and she shrieked. There came a gruff, reluctant reprimand: "Easy there! What's the good of beating her?"

I found myself coupled with an "ex-lady" in her seventies, who had been a noted musician and a friend of Rubinstein, Tchaikovsky, and other famous composers. She had been arrested the past July while strolling in a Moscow park, and hadn't been allowed to return to her room to collect any belongings. Now she stood shivering in her thin shoes, with a ragged and bloodstained army coat wrapped around her once white summer dress. In her hands she clutched a tiny suitcase, that she had somehow obtained in prison. I offered to carry it for her.

"Oh, no, thank you," she said in a nervous whisper, "it's not at all heavy. All I have in it is an old ivory fan."

"A fan?" I repeated incredulously.

"Yes," she added in the same hurried whisper, "yes, you see, I had it with me when they arrested me. It was such a hot day, that day was. Now it's all I have left. I'd hate to lose it."

For what seemed an eternity, we were kept waiting on that platform. Several more vanloads of prisoners arrived and were lined up behind us. Thieves and prostitutes quarrelled and swore; many others wept quietly. I felt sorry for the Communist "ex-ladies" who were trying to appear defiantly aloof. We others, at least, didn't have to pretend this was all the fault of some official blunder.

We looked like a herd of ragged cattle about to be shipped to a somewhat less green pasture, and when the train finally crawled in, the analogy became even stronger. As we were driven into the railway carriages, I decided that we would have probably been more comfortable if we *had* been cattle. The carriages were all alike, each with a passage running its full length. On the one side was a row of tightly sealed, whitewashed windows, and on the other—where one finds the compartments in a sleeping car—a row of wire cages. In each cage, there were three tiers of wooden bunks, four bunks to a tier, with so little space between bunks that the occupant could never sit upright. The boards were hard, but it was blissful to be able to get off our feet and lie down.

In our car, the last three cage-compartments were occupied by male prisoners. We caught glimpses of them as an armed guard escorted us on our way to the washroom. We were forbidden to look around while passing the men's area, and had to keep our eyes fixed on the floor ahead of us. The heart of every woman faltered as she went by: her own husband could possibly have been in there. One night, I thought I heard Nika's voice when a man called out for water. The sound of blows followed. Then a scream: "You have no right! There's nothing against the law in what I said!" From the sound of things, the beating went on. I shut my eyes and stuck my fingers into my ears. Was this the way Nika had lost his tooth? Soon afterwards, the guards dragged their victim through the corridor to the end of the car. Later still, we learned that he had been stripped and thrown naked into a small, unheated cell. At this news, one of the women in our cage began to sob aloud. The commander of the guards flattened his nose against the iron partition. "Do you want to join the gentleman?" he asked in an ominous voice. The woman fell silent.

This hellish journey lasted a fortnight. Our daily ration was some black bread and two cups of tepid water. I had not fully recovered from malaria, and in the stifling atmosphere, my thirst became a torture. From the corridor where our guards sat smoking, whiffs of tobacco intensified my craving for a cigarette. One evening I became slightly delirious and began to moan for a drink of water—an offence that called for the little cold cell.

Two young cage-companions of mine tried to comfort me as best they could. Both had been singers in the Moscow Grand Opera, before their husbands had been arrested and "disposed of." Now the talent and energy of these lovely young artists were destined to be buried in a forced-labour camp for the next ten years.

I saw one of them creep to the wire partition. She called out in a soft voice.

"Comrade Chief! Oh, Comrade Chief! Would you care for a little music? We're well-known singers, you know. We've been applauded by Comrade Stalin himself, and now we'd like to sing for you and your men."

There fell a prolonged silence, during which a slow, collective smile crept over the faces of the guards and ended in a broad grin on their commander: "Well, perhaps, just one or two songs. . . ." Putting their rifles aside eagerly, they all crowded in front of our cage.

Whatever their backgrounds and political shadings, Russians love music and have a soft spot for artists. That night, in the stifling heat of the rumbling train, under the ecstatic gaze of the NKVD, I heard a most amazing performance. First a cyrstal-clear, enticing soprano rose in the "Habanera" from *Carmen*. I had often heard that lovely melody, but never as I heard it that night. One of Rubinstein's duets followed, then my favourite Schubert, *Der Wanderer*. Boisterous applause broke out from every cage-compartment. The Commander reeled around as if awakening from a dream.

"Stop it! Quiet! Shut up! And you, Comrades, back to your places!" The men dispersed. Lights were lowered. But presently a hand pushed a cup of water into our cage and a rough voice said, "Eh, you singers! Here's your reward. Now keep quiet!"

As I lay in my bunk, shaking with thirst and emotion, that cup of cool, refreshing water was pressed into my hand.

"Have a drink, my poor dear," whispered a gentle voice. "We sang to get it for you."

PAUL CHAVCHAVADZE,
Pilgrimage through Hell

2. Alexander Solzhenitsyn

Dismayed by the hopeless length of my sentence, stunned by my first acquaintance with the world of Gulag, I could never have believed at the beginning of my time there that my spirit would recover by degrees from its dejection: that as the years went by, I should ascend, so gradually that I was hardly aware of it myself, to an invisible peak of the Archipelago, as though it were Mauna Loa on Hawaii, and from there gaze serenely over distant islands and even feel the lure of the treacherous shimmering sea between.

The middle part of my sentence I served on a golden isle, where prisoners were given enough to eat and drink and kept warm and clean. In return for all this not much was required of me: just twelve hours a day sitting at a desk and making myself agreeable to the bosses.

But clinging to these good things suddenly became distasteful. I was groping for some new way to make sense of prison life. Looking around me, I realized now how contemptible was the advice of the special-assignment prisoner from Krasnaya Presnya: "At all costs steer clear of general duties." The price we were paying seemed disproportionately high.

Prison released in me the ability to write, and I now gave all my time to this passion, brazenly neglecting my boring office work. There was something I had come to value more than the butter and sugar they gave me—standing on my own feet again.

Well, they jerked a few of us to our feet—en route to a Special Camp.

They took a long time getting us there—three months. (It could be done more quickly with horses in the nineteenth century.) So long that this journey became, as it were, a distinct period in my life, and it even seems to me that my character and outlook changed in the course of it.

The journey was bracing, cheerful, full of good omens.

A freshening breeze buffeted our faces—the wind of *katorga* and of freedom. People and incidents pressed in on every hand to assure us that justice was on our side! on our side! on our side! not with our judges and jailers.

The Butyrki, our old home, greeted us with a heartrending female shriek from a window—probably that of a solitary-confinement cell. "Help! Save me! They're killing me! They're killing me!" Then the cries were choked in a warder's hands.

At the Butyrki "station" we were mixed up with raw recruits of the 1949 intake. They all had funny sentences—not the usual *tenners*, but *quarters*. When at each of the numerous roll calls they had to give dates of release, it sounded like a cruel joke: "October, 1974!" "February, 1975!"

No one, surely, could sit out such a sentence. A man must get hold of some pliers and cut the wire.

These twenty-five-year sentences were enough to transform the prisoners' world. The holders of power had bombarded us with all they had. Now it was the prisoners' turn to speak—to speak freely, uninhibitedly, undeterred by threats, the words we had never heard in our lives and which alone could enlighten and unite us.

We were sitting in a Stolypin car at the Kazan station when we heard from the station loudspeaker that war had broken out in Korea. After penetrating a firm South Korean defense line to a depth of ten kilometers on the very first day, the North Koreans insisted that they had been attacked. Any imbecile who had been at the front understood that the aggressors were those who had advanced on the first day.

This war in Korea excited us even more. In our rebellious mood we longed for the storm. The storm must break, it must, it must, or else we were doomed to a lingering death! . . .

Somewhere past Ryazan the red rays of the rising sun struck with such force through the moles-eye windows of the prison car that the young guard in the corridor near our grating screwed up his eyes. Our guards might have been worse; they had crammed us into compartments fifteen or so at a time, they fed us on herring, but, to be fair, they also brought us water and let us out morning and evening to relieve ourselves, so that we should have had no quarrel with them if this lad hadn't unthinkingly, not maliciously, tossed the words "enemies of the people" at us.

That started it! Our compartment and the next pitched into him.

"All right, we're enemies of the people—but why is there no grub on the kolkhoz?"

"You're a country boy yourself by the look of you, but I bet you'll sign on again—I bet you'd sooner be a dog on a chain than go back to the plow."

"If we're enemies of the people, why paint the prison vans different colors? Who are you hiding us from?"

"Listen, kid! I had two like you who never came back from the war—and you call *me* an enemy of the people?"

It was a very long time since words like this had flown

through the bars of our cages! We shouted only the plainest of facts, too self-evident to be refuted.

A sergeant serving extra time came to the aid of the flustered youngster, but instead of hauling anyone off to the cooler, or taking names, he tried to help his subordinate to fight back.

Here, too, we saw a faint hint that times were changing—no, this was 1950, too soon to speak of better times; what we saw were signs of the new relationship between prisoners and jailers created by the new long sentences and the new political camps.

Our argument began to take on the character of a genuine debate. The young men took a good look at us, and could no longer bring themselves to call us, or those in the next compartment, enemies of the people. They tried trotting out bits from newspapers and from their elementary politics course, but their ears told them before their minds could that these set phrases rang false.

"Look for yourselves, lads! Look out the window," was the answer they got from us. "Look what you've brought Russia down to!"

Beyond the windows stretched a beggarly land of rotted thatch and rickety huts and ragged folk (we were on the Ruzayev line, by which foreigners never travel). If the Golden Horde had seen it so befouled, they would not have bothered to conquer it.

On the quiet station at Torbeyevo an old man walked along the platform in bast shoes. An old peasant woman stopped opposite the lowered window of our car and stood rooted to the spot for a long time, staring through the outer and inner bars at us prisoners tightly packed together on the top bed shelf. She stared at us with that look on her face which our people have kept for "unfortunates" throughout the ages. A few tears trickled down her cheeks. She stood there, work-coarsened and shabby, and she looked at us as though a son of hers lay among us. "You mustn't look in there, mamma," the guard told her, but not roughly. She didn't even turn her head. At her side stood a little girl of ten with white ribbons in her plaits. She looked at us very seriously, with a sadness strange in one of her

years, her little eyes wide and unblinking. She looked at us so
hard that she must have imprinted us on her memory forever.
As the train eased forward, the old woman raised her blackened
fingers and devoutly, unhurriedly made the sign of the cross
over us.

Then at another station some girl in a spotted frock, anything but shy or timid, came right up to our window and started
boldly asking us what we were in for and for how long. "Get
away," bellowed the guard who was pacing the platform.
"Why, what will you do? I'm the same as them! Here's a pack of
cigarettes—give it to the lads," and she produced them from her
handbag. (We had already realized that the girl had done time.
So many of them, now roaming around free, had received their
training on the Archipelago!) The deputy guard commander
jumped out of the train. "Get away! I'll put you inside!" She
stared scornfully at the old sweat's ugly mug. "You go and ——
yourself, you ——!" "Give it to 'em, lads," she said to encourage us. And made a dignified departure.

So we rode on, and I don't think the guards felt that they
were protecting the people from its enemies. On we went, more
and more inflamed with the conviction that we were right, that
all Russia was with us, that the time was at hand to abolish this
institution.

ALEXANDER SOLZHENITSYN,
The Gulag Archipelago
(trans. Thomas P. Whitney)

ELSEWHERE

India

1. In the days of the Raj

For the British the railway stations of upcountry India were fulcrums of Anglo-Indian security, as those cable stations were oases in the Outback of Australia. Steam, piston grease, the stuffy smell of waiting-rooms, starched white dining-room napkins, smudgily printed time-tables, soldiers at junction platforms drinking tea out of saucers—all these were basic ingredients of Anglo-India, as organic to the Raj as hill-stations or protocol. The Indian railways stimulated the Englishman's imagination, and gave him a Roman pride. In Indian cities the grandest and most ornate of the public buildings were usually the railway stations and offices, hulking mock-oriental caravanserais, Saracenic, Moghul, all domes, clocks, whirligigs, stained-glass windows, immense glass-and-girder roofs, beneath which the railway lines lay like allegories of order in chaos. There the great trains steamed and hissed: the British engine-driver grandly at the cab of the mail-train locomotive; the British conductor with his check-board at the first-class carriage door; the British stationmaster at the end of the platform, dressed splendidly in dark blue, like an admiral at the quay; the British passengers stalking down the platform in a miasma of privilege, pursued by coveys of servants and porters with bags, children, bedding, and possibly a goat to be tethered in the guard's van, and provide fresh milk for the journey. All around was the theatrical confusion of India, which Empire had tamed: a frenzy of Indians, in dhotis, in saris, in swathed torn rags, in nosecups, ankle-bangles, turbans, baggy white shorts, scarlet uniforms, yellow priestly robes, topees, bush-jackets, loin-cloths; hawkers shouting in hollow voices and peering through train windows with blazing eyes; office messengers hurrying importantly by to post their letters in the mail-coach box; entire families sitting, sleeping, clambering about, feeding babies or apparently dead on piles of baggage, tied up with string; and sometimes a desperate beggar, a man with no face or legless boy darted terrifyingly out of nowhere to seize upon a likely straggler.

The British gentry travelled first-class, usually with a servant compartment next door—on the South India Railway a little window linked them, for milord to give his orders through. The Indian gentry travelled second-class; British other ranks, commercial men and mechanics went intermediate; and pushed, levered, squeezed, squashed into the slatted wooden seats of the fourth-class compartments, travelled the Indian millions. A journey across India took anything up to a week, and the wise sahib took his own padded quilts and pillow, his own tiffin-basket (which should always be kept furnished, *Murray's Handbook* advised, "with potted meats, biscuits, some good spirit, and soda water"), and a few good books (such as, Murray suggested, Sir W. Hunter's *Indian Empire*, or Sir Alfred Lyall's *Rise and Expansion of the British Dominion in India*). There were refreshment rooms at most junctions, but the experienced traveller telegraphed his requirements ahead, and as the train drew into Chanda or Gadag, out of the shadows would leap a man in white, carrying your luncheon on a tray, covered with a napkin —fiery curry, vivid chutney and onions, chupattis, to be washed down with a draught of Scotch from your tiffin-basket. So immediate was this service that it was as though the man had been awaiting you there all morning, holding his tray: but you had to eat fast, for before you left he would want the plates back, and as the train moved off again, with a creaking of its woodwork and a distant chuffing of its engine, you might see him bowing perfunctorily still as he retreated to the Vegetarian Food Stall for the washing-up.

The Indian railways provided all sorts of social services, ancillary to their grander functions. Murray is full of their usefulness. The stationmaster at Jungshahi would arrange your camel for you. There was a comfortable Waiting Room ('with *Baths*, etc.') at Neral. Travellers to Verawal might find it convenient

Morning shave on the Bengal Express, 1910

to get permission from the stationmaster to retain their first-class railway carriage at the station, and to sleep in it at night. For the Englishman in India the railways were a reassurance, a familiar constant in an often unpredictable world. With New-man's Indian Bradshaw on one's lap, a stalwart engine-driver of the Great Northern Railway up front, and the certainty of a tonga awaiting one at Kathgodam station, one could lean back in one's seat ("unusually deep," Murray says) in rare security. Someone, somewhere, it seemed, had got the hang of the place. To travellers in the remote Himalaya, one marvellous moment of a descent into the plains was the sight of a distant plumed railway train, steaming across the flatlands with a whisper of starched linen and chilled champagne. To the new arrival at Bombay, awaiting apprehensively the plunge into the Indian hinterland, nothing could be more comforting than the Punjab Mail, glistening and eager in the gloom of Victoria station, as British as the Crown itself, and sure to be on time.

JAN MORRIS,
Pax Britannica

2. The Grand Trunk Express

The lumbering express that bisects India, a 1400-mile slash from Delhi south to Madras, gets its name from the route. It might easily have derived it from the kind of luggage the porters were heaving on board. There were grand trunks all over the platform. I had never seen such heaps of belongings in my life, or so many laden people: they were like evacuees who had been given time to pack, lazily fleeing an ambiguous catastrophe. In the best of times there is nothing simple about an Indian board-ing a train, but these people climbing into the Grand Trunk Ex-press looked as if they were setting up house—they had the air, and the merchandise, of people moving in. Within minutes the compartments were colonized, the trunks were emptied, the hampers, food baskets, water bottles, bedrolls, and Gladstones put in place; and before the train started up its character changed, for while we were still standing at Delhi Station the men stripped off their baggy trousers and twill jackets and got into traditional South Indian dress: the sleeveless gym-class undershirt and the sarong they call a *lungi*. These were scored with packing creases. It was as if, at once—in expectation of the train whistle—they all dropped the disguise they had adopted for Delhi, the Madras-bound express allowing them to assume their true identity. The train was Tamil; and they had moved in so completely, I felt like a stranger among residents, which was odd, since I had arrived earlier than anyone else.

Tamils are black and bony; they have thick straight hair and their teeth are prominent and glisten from repeated scrubbings with peeled green twigs. Watch a Tamil going over his teeth with an eight-inch twig and you begin to wonder if he isn't trying to yank a branch out of his stomach. One of the attractions of the Grand Trunk Express is that its route takes in the forests of Madhya Pradesh, where the best toothbrush twigs are found; they are sold in bundles, bound like cheroots, at the stations in the province. Tamils are also modest. Before they change their clothes each makes a toga of his bedsheet, and, hopping up and down and working his elbows, he kicks his shoes and trousers off, all the while babbling in that rippling speech that resembles the sputtering of a man singing in the shower. Tamils seem to talk constantly—only tooth-brushing silences them. Pleasure for a Tamil is discussing a large matter (life, truth, beauty, "walues") over a large meal (very wet vegetables studded with chillies and capsicums, and served with damp *puris* and two mounds of glutinous rice). The Tamils were happy on the Grand Trunk Express: their language was spoken; their food was served; their belongings were dumped helter-skelter, giving the train the customary clutter of a Tamil home.

I started out with three Tamils in my compartment. After they changed, unstrapped their suitcases, unbuckled bedrolls, and had a meal (one gently scoffed at my spoon: "Food taken with hand tastes different from food taken with spoon—sort of metal taste") they spent an immense amount of time introducing themselves to each other. In bursts of Tamil speech were English words like "reposting," "casual leave," "annual audit." As soon as I joined the conversation they began, with what I thought was a high degree of tact and courage, to speak to one another in English. They were in agreement on one point: Delhi was barbarous.

"I am staying at Lodi Hotel. I am booked months ahead. Everyone in Trich tells me it is a good hotel. Hah! I cannot use telephone. You have used telephone?"

"I cannot use telephone at all."

"It is not Lodi Hotel," said the third Tamil. "It is Delhi."

"Yes, my friend, you are right," said the second.

"I say to receptionist, 'Kindly stop speaking to me in Hindi. Does no one speak English around this place? Speak to me in English if you please!' "

"It is really atrocious situation."

"Hindi, Hindi, Hindi. *Tcha!*"

I said I'd had similar experiences. They shook their heads and added more stories of distress. We sat like four fugitives from savagery, bemoaning the general ignorance of English, and it was one of the Tamils—not I—who pointed out that the Hindi-speaker would be lost in London.

I said, "Would he be lost in Madras?"

"English is widely spoken in Madras. We also use Tamil, but seldom Hindi. It is not our language."

"In the south everyone has matric." They had a knowing ease with abbreviations, "matric" for matriculation, "Trich" for the town of Tiruchirappalli.

The conductor put his head into the compartment. He was a harassed man with the badges and equipment of Indian authority, a gunmetal puncher, a vindictive pencil, a clipboard thick with damp passenger lists, a bronze conductor's pin, and a khaki pith helmet. He tapped my shoulder.

"Bring your case."

Earlier I had asked for the two-berth compartment I had paid for. He had said they were overbooked. I demanded a refund. He said I'd have to file an application at the place of issue. I accused him of inefficiency. He withdrew. Now he had found a coupé in the next carriage.

"Does this cost extra?" I asked, sliding my suitcase in. I didn't like the extortionate overtones of the word *baksheesh*.

"What you want," he said.

"Then it doesn't."

"I am not saying it does or doesn't. I am not asking."

I liked the approach. I said, "What should I do?"

"To give or not to give." He frowned at his passenger lists. "That is entirely your lookout."

I gave him five rupees.

*   *   *

To my relief, the whistle blew and we were on our way. The engineer read the Nagpur paper, I ate my Nagpur oranges and then had a siesta. I awoke to an odd sight, the first rain clouds I'd seen since leaving England. At dusk, near the border of the South Indian province of Andhra Pradesh, broad blue grey clouds, dark at the edges, hung on the horizon. We were headed for them in a landscape where it had recently rained: now the little stations were splashed with mud, brown puddles had collected at level crossings, and the earth was reddened by the late monsoon. But we were not under the clouds until we reached Chandrapur, a station so small and sooty it is not on the map. There, the rain fell in torrents, and signalmen skipped along the line waving their sodden flags. The people on the platform stood watching from under large black umbrellas that shone with wetness. Some hawkers rushed into the downpour to sell bananas to the train passengers.

A woman crawled into the rain from the shelter of the platform. She appeared to be injured: she was on all fours, moving slowly towards the train—towards me. Her spine, I saw was twisted with meningitis; she had rags tied to her knees and woodblocks in her hands. She toiled across the tracks with painful slowness, and when she was near the door she looked up. She had a lovely smile—a girl's beaming face on that broken body. She propped herself up and lifted her free hand at me, and waited, her face streaming with rain, her clothes soaked. While I was fishing in my pockets for money the train started up, and my futile gesture was to throw a handful of rupees on to the flooded line.

At the next station I was accosted by another beggar. This was a boy of about ten, wearing a clean shirt and shorts. He implored with his eyes and said rapidly, "Please, sir, give me money. My father and mother have been at station platform for two days. They are stranded. They have no food. My father has no job, my mother's clothes are torn. We must get to Delhi soon and if you give me one or two rupees we will be able."

"The train's going to leave. You'd better hop off."

He said, "Please, sir, give me money. My father and mother—"

He went on mechanically reciting. I urged him to get off the train, but it was clear that apart from his spiel he did not speak English. I walked away.

It had grown dark, the rain was letting up, and I sat reading the engineer's newspaper. The news was of conferences, an incredible number of gatherings in the very titles of which I heard the clack of voices, the rattle of mimeographed sheets, the squeak of folding chairs, and the eternal Indian prologue: "There is one question we all have to ask ourselves—" One Nagpur conference was spending a week discussing "Is the Future of Zoroastrianism in Peril?" On the same page two hundred Indians were reported attending a "Congress of Peace-Loving Countries," "Hinduism: Are We at a Crossroads?" occupied another group, and on the back page there was an advertisement for Raymond's Suitings (slogan: "You'll have something to say in Raymond's Suitings . . ."). The man wearing a Raymond suit was shown addressing a conference audience. He was squinting, making a beckoning gesture; he had something to say. His words were, "Communication is perception. Communication is expectations. Communication is involvement."

A beggar's skinny hand appeared at my compartment door, a bruised forearm, a ragged sleeve. Then the doomed cry, "*Sahib!*"

At Sirpur, just over the border of Andhra Pradesh, the train ground to a halt. Twenty minutes later we were still there. Sirpur is insignificant: the platform is uncovered, the station has two rooms, and there are cows on the verandah. Grass tufts grow out of the ledge of the booking-office window. It smelled of rain and wood smoke and cow dung; it was little more than a hut, dignified with the usual railway signs, of which the most hopeful was TRAINS RUNNING LATE ARE LIKELY TO MAKE UP TIME.

Beggars boarding a train on the Iran-Pakistan border
Photograph by Henri Cartier-Bresson

Passengers on the Grand Trunk Express began to get out. They promenaded, belching in little groups, grateful for the exercise.

"The engine has packed up," one man told me. "They are sending for new one. Delay of two hours."

Another man said, "If there was a cabinet minister on this train they would have an engine in ten minutes' time."

The Tamils were raving on the platform. A native of Sirpur wandered out of the darkness with a sack of roasted chickpeas. He was set upon by the Tamils, who bought all the chickpeas and demanded more. A mob of Tamils gathered at the station-master's window to howl at a man tapping out Morse code with a little key.

I decided to look for a beer, but just outside the station I was in darkness so complete I had second thoughts. The smell of rain on the vegetation gave a humid richness to the air that was almost sweet. There were cows lying on the road: they were white; I could see them clearly. Using the cows as road markers I walked along until I saw a small orange light about fifty yards away. I headed towards it and came to a little hut, a low poky shack with mud walls and a canvas roof. There was a kerosene lantern on the doorway and another inside lighting the surprised faces of a half a dozen tea-drinkers, two of whom recognized me from the train.

"What do you want?" one said. "I will ask for it."

"Can I buy a bottle of beer here?"

This was translated. There was laughter. I knew the answer.

"About two kilometres down the road"—the man pointed into the blackness—"there is a bar. You can get beer there."

"How will I find it?"

"A car," he said. He spoke again to the man serving tea. "But there is no car here. Have some tea."

We stood in the hut, drinking milky tea out of cracked glasses. A joss stick was lit. No one said a word. The train passengers looked at the villagers; the villagers averted their eyes. The canvas ceiling drooped; the tables were worn shiny; the joss stick filled the room with stinking perfume. The train passengers grew uncomfortable and, in their discomfort, took an exaggerated interest in the calendar, the faded colour prints of Shiva and Ganpati. The lanterns flickered in the dead silence as our shadows leaped on the walls.

The Indian who had translated my question said under his breath, "This is the real India!"

*   *   *

The south was unexpectedly cool and lush: the greenness of the countryside matched the green on the map, the sea-level colour of this area. Because it was still early, and because Indian villagers seem to think of railway tracks as the margin of their world, there were people crouched all along the line, shitting. At first I thought they were simply squatting comfortably to watch the train go by, then I noticed the bright yellow hanks under them. I saw one man; he portended a hundred more, all facing the train for the diversion it offered, unhurriedly fouling the track. They were shitting when the train pulled in; they were still at it when the train pulled out. One curious group—a man, a boy, and a pig—were in a row, each shitting in his own way. A dignified man with his *dhoti* drawn up squatted a little distance from the tracks. He watched the train go by and he looked as if he would be there for some time: he held a large black umbrella over his head and a newspaper on his knees. Indeed, he seemed the perfect symbol for what a man in Delhi had called "The Turd World."

I think the next ten miles were the most exciting I have ever travelled in a train. We were on the coast, moving fast along a spit of land, and on either side of the train—its whistle screaming, its chimney full of smoke—white sand had drifted into magnificent dunes; beyond these dunes were slices of green sea. Sand whipped up by the engine pattered against the carriages behind, and spray from the breakers, whose regular wash dramatized the chugging of the locomotive, was flung up to speckle the windows with crystal bubbles. It was all light and water and sand, flying about the train speeding towards the Rameswaram causeway in a high wind. The palms under the scudding clouds bowed and flashed like fans made of feathers, and here and there, up to their stupas in sand, were temples flying red flags on their crooked masts. The sand covered the track in places; it had drifted into temple doorways and wrecked the frail palm-frond huts. The wind was terrific, beating on the windows, carrying sand and spray and the whistle's *hooeeee*, and nearly toppling the dhows in full sail at the hump of the spangled horizon where Ceylon lay.

"Few minutes more," said the conductor. "I think you are sorry you took this train."

"No," I said. "But I was under the impression it went to Dhanushkodi—that's what my map says."

"Indo-Ceylon Express formerly went to Dhanushkodi."

"Why doesn't it go there now?"

"No Indo-Ceylon Express," he said. "And Dhanushkodi blew away."

He explained that in 1965 a cyclone—the area is plagued with them—derailed a train, drowning forty passengers and covering Dhanushkodi with sand. He showed me what remained, sand dunes at the tip of the peninsula and the fragments of black roofs. The town had disappeared so thoroughly that not even fishermen lived there any more.

"Rameswaram is more interesting," said the conductor. "Nice temple, holy places, and tombs of Cain and Abel."

I thought I had misheard him. I asked him to repeat the names. I had not misheard.

> PAUL THEROUX,
> *The Great Railway Bazaar*

Iran before the Ayahtollahs

The train pulled out of Tehran at one o'clock precisely. I was going to Tabriz, four hundred miles away, on the Russian border, to see the American consul. His name was Carleton Coon. I shared a compartment with an Iranian who wore a black coat and pepper-and-salt trousers. His hair was parted in the middle, and he had a thin mustache. He looked like a bank clerk.

We rattled through the Tehran suburbs, and the waiter brought lunch. First there was tomato soup with an egg in it, and then grilled chicken and rice. I had already eaten Persian rice and found it the best in the world, soft and dry and very sweet. We were out in the country now; on either side was flat, sandy desert, and in the distance a range of mountains capped with snow. It was a beautiful day with sun and blue sky and an amazing purity of light. Twice we stopped at tiny brick-built stations. The first was in the middle of nowhere, with no roads leading to or from it, and no reason at all for its existence. The second was equally small; but about three miles beyond it, across the sand, lay a walled village with a squat, gleaming mosque. Here quite a lot of people got out.

After lunch I slept—and woke to see my companion in the act of waxing his mustache. Our eyes met, and we both looked away, embarrassed. He went into the corridor to gossip with another Persian, a man who hadn't shaved for days, and whose teeth were mostly gold. Then he went down the corridor, and this other man poked his head round the door.

"Hullo," he said. "How are you?"

"Fine," I said. "And you?"

"Very well, thank you."

I could see he wanted to improve his English, so I asked him in and he came and sat down.

"Is this your first visit to Azerbaijan?"

"Yes."

"You are a businessman, yes? You are going on business?"

"No, I'm a writer."

"A writer? You are a writer?"

"Yes. What are you?"

"I teach. I am a teacher."

"What do you teach?"

"Persian literature. My wife is a teacher, too."

"Is she? What does she teach?"

"Gymnastics."

"This other gentleman," I said, indicating the empty seat. "You know him?"

"Yes."

"What does he do?"

"He is a railway official. He works for the railway."

"Ah."

He gave a little smile and said, "You are American, yes?"

"No," I said, "I'm British. But I'm writing a book about the Americans. That is why I'm going to Tabriz. To see the American consul."

His eyes lit up. "You are writing a book about the Americans? That is very interesting. They are a fine people, yes? I have a son and a daughter who are studying in the United States."

Now it was my turn to look surprised. "Have you?"

"Yes. My son is studying engineering and my daughter business."

"That must cost you a lot of money," I said.

"Yes, that is so. That is why my wife and I both work. So we can send our children away to have a good education. That is what my country needs, to send more and more people away to the United States. To learn things, to teach us what to do."

I was hoping to find out more about how he had managed to send his children to America, but suddenly he got up. "Please, sir," he said, "I am taking up your time. I will go." And he went.

At seven-thirty, when it was growing dark, the waiter announced dinner at the other end of the train. I made my way there through several wooden carriages where women in *chadors* were nursing babies, and soldiers sat gossiping or playing cards. It was a bright, modern dining car, already full. They gave us the same soup as at lunch and a delicious *chello-kebab*, and a pot of yoghurt, and masses more rice with about two ounces of butter laid on top. Opposite me was a family in which were two small girls in identical dresses, red with green spots. One looked quite normal, but the other had huge cheeks and great bushy eyebrows and an unusually dark skin. She shoveled her food into her mouth with both hands like a demented old woman. Next to me was a policeman with his cap on, and then the railway official came in wearing a green felt hat. Headgear in Persian dining cars seemed to be *à la mode*.

When I returned to the compartment, I found the door locked. The teacher was standing outside.

"The railway official," he said, "has locked the door. Against robbers, yes?" He took out his wallet and showed me photographs of his son and his daughter, an enchantingly pretty girl of twenty-one. I showed him photographs of my wife and children.

"Your wife is beautiful," he said.

"Yes," I said. "She used to be a ballet dancer."

He seemed surprised.

"Yes. She made a film called *The Red Shoes*. It was very famous. Did you see it?"

"No. I do not often see the films."

We chatted some more, and then the railway official came back and opened the door. But he didn't stay long. An inspector arrived and bundled him out. He was followed by a man in blue dungarees, who made up three beds. Then an army officer wearing dark glasses came in, and behind him a charming Iranian of about thirty, who said he had been four years at college in Denver, Colorado. "My friend and I," he said, "are traveling second class, but we have paid the difference in order to get a good night's rest."

He told me that he was an official in local government and was going to take up a post at a small town near Tabriz. I told him what I was doing, and he said, "A great many people in Iran don't know there are Americans here. Almost as many know there are some here but they don't meet them, and the fact makes no impact. A small number, students and Communists mostly, resent them. An even smaller number realize it is better to have them with you than to be alone. There have been times in our country when we were alone and it was no good. If we have to be on a side, it is better we should be on the American side than the other."

Before turning in, I went down the corridor to the washroom. On the way I passed the teacher and the railway official chatting together. The teacher said, "I am telling my friend here what you are telling me, that your wife is a belly dancer. Like me, he finds it interesting, yes?"

LUDOVIC KENNEDY,
Very Lovely People

An unusual death in Africa

Towards the end of my stay in British East Africa, I dined one
evening with Mr. Ryall, the Superintendent of the Police, in his
inspection carriage on the railway. Poor Ryall! I little thought
then what a terrible fate was to overtake him only a few months
later in that very carriage in which we dined.

A man-eating lion had taken up his quarters at a little roadside station called Kimaa, and had developed an extraordinary
taste for the members of the railway staff. He was a most daring
brute, quite indifferent as to whether he carried off the station-
master, the signalman, or the pointsman; and one night, in his
efforts to obtain a meal, he actually climbed up on to the roof
of the station buildings and tried to tear off the corrugated-iron
sheets. At this the terrified *baboo* in charge of the telegraph instrument below sent the following laconic message to the Traffic Manager: "Lion fighting with station. Send urgent succour."
Fortunately he was not victorious in his "fight with the station"; but he tried so hard to get in that he cut his feet badly on
the iron sheeting, leaving large blood-stains on the roof. Another night, however, he succeeded in carrying off the native
driver of the pumping-engine, and soon afterwards added several other victims to his list. On one occasion an engine-driver
arranged to sit up all night in a large iron water-tank in the
hope of getting a shot at him, and had a loop-hole cut in the side
of the tank from which to fire. But as so often happens, the
hunter became the hunted; the lion turned up in the middle of
the night, overthrew the tank and actually tried to drag the
driver out through the narrow circular hole in the top through
which he had squeezed in. Fortunately the tank was just too
deep for the brute to be able to reach the man at the bottom; but
the latter was naturally half paralysed with fear and had to
crouch so low down as to be unable to take anything like proper
aim. He fired, however, and succeeded in frightening the lion
away for the time being.

It was in a vain attempt to destroy this pest that poor Ryall
met his tragic and untimely end. On June 6, 1900, he was trav-

elling up in his inspection carriage from Makindu to Nairobi, accompanied by two friends, Mr. Huebner and Mr. Parenti. When they reached Kimaa, which is about two hundred and fifty miles from Mombasa, they were told that the man-eater had been seen close to the station only a short time before their train arrived, so they at once made up their minds to remain there for the night and endeavor to shoot him. Ryall's carriage was accordingly detached from the train and shunted into a siding close to the station, where, owing to the unfinished state of the line, it did not stand perfectly level, but had a pronounced

". . . and always there is the counterpoint between
life within the train and life without . . ."
Passengers on the Uganda Railway, 1903

list to one side. In the afternoon the three friends went out to look for the lion, but finding no traces of him whatever, they returned to the carriage for dinner. Afterwards they all sat up on guard for some time; but the only noticeable thing they saw was what they took to be two very bright and steady glow-worms. After events proved that these could have been nothing else than the eyes of the man-eater steadily watching them all the time and studying their every movement. The hour now growing late, and there being apparently no sign of the lion, Ryall persuaded his two friends to lie down, while he kept the first watch. Huebner occupied the high berth over the table on the one side of the carriage, the only other berth being on the opposite side of the compartment and lower down. This Ryall offered to Parenti, who declined it, saying that he would be quite comfortable on the floor; and he accordingly lay down to sleep, with his feet towards the sliding door which gave admission to the carriage.

It is supposed that Ryall, after watching for some considerable time, must have come to the conclusion that the lion was not going to make its appearance that night, for he lay down on the lower berth and dozed off. No sooner had he done so, doubtless, than the cunning man-eater began cautiously to stalk the three sleepers. In order to reach the little platform at the end of the carriage, he had to mount two very high steps from the railway line, but these he managed to negotiate successfully and in silence. The door from this platform into the carriage was a sliding one on wheels, which ran very easily on a brass runner; and as it was probably not quite shut, or at any rate not secured in any way, it was an easy matter for the lion to thrust in a paw and shove it open. But owing to the tilt of the carriage and to his great extra weight on the one side, the door slid to and snapped into the lock the moment he got his body right in, thus leaving him shut up with the three sleeping men in the compartment.

He sprang at once at Ryall, but in order to reach him had actually to plant his feet on Parenti, who, it will be remembered, was sleeping on the floor. At this moment Huebner was suddenly awakened by a loud cry, and on looking down from his berth was horrified to see an enormous lion with his hind feet on Parenti's body, while his forepaws rested on poor Ryall. Small wonder that he was panic-stricken at the sight. There was only one possible way of escape, and that was through the second sliding door communicating with the servants' quarters, which was opposite to that by which the lion had entered. But in order to reach this door Huebner had literally to jump on to the man-eater's back, for its great bulk filled up all the space beneath his berth. It sounds scarcely credible, but it appears that in the excitement and horror of the moment he actually did this, and fortunately the lion was too busily engaged with his victim to pay any attention to him. So he managed to reach the door in safety; but there, to his dismay, he found that it was held fast on the other side by the terrified coolies, who had been aroused by the disturbance caused by the lion's entrance. In utter desperation he made frantic efforts to open it, and exerting all his strength at last managed to pull it back sufficiently far to allow him to squeeze through, when the trembling coolies instantly tied it up again with their turbans. A moment afterwards a great crash was heard, and the whole carriage lurched violently to one side; the lion had broken through one of the windows, carrying off poor Ryall with him. Being now released, Parenti lost no time in jumping through the window on the opposite side of the carriage, and fled for refuge to one of the station buildings; his escape was little short of miraculous, as the lion had been actually standing on him as he lay on the floor. The carriage itself was badly shattered, and the woodwork of the window had been broken to pieces by the passage of the lion as he sprang through with his victim in his mouth.

All that can be hoped is that poor Ryall's death was instantaneous. His remains were found next morning about a quarter of a mile away in the bush, and were taken to Nairobi for burial. I am glad to be able to add that very shortly afterwards the terrible brute who was responsible for this awful tragedy was caught in an ingenious trap constructed by one of the railway staff. He was kept on view for several days, and then shot.

J. H. PATTERSON,
Man-Eaters of Tsavo

Australia

1. Across the Outback

My health had broken down in New York in May; it had remained in a doubtful but fairish condition during a succeeding period of 82 days; it broke again on the Pacific. It broke again in Sydney, but not until after I had had a good outing, and had also filled my lecture engagements. This latest break lost me the chance of seeing Queensland. In the circumstances, to go north toward hotter weather was not advisable.

So we moved south with a westward slant, 17 hours by rail to the capital of the colony of Victoria, Melbourne—that juvenile city of sixty years, and half a million inhabitants. On the map the distance looked small; but that is a trouble with all divisions of distance in such a vast country as Australia. The colony of Victoria itself looks small on the map—looks like a county, in fact—yet it is about as large as England, Scotland, and Wales combined. Or, to get another focus upon it, it is just 80 times as large as the State of Rhode Island, and one-third as large as the State of Texas.

Outside of Melbourne, Victoria seems to be owned by a handful of squatters, each with a Rhode Island for a sheep farm. That is the impression which one gathers from common talk, yet the wool industry of Victoria is by no means so great as that of New South Wales. The climate of Victoria is favorable to other great industries—among other, wheat-growing and the making of wine.

We took the train at Sydney at about four in the afternoon. It was American in one way, for we had a most rational sleeping car; also the car was clean and fine and new—nothing about it to suggest the rolling stock of the continent of Europe. But our baggage was weighed, and extra weight charged for. That was continental. Continental and troublesome. Any detail of railroading that is not troublesome cannot honorably be described as continental.

The tickets were round-trip ones—to Melbourne, and clear to Adelaide in South Australia, and then all the way back to Sydney. Twelve hundred more miles than we really expected to make; but then as the round trip wouldn't cost much more than the single trip, it seemed well enough to buy as many miles as one could afford, even if one was not likely to need them. A human being has a natural desire to have more of a good thing than he needs.

Now comes a singular thing: the oddest thing, the strangest thing, the most baffling and unaccountable marvel that Australasia can show. At the frontier between New South Wales and Victoria our multitude of passengers were routed out of their snug beds by lantern-light in the morning in the biting cold of a high altitude to change cars on a road that has no break in it from Sydney to Melbourne! Think of the paralysis of intellect that gave that idea birth; imagine the bowlder it emerged from on some petrified legislator's shoulders.

It is a narrow-gauge road to the frontier, and a broader gauge thence to Melbourne. The two governments were the builders of the road and are the owners of it. One or two reasons are given for this curious state of things. One is, that it represents the jealousy existing between the colonies—the two most important colonies of Australasia. What the other one is, I have forgotten. But it is of no consequence. It could be but another effort to explain the inexplicable.

All passengers fret at the double-gauge; all shippers of freight must of course fret at it; unnecessary expense, delay, and annoyance are imposed upon everybody concerned, and no one is benefited.

Each Australian colony fences itself off from its neighbor with a custom-house. Personally, I have no objection, but it must be a good deal of inconvenience to the people. We have something resembling it here and there in America, but it goes by another name. The large empire of the Pacific coast requires a world of iron machinery, and could manufacture it economically on the spot if the imposts on foreign iron were removed. But they are not. Protection to Pennsylvania and Alabama forbids it. The result to the Pacific coast is the same as if there were several rows of custom-fences between the coast and the East. Iron carted across the American continent at luxurious railway rates would be valuable enough to be coined when it arrived.

We changed cars. This was at Albury. And it was there, I think, that the growing day and the early sun exposed the distant range called the Blue Mountains. Accurately named. "My word!" as the Australians say, but it was a stunning color, that blue. Deep, strong, rich, exquisite; towering and majestic masses of blue—a softly luminous blue, a smouldering blue, as if vaguely lit by fires within. It extinguished the blue of the sky— made it pallid and unwholesome, whitey and washed-out. A wonderful color—just divine.

A resident told me that those were not mountains; he said they were rabbit-piles. And explained that long exposure and the over-ripe condition of the rabbits was what made them look so blue. This man may have been right, but much reading of books of travel has made me distrustful of gratis information furnished by unofficial residents of a country. The facts which such people give to travelers are usually erroneous, and often intemperately so. The rabbit-plague has indeed been very bad in Australia, and it could account for one mountain, but not for a mountain range, it seems to me. It is too large an order.

We breakfasted at the station. A good breakfast, except the coffee; and cheap. The government establishes the prices and placards them. The waiters were men, I think; but that is not usual in Australasia. The usual thing is to have girls. No, not girls, young ladies—generally duchesses. Dress? They would attract attention at any royal levée in Europe. Even empresses and queens do not dress as they do. Not that they could not afford it, perhaps, but they would not know how.

All the pleasant morning we slid smoothly along over the plains, through thin—not thick—forests of great melancholy gum trees, with trunks rugged with curled sheets of flaking bark—erysipelas convalescents, so to speak, shedding their dead skins. And all along were tiny cabins, built sometimes of wood, sometimes of gray-blue corrugated iron; and the doorsteps and fences were clogged with children—rugged little simply-clad chaps that looked as if they had been imported from the banks of the Mississippi without breaking bulk.

Notice to passengers at a halt in the Australian interior:
"To stop express, wave the tin flag. At night,
light candle in lantern."

And there were little villages, with neat stations well plac-
arded with showy advertisements—mainly of almost *too* self-
righteous brands of "sheep-dip," if that is the name—and I think
it is. It is a stuff like tar, and is dabbed on to places where the
shearer clips a piece out of the sheep. It bars out the flies, and
has healing properties, and a nip to it which makes the sheep
skip like the cattle on a thousand hills. It is not good to eat. That
is, it is not good to eat except when mixed with railroad coffee.
It improves railroad coffee. Without it railroad coffee is too
vague. But with it, it is quite assertive and enthusiastic. By itself,
railroad coffee is too passive; but sheep-dip makes it wake up
and get down to business. I wonder where they get railroad
coffee?

We saw birds, but not a kangaroo, not an emu, not an orni-
thorhyncus, not a lecturer, not a native. Indeed, the land seemed
quite destitute of game. But I have misused the word native. In
Australia it is applied to Australian-born whites only. I should
have said that we saw no Aboriginals—no "blackfellows." And
to this day I have never seen one. In the great museums you will
find all the other curiosities, but in the curio of chiefest interest
to the stranger all of them are lacking. We have at home an
abundance of museums, and not an American Indian in them.
It is clearly an absurdity, but it never struck me before.

MARK TWAIN,
Following the Equator (1897)

2. The Ghan Express

From Quorn I caught the Ghan to Alice Springs, the oasis
town in the centre of the continent. The Ghan was a train which
ran once a week, and at the Alice the railroad ended. The name
commemorated the outmoded camel trains which had been run
by Afghans. The moment you stepped aboard the Ghan you
entered a new world, where inhibitions dropped to zero and
mateship soared. It became the only world for you where you
were safe from the arid wastes and burning ridges outside. My
carriage was one of those long ones with seats down the sides. At

least, there were seats until some of my fellow-passengers tore them up to make room to dance in, to the music of the bagpipes which one of them played. The only lady in the carriage was the bundled-up *lubra* of a black-tracker employed by the police, and she had a moustache. So the passengers, who were tough-looking miners and stockmen, chose partners among themselves, assumed the embrace of the ballroom, and went jigging and yelping and hoo-roo-ing up and down the aisle as the train bounded and rattled and bored its way into the empty night, and the bagpipes wailed and shrieked. I huddled in a corner, pretending not to notice. The journey was to take three days and two nights. Presently one of the cattlemen, as tall as Chips Rafferty, but aggressive and red-haired, loomed over me and demanded my name. "Thomas," I said. "Good-oh," he said, "mine's Bluey. Your hair's too long—what are you, a musician or something?" I confessed that I had been a singer, so he turned to the others and shouted, "Shut up, all youse, Tom's going to sing us a song." I cleared my throat and delivered a verse and chorus of "Stick to me, Bill." Bluey called the meeting to order and announced, "Now listen, Tom 'ere's my mate. Anybody wants to sling off at his hair gotta do it to me, see?" There was a murmur of agreement and dancing was resumed. "Where's your swag, Tom?" asked my self-elected protector. The bushman travels with his possessions rolled in a blanket. I had to confess that I had no blanket. Bluey leaned down closer, which was alarming. He was unsteady on his feet, not only because of the lurching of the train, but because he had drunk a lot of methylated spirits and he had the breath to prove it. "Leave it to me, cobber," he whispered hoarsely. "You gotta bash the old spine in comfort. I'll scrounge you a blanket and we'll snore off on the floor. Right?" I said "Right," and Bluey rolled away, shoving through the dancing couples, past the happy bagpiper, out of the carriage. Soon he was back with a blanket for me and we all lay down on the floor and slept. Like most of the fellows, Bluey had no money and was cheerfully making the journey on spec, hoping to get a job somewhere in the Northern Territory. He was too proud to let me buy him meals in the dining-car, so I smuggled food out under my shirt.

At one of the lengthy stops, the engineer invited me to drive
the train for an hour or two through the roadless, fenceless land.
I got up there amongst the roaring steam, the fire-eating furnace, the rattle and roll. No houses or tall trees, a world of sparse
mulga scrub; once a dead horse by the line, a couple of emus
racing away from us, a tall, brown kangaroo bounding alongside, a lonely prospector's grave. All the way empty beer bottles
sparkled in the sun, cast there by passing travellers. The fireman
had a wonderful theory that they may affect the chemical com-
position of the soil, and in turn the vegetation grown in it, the
animals which feed upon it, and in due course the local humans.
We snorted and swayed over the dry, pebbly bed of a river with
white ghost gums on its banks, at a full thirty miles an hour.
There are only two seasons here—the Dry and the Wet. When
the rains come, sudden and heavy, the dry river beds change
into raging torrents and men crossing them are sometimes swept
to their death. The Overland Telegraph, 2,230 miles from south
coast to north coast, paced beside the railway track. Some of the
poles had to be carried 350 miles and were then gnawed away
by insects, and aborigines stole the insulators to make spear tips.
Men gave their lives to put those wires across the continent.

Some time after midnight, unless the train is on schedule,
the steep red sides of Heavitree Gap tower above the track, and
on a plateau 2,000 feet above the sea you reach the terminus,
Alice Springs, population 3,000. I said good-bye to Bluey and
the piper and checked in at one of the two pubs. I had a job to
do; they would camp under the stars till they found one. I had
an itinerary to follow, their only obligation was to their appe-
tites.

WILFRID THOMAS,
Living on Air

OUT OF THE WINDOW

In the middle of countries, far from hills and sea,
Are the little places one passes by in trains
And never stops at; where the skies extend
Uninterrupted, and the level plains
Stretch green and yellow and green without an end.
And behind the glass of their Grand Express
Folk yawn away a province through,
With nothing to think of, nothing to do,
Nothing even to look at—never a "view"
In this damned wilderness.
But I look out of the window and find
Much to satisfy the mind.
Mark how the furrows, formed and wheeled
In a motion orderly and staid,
Sweep, as we pass, across the field
Like a drilled army on parade.
And here's a market-garden, barred
With stripe on stripe of varied greens . . .
Bright potatoes, flower starred,
And the opacous colour of beans.
Each line deliberately swings
Towards me, till I see a straight
Green avenue to the heart of things,
The glimpse of a sudden opened gate
Piercing the adverse walls of fate . . .
A moment only, and then, fast, fast,
The gate swings to, the avenue closes;
Fate laughs, and once more interposes
Its barriers.
                    The train has passed.

ALDOUS HUXLEY

A Chinese train

Two days later, at seven o'clock in the morning, we left Hankow by train for Cheng-chow.

Our servant Chiang accompanied us to the station. Already before dawn he had arrived at the Consulate to report for his first day of duty—a demure and dignified figure, in his patent leather shoes, black silk robe, spotless linen and European felt hat. His grandeur tacitly reproved our shabbiness—Auden's out-at-elbow sportscoat, my dirty, baggy flannels. We were unworthy of our employee. He was altogether a gentleman's gentleman.

At the ticket-barrier, Chiang began to exhibit his powers. Herding the coolies with our baggage ahead of him he flourished our Government passes (stamped with the Generalissimo's own chop) beneath the awed nose of the sentry. We should have lost face, no doubt, had we deigned to present them ourselves. Then, when everything was arranged, Chiang stepped aside, with a smiling bow, to let us pass. This, his unctuous gesture seemed to say, is how Big Shots board a train.

No sooner had we settled into our compartment, than Chiang bustled off, to carry on the process of face-making among the car-boys. "My masters," he undoubtedly told them, "are very important personages. They are the friends of the Generalissimo and the King of England. We are travelling to the front on a special mission. You had better look after us well, or there might be trouble." The car-boys, no doubt, knew just how much of this to believe; but their curiosity was aroused, nevertheless, and they all came to peep and smile at us through the corridor window. We may have undone Chiang's work a little by winking and waving back. But perhaps we were not unimposing figures, with our superbly developed chests—padded out several inches by thick wads of Hankow dollar-bills stuffed into every available inner pocket. This seemed a dangerous way to carry money, but traveller's cheques would have been useless in many of the places to which we were going.

The Manchurian frontier, 1911. Porters, clearly marked,
transfer baggage that includes umbrellas, canes, and golf clubs
between the Russian-owned Chinese Eastern Railway and the
American-equipped by Japanese-owned South Manchurian Railway.

This train was in every way superior to those running on the Canton–Hankow line. In peace-time it would have taken you through to Peking. Nowadays it went no further than Cheng-chow: the railway bridge over the Yellow River had been blown up to check the Japanese advance. There was a handsome dining-car, with potted plants on the tables, in which we spent most of the day. This dining-car had only one serious disadvantage: there were not enough spittoons. Two of the available five were placed just behind our respective chairs, and the passengers made use of them unceasingly, clearing their throats before doing so with most unappetizing relish. In China, it seems, children learn to spit when they are two years old, and the habit is never lost. True, the New Life Movement discourages it, but without any visible effect. Even high government officials of our acquaintance hawked and spat without the least restraint.

Our journey was quite uneventful, despite the usual prophecies of air-attack. The train ran steadily on through the golden-yellow landscape. The snow had all disappeared, and the sun was hot; but it was still winter here, the trees were leafless and the earth bare and dry. All around us spread the undulating, densely inhabited plain. At a single glance from the carriage-window, one could seldom see less than two hundred people dotted over the paddy-fields, fishing with nets in village ponds, or squatting, on bare haunches, to manure the earth. Their gestures and attitudes had a timeless anonymity; each single figure would have made an admirable "condition humaine" shot for a Russian peasant-film. What an anonymous country this is! Everywhere the labouring men and women, in their clothes of deep, brilliant blue; everywhere the little grave-mounds, usurping valuable square feet of the arable soil—a class-struggle between the living and the dead. The naked, lemon-coloured torsos, bent over their unending tasks, have no individuality; they seem folded and reticent as plants. The children are all alike—gaping, bleary-nosed, in their padded jackets, like stuffed mass-produced dolls. Today, for the first time, we saw women rolling along, balanced insecurely as stilt-walkers on their tiny bound feet.

We arrived in Cheng-chow after midnight, two hours behind time. The moon shone brilliantly down on the ruined station, smashed in a big air-raid several weeks before. Outside, in the station-square, moonlight heightened the drama of the shattered buildings; this might have been Ypres in 1915. An aerial torpedo had hit the Hotel of Flowery Peace; nothing remained standing but some broken splinters of the outer walls, within which people were searching the débris by the light of lanterns. All along the roadway street-vendors were selling food, under the flicker of acetylene flares. Chiang told us that Cheng-chow now did most of its business by night. In the daytime the population withdrew into the suburbs, for fear of the planes.

A few yards down the main street from the square we found an hotel with an intact roof and an available bedroom. The proprietor warned us that we should be expected to leave it at 8 A.M.; during the daytime all the hotels were closed. Chiang bustled about, giving orders to everybody, admirably officious to secure our comfort. The beds were unpacked and erected, tea was brought; with his own hands he steadied the table by placing a piece of folded toilet-paper under one of the legs. Where would he sleep himself, we asked. "Oh, it doesn't matter," Chiang replied, modestly smiling. "I shall find a place." He seemed positively to be enjoying this adventure. We both agreed that we had got a treasure.

I slept very badly that night, dozing only in five-minute snatches until dawn. From the station-sidings came the mournful wail of locomotives, mingling with cries of the nocturnal street-hawkers and the constant shuffling and chatter of people moving about downstairs. Through a window beside my bed I could see the ragged bomb-hole in the roof of the next-door house, and the snapped beam ends poking up forlornly into the clear moonlight. Why should the people of this town assume that the Japs would only attack during the daytime? Tonight, for example, would be ideal. . . . And I remembered how Stephen Spender had told me of a very similar experience he had had during a visit to wartime Spain. Meanwhile, in the opposite bed, Auden slept deeply, with the long, calm snore of the truly strong.

W. H. Auden and
Christopher Isherwood,
Journey to a War

WAR

Hitler's train

L ate on the evening of September 3, 1939, Hitler exchanged
the elegant marbled halls of the Chancellery for the special
train, *Amerika*, parked in a dusty Pomeranian railroad station
surrounded by parched and scented pine trees and wooden barrack huts baked dry by the central European sun.

Never before had Germany's railroads conveyed a train like
this—a cumbersome assemblage of twelve or fifteen coaches
hauled by two locomotives immediately followed by armored
wagons bristling with 20-millimeter antiaircraft guns; a similar
flak wagon brought up the rear. Hitler's personal coach came
first: a drawing room about the size of three regular compartments, a sleeping berth, and a bathroom. In the drawing room,
there was an oblong table with eight chairs grouped around it.
The four remaining compartments in Hitler's coach were occupied by his adjutants and manservants. Other coaches housed
dining accommodations and quarters for his military escort,
private detectives, medical staff, press section, and visiting
guests. Joachim von Ribbentrop, Hans Lammers, and Heinrich
Himmler followed in a second train code-named *Heinrich*.
Göring's private—and considerably more comfortably furnished
—train, *Asia*, remained with him at Luftwaffe headquarters
near Potsdam.

The nerve center of Hitler's train was the "command coach"
attached to his own quarters. One half was taken up by a long
conference room dominated by a map table, and the other half
by Hitler's communications center, which was in constant touch
by teleprinter and radio-telephone with the OKW and other
ministries in Berlin, as well as with military headquarters on
the front. Hitler was to spend most of his waking hours in this

hot, confined space for the next two weeks, while Colonel Rudolf
Schmundt, Hitler's chief adjutant, valiantly kept the stream of
importunate visitors to a minimum. Here General Wilhelm
Keitel introduced to the Führer for the first time his chief of
operations, Major General Alfred Jodl, a placid, bald-headed
Bavarian mountain-warfare officer a year younger than Hitler,
whose principal strategic adviser he was to be until the last days
of the war. (Jodl was to be called upon by the Americans in the
postwar period for his advice on the defense of western Europe,
then hanged as a war criminal at Nuremberg.) Jodl took one of
the chairs in the middle of the long map-table, while Keitel

Trains played a vital part in Hitler's war. Here the
Führer receives Admiral Horthy, Regent of Hungary (*left*),
at his headquarters, where Horthy was detained while
six divisions marched into Hungary.

regularly sat at one end and Colonel Nikolaus von Vormann, the army's liaison officer, sat next to the three telephones at the other.

In the train, as at the Chancellery, the brown Nazi party uniform dominated the scene. Generally speaking, Hitler's adjutants were the only others who found room there. Even Rommel, the new commandant of the Führer's headquarters, could not live in this train. Hitler hardly intervened in the conduct of the Polish campaign anyway. He would appear in the command coach at 9 A.M. to hear Jodl's personal report on the morning situation and to inspect the maps that had been flown in from Berlin. His first inquiry of Colonel von Vormann was always about the dangerous western front situation, for of 30 German divisions left to hold the three-hundred-mile line, only 12 were up to scratch; and against them France might at any time unleash her army of 110 divisions. But contrary to every prediction voiced by Hitler's critics, the western front was curiously quiet. On September 4, an awed Colonel von Vormann wrote: "Meanwhile, a propaganda war has broken out in the west. Will the Führer prove right after all? They say that the French have hung out a banner at Saarbrücken reading *We won't fire the first shot*. As we've strictly forbidden our troops to open hostilities, I can't wait to see what happens now."

*   *   *

His heavy special train, *Amerika*, had left for Upper Silesia on the ninth. It finally halted in a railway siding at Illnau. The pleasing draft in the corridors ceased, and the temperature within the camouflage-gray walls and roofs rose. The air outside was thick with the hot dust-particles of mid-September. His secretary Christa Schroeder wrote plaintively:

We have been living in this train for ten days now. Its location is constantly being changed, but since we never get out the monotony is dreadful. The heat here is unbearable, quite terrible. All day long the sun beats down on the compartments, and we just wilt in the tropical heat. I am soaked to the skin, absolutely awful. To top it all, there is hardly anything worthwhile to do. The Chief drives off in the morning leaving us condemned to wait for his return. We never stay long

enough in one place. Recently we were parked one night near a field
hospital through which a big shipment of casualties was just passing.
. . . Those who tour Poland with the Chief see a lot, but it's not easy
for them because the enemy are such cowards—shooting in the back
and ambushing—and because it is difficult to protect the Chief, who
has taken to driving around as though he were in Germany, standing
up in his open car even in the most hazardous areas. I think he is
being reckless, but nobody can persuade him not to do it. On the very
first day he drove through a copse still swarming with Polacks—just
half an hour earlier they had wiped out an unarmed German medical
unit. One of the medics escaped and gave him an eyewitness account.
. . . Once again, the Führer was standing in full view of everybody
on a hummock, with soldiers streaming toward him from all sides. In
a hollow there was this Polish artillery; obviously they saw the sudden flurry of activity and—since it's no secret that the F. is touring
the front—they guessed who it was. Half an hour later the bombs
came raining down. Obviously it gives the soldiers' morale a colossal
boost to see the F. in the thick of the danger with them, but I still
think it's too risky. We can only trust in God to protect him.

DAVID IRVING,
Hitler's War

A London evacuee

We said goodbye at home, after a breakfast I had barely
touched, and then again in the school playground before the
lines were formed. I saw her once more, standing with other
mothers on the corner of Devas Street as I passed, stiff in my
new clothes, stiff card in my lapel, gasmask clumsy against my
body, and the hard handle of the suitcase burning my fingers.
She waved, and smiled. I smiled back, equally forlorn, and then
the curved wooden wall of the goods-yard hid her, and I turned
to face the station.

I was two months short of my fourteenth birthday, and I had
had one holiday in my life: a day at Southend. The country to
me was the scuffed grass of Blackheath, the tin urinals of its
Fair-Day; or Victoria Park with old men careful over model
boats, and grit in sulphur-tasting drinking-mugs chained to the
foot of a broken-nosed cherub. My father was dead two years,

and there were three other children. Only the rich went to
Bognor.

So, as the train left Bromley South Station, I had started my
longest journey, far longer than that never-forgotten day-excur-
sion to cockle-and-eel land. And I was scared and appalled at my
loneliness, sitting there in a carriage full of children and comics
and the smell of oranges. I watched the shuttling slums with a
sudden desperate love, staying longest at open windows: a hand
shaking a duster, a canary in a cage, a shirt-sleeved man reading
a newspaper. These were my people, my sights and my sounds.
I loved every scruffy plane tree, every blatant cinema, every
hoarding shouting *News of the World* and *Lifebuoy Soap*.

London children about to be evacuated to the country.
A familiar sight on main line platforms at
the beginning of the war.

We were bound for the West Country, but I felt no sense of adventure. The suburbs came and went with their prissy superiority, their sharp hedges and clean paint. The real country took over from tamed copses and golf-courses, sports-clubs and allotments; and it came with the late afternoon, sending its woods and farmlands out to meet us, darker out of darkness, an animality made manifest in cows, bulls and horses, no longer storybook and domestic, but free and strangely savage.

We arrived at early evening, standing on the platform, tired under the first stars, breathing a different air. Always the memory of that smell: of grass and animals and manure and apples and hay—a cloying, heady scent to a city-child: the breath of a Pagan God. And, although I did not know it then, it was the presence of this God which was to awake in me a nature stifled by concrete and stone and asphalt, which before had stirred only spasmodically at a freshet of leaves in a backyard, the whirr of a racing-pigeon. A bronzed, loose-limbed, freedom-loving God, who was soon to do battle with One who spoke of original sin and eventual judgement, and who pointed not to the flourishing virile oak, but to a different kind of tree.

B. S. JOHNSON,
The Evacuees

The Final Solution

The day was clear; a cold, early February sun hung weakly in the sky. I glanced at the long lines of people. Among us were many different nationalities, but we were all Jews, and all shared the same suffering. Spring was coming, and like some strange flock of birds we were proceeding to another stopping place. Our flight had been long, continuous, terrible. Out we went through the main gate. We trudged under the sign surmounting the wire fencing: Bergen-Belsen. I had come in, puzzled about what possible new evil those words could represent

and now I was leaving, sickened with the knowledge. Death itself meant little at Bergen-Belsen—it was the suffering that
went before that made it so awful. *Krepierenslager*. That was
the proper word.

We stood silently outside the gates, waiting for the full transport to be formed. It was late in the morning before we finally
started marching away from Bergen-Belsen. I was marching
with shadows, not people. Two thousand of us, shambling a few
miles to the railway siding. The SS men hit us incessantly with
clubs and whips. From time to time they would separate a particularly weak person and beat her senseless and leave the body
in the snow, as an example to those following. "Fast! Fast!" they
shouted constantly. There was one Kapo who took it upon himself to manhandle our group. He was tall and wore a white
turtle-necked sweater which he kept adjusting upon himself. He
had carved a short, heavy stick with a bulbous end, which he
swung viciously about, striking girls in the back. One blow was
enough to drop a person. If a girl lay on the ground more than a
few seconds, he kicked her and walked on.

There were almost as many men as women marching with
this transport. I was struck by the similarity between them and
us. We all looked alike. The men were as thin, as weak as we
were, and not one of them raised a hand to protest the beatings.
They slogged along, heads bent low, as if dragging great weights
behind them. I found myself thinking about my benefactor and
wondering if he had been reduced to the state of these men. Did
he still live?

There was something new waiting for us at the railway siding: most of the trucks were high-walled and open, without
roofs. Luckily, I was shoved into one of the few closed freight
trucks, with about seventy other people. Most of the men were
put into the open trucks. It was close and incredibly filthy in our
truck, but at least the rain and snow would not come down on
us. When the doors were slammed shut, a wave of panic swept
over the prisoners, and a high wailing and shrieking started. In
the semi-darkness we were terrified by our own numbers. Some
people went berserk and bit each other in a rage. I pressed myself against a wall, and listened in horror as the sounds of their

tussling filled the car. They writhed and screamed and even growled, for many minutes. And then, slowly, the madness subsided and all was quiet. I felt the tension lessen; we relaxed and waited.

I tried to think where we might be going . . . another ammunition factory, Stefa had said. It was not to be Hassag-Pelcery, that was certain. I supposed it must be some place in Germany, but where? I did not know where the central industrial area of Germany was. I hoped it was closer to the advancing armies, if indeed they were advancing. The Germans did not seem to be aware of any difficulties. They beat us as savagely as ever, and they were as cruel and harsh as ever. If the Germans were truly in danger of defeat, it seemed to me that they would try to treat their prisoners as well as possible, so that they might not be punished for cruelty. At last the train got under way, and I fell asleep.

This transport was conducted in the same way as the one into Bergen-Belsen. The train stopped about three times that day. Storm troopers banged on the doors, and demanded to know how many dead there were. Then they jumped in and threw out the bodies. Once I got a look at the tracks. The right-of-way was littered with corpses. On the second morning, without warning, the Germans suddenly began firing into the car with machine guns. The wood splintered and ripped as shells exploded and ricocheted, and the car was filled with the cries of the wounded. A piece of wood struck my cheek and stunned me for a few minutes. After the attack we could hear the Germans laughing. A few seconds later, as they moved on, we heard them fire into the adjoining car.

In the afternoon of that second day, the train was stopped again, and the guards came in and gave us some food. After all, they said, we were workers! One small loaf of hard black bread was divided among ten of us. And some oily liquid from raw fish was given out. People gulped down the horrid stuff without tasting it, and then they were nauseated by the salt water and entrails. I did not have any. I ate the thin piece of bread given to me, which only served to make me more hungry and aware of the starvation-shrunken faces about me. The poor people who

The final solution. Jewish prisoners being taken to
a concentration camp.

had eaten the fish oil were sick through the night; the sounds of their retching and gagging continued for hours.

We spent five days travelling in the railway truck. The last night we stopped at another rail siding. I could hear people tramping about outside. Suddenly, I felt the car shake as explosions rumbled and crashed in the distance. I could make no sense of these sounds for a long time, and then I thought they must be bombs. Bombs! From Allied planes. What if they bombed this train—how could they know it was filled with people? The explosions seemed to come nearer. One bomb falling quickly on this truck: we would all go, Nazis and prisoners alike, all the miserable people in the world. Chanka awoke and we hugged each other.

"What is it? Are the Germans killing us?"

"It's a bomber, I think. It must be the British. The enem—I mean the British—are coming, I'm sure." To call the Allies the enemy! I was ashamed of my words, but after so many years as a German prisoner, working for them, listening to them, and being told what to believe, I had almost come to think of the Allies as the enemy. I resolved not to make the same mistake again. The bombing passed and the night was silent once more.

A day and another night we were by the siding. The engine of the train seemed to have been taken away, for I could hear no hissing steam, no mechanical life of any kind. Aside from the black bread, we had had nothing for about six days, by my hazy count. People were dying at a greater rate than before. Less than half the original seventy remained alive in our car.

The next morning, the doors were flung open and we were counted and beaten in the usual manner. But this time, when the SS men left, the doors were left open. We looked out dully. On the other side of the tracks stretched a wide, flat field. It was a potato field, and here and there the wind had blown away the snow, leaving the hard, brown earth exposed. At the near edge of the field, a small boy was walking through the snow. He was thickly bundled against the February cold, and concentrated so hard on walking that he did not even notice us staring at him.

He held a large wicker basket of potatoes in his hand. I thought I was in some kind of odd dream, where even the innocent passing of a child was twisted into the most acute suffering imaginable. We began shouting weakly to the little boy to come over and give us his basket. Cracked voices strained in shrunken throats. The wind sang and blew away our croakings, but at last the boy stopped and turned and looked at us in amazement. We could not realize how terrible we must have looked to him. Frightened by such apparitions from the grave, he dropped the basket and ran across the fields and soon was gone.

Lying scattered in the field were some potatoes. A huge German guard put his head in the car. "Go ahead," he smiled. "Go on—get them. You need them." He waved to us casually. "There they are," he said, pointing to the potatoes lying in the snow. Vaguely, a warning sounded in the back of my mind, but no matter—we must have food!

As if moved by the same hand, we started for the wide doors. Just outside, the guards laughed and talked among themselves. I got up, then fell back, stunned by my weakness. I could barely stand. Others were finding the same thing true, and figures wobbled and flopped on the floor, then started crawling and clawing at each other as they fought their way to the door and dropped over the edge to the ground. I was too weak. I dragged myself half-way across the floor then collapsed and could not move any farther.

About fifteen people were able to get through the doors. They gathered their strength and started running silently across the field, a stumbling group of the dead, intent upon some cold, raw potatoes. I watched helplessly. They would have the food for themselves, and I would go hungry again! Laughing and cackling, they fell on the ground, grovelling after the potatoes and pulling at one another to wrest the food from desperate fingers. And then the machine guns started up. The truck shook and shuddered and filled with acrid smoke. People were crying out again in fear and anguish, and the field was filled with falling bodies and the snow stained with blood. The guards shouted —what, what were they shouting? What was it they screamed so lustily? "Go ahead. Get the potatoes."

I looked round wildly for Chanka. She was lying against the wall of the car. She had not seen the potatoes.

The guards killed everyone in the field. Those who were as weak as I and unable to run for the food barely understood the awful quirk of fate that we should survive because of our own weakness.

At last, we were removed from the train and assembled. No one, as far as I could see, had survived the trip in the open cars. And less than a third of our car had survived.

SALA PAWLOWICZ with KEVIN KLOSE,
I Will Survive

An escape in Canada

Franz von Werra of the German Luftwaffe was shot down over Britain in his Messerschmidt on September 5, 1940. After two unsuccessful attempts to escape from a British prison camp, he was transferred to Canada. There he planned to make a further escape from the train that was taking him into the interior.

Von Werra decided that it would be best to try to escape as late as possible in the journey. This would give a chance for the excitement of any other escape attempt to die down. Above all, he did not want to get off the train in the backwoods. The point where he escaped must be reasonably close to the U.S. border, within reach of main roads, and not too far from human habitation. The obvious choice was somewhere between Montreal and Ottawa.

There was no chance of getting out of the lavatory window. The door was wedged wide open and a guard stood near the doorway all the time the prisoner was inside. It would have to be the coach window. But with a guard standing only a few yards away, this looked impossible.

The attempt would have to be made while the train was in motion. As soon as it stopped, at signals or in stations, the three guards on duty in the coach were immediately on the alert, and other guards kept both sides of the train under observation. The other prisoners would have to stage a diversion at the critical time for the benefit of the three guards on duty; a quarrel farther along the coach might be the thing.

Owing to the height of the window above the floor, and the narrowness of the aperture, he could not jump out feet first, but would have to dive out, head first. But to do so while the train was travelling at speed would be suicidal. He would have to choose a moment when the train was travelling slowly, preferably just after it started following a halt. He would need the cover of darkness; the best time would be shortly before dawn.

But how was he to get the windows opened unnoticed? He observed that when the train halted for any length of time, the heat inside the coach partly melted the frost on the inner panes and the ice on the frame between them. After a long stop it should be possible to open the inner window fairly easily. If he opened it just a little way—less than a centimetre would do—the heat from the carriage would melt some of the ice on the frame between the two windows, and make it possible to open the outer window.

After the next long halt this plan was put into effect. Wagner stood up and kept an eye on the guards while von Werra, hidden by the backs of the seats, knelt down in front of the window and raised it a quarter of an inch. He wedged it with paper in case the vibration of the train closed it again.

Thereafter, whenever a guard happened to pass by the bay in which they were sitting, von Werra or Wagner would lay his arm negligently along the window sill, thus concealing the opening.

During the next long halt they had the satisfaction of seeing water from the melting ice trickle from the gap.

The volume of ice between the windows was greatly reduced in the next twenty-four hours. The process of freeing the frame would probably be accelerated if the coach temperature was raised to maximum. Von Werra therefore arranged with other prisoners to open all heat regulators to "Full" as soon as the train left Montreal.

There were several other difficulties to overcome: how to keep watch on three guards at once and to open the window when their attention was distracted; how to conceal the open window; how to shut both windows afterwards, for it would make all the difference if his disappearance were not discovered for some time; he must be wearing his overcoat when he dived out, but how, having been sitting in his shirt-sleeves, could he put it on without arousing the guards' curiosity?

An escaper must have luck, and luck solved most of these problems for von Werra.

The train reached Montreal late the following night. There was a long halt during which the heat was cut off while the locomotive was changed. The temperature in the coach dropped rapidly, and thus it was quite natural for the regulators to be fully opened when the heating was reconnected.

At the evening meal that night they had tomato soup, goulash, and a whole case of dessert apples. The prisoners were starved of fresh fruit, and they ate the lot.

This surfeit of apples following the unaccustomedly rich and plentiful food of the past twenty-four hours proved too much for their systems. In von Werra's coach from midnight onwards there was a long queue for the toilet, and some of the traffic had to be diverted to the guards' toilet at the other end of the coach. The three guards on duty were highly amused. Their attention was diverted, and at times there was only one guard left in the coach.

In spite of the stifling heat in the coach, one or two of the prisoners, white-faced and shivering from sickness, wrapped their coats or blankets about them, and sat hugging their stomachs. Von Werra was able to put on his overcoat without arousing the slightest suspicion. Afterwards he sat with his head in his hands. The guards were not expecting any of the prisoners to escape in their present condition.

But the train would not slow down. It went on and on exasperatingly at high speed. It was hours before the brakes were applied with a gradually increased pressure that indicated a coming halt at a station.

Through his fingers von Werra glanced at his three companions. All were wide awake and looking at him questioningly. Manhard and Wilhelm sat facing one another in the seats beside the gangway, each watching a guard. Their thumbs protruded from the blankets above their knees. Von Werra watched those thumbs. One thumb was horizontal, the other vertical.

Now both were sticking up. Von Werra stood up, opened out his blanket and shook it. Wagner knelt down behind it in front of the window. A second later he was back in his seat. Von Werra finished folding his blanket and sat down again.

The inner window was wide open. No word had been spoken.

The train stopped at a station. The remaining ice on the window frame and the frost on the glass were now fully exposed to the heat of the carriage. The guards stretched their limbs on the platform. The frost quickly melted on von Werra's outer window; through it he could see their silhouettes, massive against the station lights. If he could see them, they could see him. All the other windows were pearl-grey and opaque from frost. His was black and must be as noticeable as a gap in a row of teeth!

Would the guards spot it? The minutes dragged interminably. The halt was much too long.

A bell clanged, the engine whistle sounded. The guards climbed aboard, banging the snow off their boots on the steps. Two of them got in the prisoners' end of the coach and had to walk back down the gangway to their seats. They would have to pass the defrosted window. Von Werra held his breath, keeping his head in his hands, peering between his fingers. The train was already moving. The first guard passed by looking straight ahead. The second approached more slowly. He was feeling his way. His spectacles were misted and he was squinting over the rims. He passed by.

Von Werra glanced at his friends. They were ready.

There were several prisoners now with raised hands, for during the halt there had been no visits to the toilet. A guard escorted the first man out. Two guards were left.

The train clanked and lurched over points outside the station. It was gathering speed rapidly. Manhard's thumb was up.

Wagner, holding two corners of his blanket in his lap,

looked at von Werra in anxious inquiry. Von Werra nodded. Wagner stood up, and opened out the blanket. Wilhelm slid along into Wagner's corner seat.

Masked by the blanket, von Werra stood up, caught hold of the outer window, and jerked upwards. It did not move. Another fierce jerk and then a steady, sustained lift. The window opened smoothly.

A rush of cold air pressed the blanket against Wagner's body. He continued to shake the corners up and down, looking up the coach towards the two guards.

Von Werra felt the icy blast on his face, heard the unexpectedly loud and hollow beat of the wheels over the rail joints. Snowdrifts flashed by at a terrifying speed. The train was still accelerating.

It was sheer madness. Suicide. He couldn't possibly do it.

The next moment Wilhelm saw von Werra's jack-boots disappear through the middle of the open window. For a split second, which he will never forget, he saw von Werra's body, rigid, arms straight out above his head, suspended almost horizontally a foot or so outside the coach.

It dropped back and was gone. There was nothing but the icy draught and the whine and the beat of the wheels on the rails.

Wilhelm shut the outer and inner windows and slid back along the seat. Wagner folded the blanket deliberately, slowly, and sat down.

No word was spoken.

All three were aghast, incredulous.

A few brief seconds ago von Werra had been sitting there with his head in his hands. Now he was gone.

The three of them watched ferns of frost sprout rapidly over the window. Inside a minute the glass was completely covered. It was as though the window had never been opened.

They never saw von Werra again. They had not even had time to wish him luck.

At daybreak, Major Cramer, who was officer-in-charge of the prisoners in that coach, walked down the gangway to see how the men who had been ill during the night were getting on.

When he reached the bay occupied by Wagner, Manhard and Wilhelm, he paused. All three were lying on their bunks. Von Werra's was empty. He raised his eyebrows interrogatively. Wagner nodded his head slowly.

Cramer passed on, smiling.

It was not until late the following afternoon that von Werra's absence was discovered. The train was then several hundred miles from the point where he had dived out of the window.

KENDAL BURT AND
JAMES LEASOR,
The One That Got Away

Von Werra succeeded in crossing the border, and eventually reached New York City. He flew back to Europe from Rio in an Italian flying-boat, and on arrival in Germany was received by Hitler. On October 25, 1941, on a mission over the North Sea, he was killed when his plane developed engine trouble and crashed into the sea.

TROOP TRAIN

It stops the town we come through. Workers raise
Their oily arms in good salute and grin.
Kids scream as at a circus. Business men
Glance hopefully and go their measured way.
And women standing at their dumbstruck door
More slowly wave and seem to warn us back,
As if a tear blinding the course of war
Might once dissolve our iron in their sweet wish.

Fruit of the world, O clustered on ourselves
We hang as from a cornucopia
In total friendliness, with faces bunched
To spray the streets with catcalls and with leers.
A bottle smashes on the moving ties
And eyes fixed on a lady smiling pink
Stretch like a rubber-band and snap and sting
The mouth that wants the drink-of-water kiss.

And on through crummy continents and days,
Deliberate, grimy, slightly drunk we crawl,
The good-bad boys of circumstance and chance,
Whose bucket-helmets bang the empty wall
Where twist the murdered bodies of our packs
Next to the guns that only seem themselves.
And distance like a strap adjusted shrinks,
Tightens across the shoulder and holds firm.

Here is a deck of cards; out of this hand
Dealer, deal me my luck, a pair of bulls,
The right draw to a flush, the one-eyed jack.
Diamonds and hearts are red but spades are black,
And spades are spades and clubs are clovers—black.
But deal me winners, souvenirs of peace.
This stands to reason and arithmetic,
Luck also travels and not all come back.

Trains lead to ships and ships to death or trains,
And trains to death or trucks, and trucks to death,
Or trucks lead to the march, the march to death,
Or that survival which is all our hope;
And death leads back to trucks and trains and ships,
But life leads to the march, O flag! at last
The place of life found after trains and death
—Nightfall of nations brilliant after war.

KARL SHAPIRO

Capture of an ammunition train

I forget which of us it was who found the ammunition train. There were two of them, as a matter of fact, lying forlornly in a railway siding outside the town of Larissa. Larissa in the great empty plain of Thessaly was the main British supply base in northern Greece, from which, in April 1941, we were withdrawing under heavy German pressure.

The town had been bombed by the Italians, then it had been badly damaged by an earthquake, and now it was receiving regular attention from the Luftwaffe. It was an awful mess. The Greek railway staff had run away and it was obvious that the two ammunition trains had been abandoned. I knew that we were seriously short of ammunition further down the line so I went to the Brigadier in charge of the base and asked permission to try to get one of the trains away. It was given with alacrity.

I don't want you to think that this action on my part was public-spirited, or anything like that. My motives were purely selfish. We wanted a job. We were a small unit which had been carrying out various irregular activities further north; but now the sort of tasks for which we were designed had become impossible, and we were in danger of becoming redundant. We felt that if we could get this train away we should be doing something useful and justifying our existence. Besides, one of us claimed that he knew how to drive an engine.

This was Norman Johnstone, a brother officer in the Grenadier Guards. One of our jobs earlier in the campaign had been to destroy some rolling stock which could not be moved away. Norman had a splendid time blowing up about twenty valuable locomotives and a lot of trucks, but towards the end we ran out of explosives. At this stage a sergeant in the 4th Hussars turned up, who was an engine-driver in civilian life. With Norman helping him, he got steam up in the four surviving engines, drove them a quarter of a mile down the line, then sent them full tilt back into the station, where they caused further havoc of a spectacular and enjoyable kind.

These were perhaps not ideal conditions under which to learn how to drive an engine, especially as the whole thing was carried out under shell-fire; all we knew for certain about Norman's capabilities as an engine-driver was that every single locomotive with which he had been associated had become scrap metal in a matter of minutes. Still, he is a determined and methodical chap, and there seemed no harm in letting him have a go. So early in the morning we made our way to the railway station, just in time for the first air-raid of the day. Except for occasional parties of refugees and stragglers from the Greek army the station was deserted. There were two excellent reasons for this. First of all there were no trains running, so there was no point in anybody going there. Secondly, the station was practically the only thing left in the ruins of Larissa that was worth bombing; we had ten air raids altogether before we left in the afternoon, and they always had a go at the station.

The first thing we had to do was to get steam up in a railway engine. There were plenty of these about but all except two had been rendered unserviceable by the Luftwaffe. We started work on the bigger of the two. After having a quick look round, Norman explained to us that one of the most popular and probably in the long run the soundest of all methods of making steam was by boiling water, but that we might have to devise some alternative formula as the water mains had been cut by bombs and there was very little coal to be found. However, in the end we got together enough of these two more or less essential ingredients, and all was going well when one of the few really large bombs that came our way blew a hole in the track just outside the shed we were working in, thus, as it were, locking the stable door before we had been able to steal the horse. Greatly disgusted, we transferred our attention to the other sound engine.

There were more air-raids, and it came on to rain, and two Greek deserters stole my car, and altogether things did not look very hopeful, especially when somebody pointed out that there was now only one undamaged and navigable set of tracks leading out of the battered marshalling yard. But the needle on the pressure-gauge in the cabin of our engine was rising slowly, and at last, whistling excitedly, the ancient machine got under way.

She was a majestic sight, and would have been even more majestic if she had not gone backwards instead of forwards.

It was at this point that a certain gap in Norman's education as an engine-driver became evident. The sergeant in the 4th Hussars had taught him how to start a locomotive and how to launch it on a career of self-destruction; but Norman's early training in how to stop an engine had been confined entirely to making it run violently into a lot of other rolling stock. We trotted anxiously along the cinders, hanging, so to speak, on to Norman's stirrup leathers. "Do you know how to stop?" we shouted. "Not yet," replied Norman, a trifle testily. But he soon found out and presently mastered the knack of making the engine go forward as well as backwards, and we steamed rather incredulously northwards towards the siding where the ammunition trains lay.

We chose the bigger of the two. It consisted of twenty-six trucks containing 120 tons of ammunition and 150 tons of petrol. It was not what you might call an ideally balanced cargo from our point of view, and nobody particularly wanted the petrol, but the train was made up like that and we had to lump it.

It really was rather a proud moment when we steamed back through Larissa with this enormous train clattering along behind us, and out into the broad plain of Thessaly. Norman drove, the stoker was Oliver Barstow—a young officer in the Royal Horse Artillery who was killed a few days later—and Guardsman Loveday and I, armed with our only tommy-gun, prepared to engage any hostile aircraft who might be so foolhardy as to come within range. It was a lovely evening, and we all felt tremendously pleased with ourselves. Driving a train, once you have got the beastly thing started, seemed to be extraordinarily easy. No steering, no gear-changing, no problems of navigation, no flat tyres, none of those uncomfortable suspicions that perhaps after all you ought to have taken that last turning to the left. There's nothing in it, we told each other.

Almost as soon as we had left Larissa we had begun to climb up a long, gentle slope; and we had only done about five miles when the needle on the pressure gauge began slowly but firmly

to fall. We stoked like mad. Norman pulled, pushed and twid-
dled the various devices on what we incorrectly called the dash-
board. Pressure continued to fall, and the train went slower and
slower. At last it stopped altogether. "We'd better get out," said
Norman, "and have a look at the injector-sprockets." He may
not actually have said "injector-sprockets" but anyhow it was
some technical term which meant nothing to us and may not
have meant a very great deal to him. It was at this point that we
realized that the train had not merely stopped but was beginning to run slowly backwards down the hill. The thought of
free-wheeling backwards into Larissa was distasteful to all of us.
In the hurry of departure we had had no time to organize our
ten brakesmen, who were all confined in the guards' van instead
of being dispersed along the train so that they could operate the
brakes on individual goods wagons. There was only one thing
to do. I leapt off the engine and ran back down the train as fast
as I could, like an old lady running for a bus: jumped on the
back of the nearest goods van, swarmed up a little ladder on to
its roof and feverishly turned the wheel which put the brake on.
The train continued to go backwards, but it seemed to be losing
speed and at last, after I had repeated this operation several
times, it came reluctantly to a stop.

We were really having a great deal of fun with this train.
We had got a tremendous kick out of starting it, and now we
were scarcely less elated at having brought it to a standstill. But
we had to face the facts, and the main fact was that as engine-
drivers, though we had no doubt some excellent qualities—orig-
inality, determination, cheerfulness, and so on—we were open
to the serious criticism that we did not seem to be able to drive
our engine very far. A run of five miles, with a small discount
for going backwards unexpectedly, is not much to show for a
hard day's work. At this point, moreover, it suddenly began to
look as if we were going to lose our precious train altogether. As
we tinkered away at the engine, the air grew loud with an expected but none the less unwelcome noise, and a number of
enemy bombers could be seen marching through the sky towards
us. We were a conspicuous object in the middle of that empty
plain and I quickly gave orders for the ten soldiers in the

guard's van to go and take cover 500 yards from the train. In point of fact there was no cover to take, but they trotted off with alacrity and sat down round a small tree about the size of a big gooseberry bush in the middle distance. We ourselves couldn't very well leave the engine because the fire might have gone out (or anyhow we thought it might) and we should have had to start all over again.

But if we had our troubles, the enemy, as so often happens, had his too. The bombers were obviously interested in us, but it soon became equally obvious that they had no bombs, having wasted all theirs on the ruins of Larissa earlier in the day. They still, however, had their machine-guns and three or four of the aircraft proceeded to attack us, coming in very low one after the other. But they all made the same mistake, which they might not have made if we ourselves had taken evasive action and left the train. They all attacked the engine, round which they could see signs of life, instead of flying up and down the twenty-odd wagons full of petrol and high explosive and spraying them with bullets, which could hardly have failed to produce results of some sort. They concentrated on putting the engine out of action; and the engine, as we ourselves were just beginning to realize, was out of action already, all the water in the boiler having somehow disappeared.

We used the engine in much the same way as one uses a grouse-butt. Whichever side the attack was coming from, we got the other side. The flying-machine, making a terrible noise and blazing away with its machine-guns, swept down on us, and as it roared overhead—much bigger, much more malevolent but not really very much higher than the average grouse—we pooped off at it with our tommy-gun, to which the German rear-gunner replied with a burst that kicked up the dust a hundred yards away or more. It got rather silly after a bit. I am quite sure we never hit the Luftwaffe, and the only damage the Luftwaffe did to us was to make a hole in a map somebody had left in the cab. And one of the things about driving a train is that you don't need a map to do it with. They gave it up quite soon—it was getting late anyhow—and went home to Bulgaria. We climbed back into our engine again and as I looked at our only casualty—the map, torn by an explosive bullet and covered with coal dust—I couldn't help rather envying the Luftwaffe, who almost certainly believed that they had succeeded in doing what they set out to do. It was only too obvious that we had not. Night fell, and it was fairly cold.

Then, all of a sudden, out of the darkness, another train appeared. It was full of Australian gunners whose guns were supposed to have come on by road. They towed us back to the next station. Here we picked up a good engine with a Greek driver and set off for the south. It was ideal weather all next day —pouring rain and low cloud—and we never saw a German aeroplane at all. Forty-eight hours after we had started work on this unlikely project we reached our—or rather the ammunition's—destination. It was a place called Amphykleion and here I formally handed over the train—twenty-six coaches, 150 tons of petrol, 120 tons of ammunition—to the supply people. Everyone was delighted with it. "This really will make a difference," they said. We felt childishly pleased. The sun shone, it was a lovely morning. And this marked improvement in the weather made it comparatively easy for a small force of German dive-bombers, a few hours later, to dispose of the train and all its contents with a terrible finality.

So you see this is not a success story. Nor is it a story which can have—from me, at any rate—a moral; for the only possible moral anyone can draw from it is that human endeavour is always likely to be futile, that it is better to leave ammunition trains in their sidings. And I hope the nonsense I have talked has not included anything as nonsensical as that.

PETER FLEMING,
With the Guards to Mexico

An English girl
in Hitler's Germany

In 1934 Christabel Burton, a niece of Lord Northcliffe, married
Peter Bielenberg, a Hamburg lawyer. She was in Germany
throughout the war, and in this excerpt from her book *The
Past Is Myself*, she describes a train journey out of Berlin late
in 1944. The "Adam" and "Carl" referred to are Adam von
Trott and Carl Langbehn, both friends who were executed by
the Nazis for their part in the German Resistance. While waiting for the train, Christabel Bielenberg is befriended by a
Herr Lemke, who helps find her a seat.

We sat together in the deathly quiet which always seemed
to descend before an air-raid; an involuntary, almost reverent
silence, a tribute, a fleeting prayer for those who were about to
die. An occasional dull booming was the only sound to be heard,
and Herr Lemke whispered out of the darkness that he thought
it was not anti-aircraft as yet, but the Russian guns from the
Eastern front. My countrymen were taking longer than usual to
arrive this time, I thought vaguely; sometimes they did seem to
wait around for a bit before coming in to the kill. Slowly then,
one after another, the searchlights soared up into the darkness
and began their ritual dance across the clear starlit sky; the
reception committee—it could not be long now.

Then, quietly, without warning the train began to move,
slowly, almost hesitantly at first, clanking over the points, out
from under the domed roof it began to gather speed. Herr Lemke
was jubilant. "What did I say, you see, *Gnä' Frau*, what did I
say? A combination of German planning and English calm and
Irish luck could run the world. Oh dear, I must laugh. How
pleased Mutti will be when I tell her this story. 'Papi,' she will
say, 'I knew you would get home somehow.' But this calls for a
little celebration. Wait now, I must find the glasses."

He was on his feet, fussing about, feeling for his suitcases,
seemingly quite oblivious of the fact that we were still in the
target area. He seemed to be taking off his boots and I could almost imagine him putting on his bedroom slippers—carpet slippers, I'd be bound. A rustle of paper, either the promised glasses

or a neat packet of sandwiches—a smell of smoked ham—it was sandwiches.

Suddenly a blinding light filled the carriage. A searchlight sweeping upwards from just beside the track, shone for a few fleeting seconds straight through our window and threw our small world into brilliant relief; every detail stood out as in a flashlight photograph. Papi Lemke's stockinged feet resting neatly side by side on a folded newspaper, next door to his opened suitcase. My rucksack, and above it hanging from the rack, the usual yellow and black notice, *"Achtung Feind hört mit"*—"Beware an enemy may be listening." Helmuth Moltke had had such a warning hanging in his library, Freya had pinched it from somewhere and given it to him as a joke. On the rack to the right of this one, though, lay a black peaked army cap, decorated with the skull and crossbones, a Sam Browne belt too, and in the corner next to the window opposite, staring straight at me, sat a tall figure in black uniform, motionless as a statue. I had time to register fair short-clipped hair, a pale long rather handsome face, even a curious twitch in one cheek, once— twice, it forced him to wink with one eye and it was the only sign he gave of being alive.

Then the searchlight swung away from the train and the picture faded slowly into darkness. I slid back along the seat and nudged Herr Lemke, and told him perhaps we should tidy our luggage as we were not alone in the compartment. In case he should not have seen the cap on the rack opposite, I drew the sign of the Swastika on his knee with my finger. I need not have bothered. Poor Herr Lemke, he had seen it all right and, no doubt, the forked lightning insignia on the uniform as well. He kept clearing his throat and I could almost sense his sitting to attention. *"Gestatten Sie,* excuse me—Sir—would you allow me to offer you a sandwich?" "No—I would not," the answer came in a slow, insulting drawl. "A little *cognac* perhaps?" "No." This was terrible, I could hear my friend shuffling about in his corner —finally "But you, *Fräulein, Gnädige Frau*, perhaps you would give me the pleasure?" I would have liked to come to his rescue, as I knew he was suffering, wondering desperately if he had said anything he shouldn't have, and wishing to goodness that he had closed his suitcase with the forbidden brandy. But I dared

not help him out. I had eaten practically nothing all day and
something told me I might need a clear head. "I'm sorry, Herr
Lemke, but I don't think I will just now." That settled it. He
cleared his throat again and murmured something about having
left his bedroom slippers in the hotel. I heard him fold up his
sandwich paper and his suitcase clicked shut. Then he slid open
the door to the corridor and shut it firmly behind him. He returned some minutes later to grab his other suitcase, moving so
quietly that I supposed he must be carrying even his carpet slippers. In his agitation he even forgot to say goodbye.

The silence was broken by a short laugh from the opposite
bench. "A brave little fellow, our erstwhile travelling companion." The voice was quiet and cultivated, with an accent I could
not locate. "I expect he wanted to stretch out in a carriage to
himself." In truth I felt a bit deserted, but it seemed only fair to
try and rustle up some remnant of loyalty.

"With his bottles of loot, no doubt."

I did not answer, hoping that he would leave it at that, but
no—"You are travelling far, *Gnädige Frau?*" "Far? Well, not so
far really, it all depends what one calls far—" the old technique,
an answer and no answer.

"It's very cold in this compartment isn't it? Would you care
to have my army coat over your knees? I don't need it as I have
my sheepskin affair."

"That's very nice of you, but actually I have on my skiing
clothes and I am fairly all right as yet."

How I wished he would leave me alone; I was so tired, I was
finding it so hard to concentrate, but his next question had me
wishing sincerely that I had followed Herr Lemke's good example and left the carriage.

"Would you mind my asking where you come from?"

I supposed I had made some mistake with my German, but
there was a chance that the question was put quite innocently,
so I told him I didn't mind his asking a bit, but wondered could
he guess. After a moment's pause he said he did not know. Sweden? Holland, perhaps? But then a little while back I had made
some remark in unmistakable Black Forest dialect. "I am living
in the Black Forest at present, with my children," I said. "I am
neither Swedish nor Dutch. By the way, where do you come

from?" In order to evade a straight answer I knew that I was
getting drawn into a wretched conversation, but I was too tired
to think up a way out.

"Me? Aha!" he gave a short rather brittle laugh. "I come
from Riga. Do you know Riga? It is very beautiful. We Latvians
are what is called a border people, which means that we have
been 'liberated' very often. You know, perhaps, the story of the
Alsatian boy who was recruited for the German army in 1942
and he was asked which side he thought would win the war. He
answered that his great-grandfather had fought in 1870 for the
French and lost, and his grandfather in 1914 for the Germans
and lost, and his father in 1940 for the French and lost, and now
he was going to fight for the Germans and he didn't really know
what to think. It was much the same with us, sometimes we
were 'liberated' by the Poles, then by the Swedes, just lately by
the Russians, and then lastly by the Germans. We were glad,
very glad, for the Russian occupation had been very hard. My
father was killed by the Russians and my mother died of grief—
I think it must have been. Our people baked cakes and stood by
the roadside and gave them to the German troops as they
marched through our villages. The troops looked splendid, crack
German regiments, and each soldier had a flower in his cap, and
as I watched I knew that I had only one wish in the world and
that was to get into uniform as soon as possible and to march
with them. You see, I felt that this would be the only chance to
take my revenge for what the Russians had done to my home. So
I volunteered and, as my head had the correct Aryan measure-
ment—my shoulders, my chest, the shape of my nose, truly
Aryan, also I hadn't flat feet—I had the particular honour of
being recruited for the SS."

His slow voice had quickened, and I could hear him move in
the darkness. He seemed to be leaning forward for his voice
sounded nearer as he asked suddenly: "But where *do* you come
from, *Gnädige Frau?* Are you German?" "No," I said, "I'm
not, my people come from Ireland." "Ach, now I understand,
the Irish, they are musical, hence your voice. You have a very
sympathetic voice, *Gnädige Frau.* Perhaps it is because of your
voice that I'm telling you these things—that and the funny expression you had on your face as you stood on the barrow out-

side the window. Then perhaps you can understand a bit the feeling. Your country, too, was occupied by the British. Your people were insulted, starved, murdered—but where was I?—oh yes, my Aryan contours, my hopes for revenge. Well, they told us that we could revenge ourselves on our enemies and they sent us to Poland. Not to fight the Poles, oh no, they had been defeated long ago—but to kill Jews. We just had the shooting to do, others did the burying," he drew a deep, sighing breath. "Do you know what it means—to kill Jews, men, women, and children as they stand in a semicircle around the machine guns? I belonged to what is called an *Einsatzkommando*, an extermination squad—so I know. What do you say when I tell you that a little boy, no older than my youngest brother, before such a killing, stood there to attention and asked me, 'Do I stand straight enough, Uncle?' Yes, he asked that of me; and once, when the circle stood round us, an old man stepped out of the ranks, he had long hair and a beard, a priest of some sort I suppose. Anyway, he came towards us slowly across the grass, slowly step by step, and within a few feet of the guns he stopped and looked at us one after another, a straight, deep, dark and terrible look. 'My children,' he said, 'God is watching what you do.' He turned from us then, and someone shot him in the back before he had gone more than a few steps. But I—I could not forget that look, even now it burns into me."

The window I had climbed through would not close properly and a numbing cold seemed to be creeping upwards from my feet, but the voice, just a voice in the darkness, went on and on, sometimes pitched so low that I could hardly hear it above the creaking and rumbling of the train, sometimes raised to a note of near hysteria. He told me that he had resigned from the Death Commandos and joined the *Waffen SS*, the fighting SS units, and he told me of how he had tried to be killed, but his comrades had fallen around him and each time, by some miracle, he had lived. The ones with the photographs in their wallets, the frightened ones, and the ones with the dreams of the future, they were the ones who got killed, he said. Only those who didn't care, got the Iron Crosses. Now he was going to the front, to his unit if he could reach it, otherwise anywhere, *anywhere*, did I hear, where he would be allowed to die.

During his story I had found it increasingly difficult to listen. I had eaten practically nothing all day and the cold in the carriage was intense. As I fought wave after wave of exhaustion, my head kept falling forward and only the most startling points of his story penetrated the fog of sleep. The little fair-haired Jewish boy—the old Rabbi. Oh God, was it for these that Adam had done penance and maybe now, Peter, too?

Some two years back I had been in a tram with Nicky when an elderly lady, with the Jewish star pinned to her coat had got up from her place so that my Aryan eight-year-old son could sit down. I had got up too and the three of us had stood silently looking at the empty seats. I had felt quite proud of my little gesture at the time. How utterly feeble it seemed now. Too much—too much. "You are silent, *Gnädige Frau?* You are horrified at my story?" He seemed very near. "No—no," my own voice from somewhere far away; it seemed no longer my own. "I am not horrified, I think I pity you, for you have more on your conscience than can be absolved by your death."

And suddenly, for a second in time, the fogs cleared and it was as if Adam's and Carl's dying and Peter's imprisonment seemed a splendid, glowing, real thing, absolutely necessary and right. "But others have died and may have to die for you," I heard myself murmuring. I do not know if he heard, as I was already nearly asleep. The train rumbled rhythmically onwards into the night. Totteridge, where I was born—a village church— a small Chris collecting her weekly text at children's service. Miss Osborne at the organ. "He died that we might be forgiven. He died to make us good. He died—He died—"

I awoke twice before reaching Tuttlingen. Once, when the train jerked to a stop at a half-lit station, I realized that I was warmer and that my head was resting on something hard and uncomfortable. The man had moved and was sitting beside me, his greatcoat was over my knees and my head had fallen on to his shoulder. His SS shoulder tabs had been pressing into my cheek. In the half light I saw his face for the second time: perhaps I had been mistaken about that twitching nerve; it looked peaceful enough now anyway, almost childlike. His hand, with the signet ring of the SS, was resting on mine, and as I moved it closed with an almost desperate grip and then relaxed. I put my head back on his shoulder gently, so as not to waken him, and I slept again. The next time I woke, the carriage was empty and the train was moving. A grey, cold dawn lightened the window. I glanced involuntarily at the sky and the low snow-clouds scudding past. It was not going to be a very good day for an air-raid I thought, and so there was a chance that I might be home in my valley before evening.

CHRISTABEL BIELENBERG,
The Past Is Myself

Kindness to a prisoner of war

I think we were all glad to be paraded on the eighth of June, searched and marched to the station. I don't think I shall ever forget the preliminaries to our departure: we must have been kept on the barrack square in the boiling sun for about three hours, every few minutes having to pick up our bundles and shift a few yards, all in accordance with some incredible system, quite incomprehensible to us, of counting us. The German Army, with all its qualities, cannot count; a squad of twenty prisoners will defeat any German NCO who will invariably find they are nineteen or twenty-one—and the officers don't seem to be any better.

Finally rations were issued for what we were told was to be probably a week's journey. They consisted of 800 grammes of preserved meat between three, three Greek biscuits and half a loaf, short commons indeed for two days let alone seven. Fortunately we had still a small amount of bully which we had carried from Corinth, but the prospects didn't appear bright. And indeed they would not have been had it not been for the generosity of the Serbian town of Kralejvo through which we passed on the third day of our journey. By that time our rations had to all intents and purposes been consumed, except perhaps for a Greek biscuit or two which may have still remained uneaten. The front part of our long train was occupied by some Serbs who had been with us at Corinth. They, poor devils, were passing through their own country on their way to the prison camps.

Vienna 1945: a German prisoner of war returns home.
An anxious mother asks if he has seen her son.

They, too, were short of food and knew that we were also and they managed to get a message sent on ahead to Kralejvo where we arrived with empty larders. There on the platform the full length of the train we found men and women with baskets of bread, cheese, bacon, butter and fruit, and as the train pulled up they started to pelt us with their gifts. Someone had organized well. The town had turned out in force and had spared none of its possessions, and as we caught the loaves which were being thrown at us like Rugby footballs we probably thought (if we had time under the hail of bread) that all this food could ill be spared from an impoverished Balkan town. The German guards didn't know what to do. For some reason, difficult to explain, the young German officer in charge of the train did not want us to receive the food. I cannot understand why unless he was intent on starving us. He knew exactly how inadequate was the ration issue for the journey, but perhaps he resented the obvious sympathy of the Serbs. He stormed up and down the length of the train shouting his ineptitudes but no sooner had this ridiculous cocky military squall passed by than the guards closed their eyes and the stream of food started again. No one of us will ever forget the generosity of these kind people: had it not been for them we should have arrived at our Bavarian destination in a sorry plight. In our truck alone we caught fifty-one good sized loaves warm from the bakehouse as well as a quantity of most nourishing fat bacon full of everything which we were lacking in our diet. Men, women and children provided this manna in our desert and as the baskets emptied so the children ran back into the town for more, and before long others came with baskets of delicious ripe black cherries. One small girl with her mother, who was in tears, threw us some money. They would have given all they had, these poor people, I believe. They showered on us what we most wanted, food and sympathy, and as the train drew out of the station a group of women followed it waving their handkerchiefs, their eyes brimming with tears. No one of us will ever forget this last contact with humanity and, even though the incident is now a year old, it lives in my mind a vivid companion to a desire one day to be able to tell these people what their kindness meant.

MILES REID,
Last on the List

The courage of Driver Gimbert

It happened in the small hours of June 2, 1944. A March driver, Benjamin Gimbert by name, was rostered to take a trainload of bombs from March to Whitemoor by way of Ely and Ipswich. He had forty 500 lb. bombs in the first wagon, seventy-four more in the second, a load of detonators in the third, and after that some forty-eight more wagons all filled with high explosives. For an engine they had one of the War Department eight-coupled locomotives, one of the ugliest creatures that ever ran on a British railway.

They started at 12.15 A.M. and made their slow way to Ely, through the Junction, and then on by single line through Soham to Fordham. All went well until they were approaching Soham, when the driver looked out and saw that the first wagon was on fire. He knew well enough what the train contained, and he and his mate might just have had time to get down and run for it. But they did not choose to do so for they were not that kind of men. He stopped the train carefully, well short of the station, and sent his fireman to uncouple the burning wagon from the rest of the train, remembering to tell him to take a coal hammer with him in case the coupling was too hot to touch. This was successfully done, and driver Gimbert then proceeded with his blazing wagon into the station, intending to take it some distance along the line, where it would be well clear of all buildings, to uncouple it from the engine there, while he and his mate hoped to be able to take the engine on to Fordham. The signal-box at Soham is on the station, and the signalman, seeing that something was wrong, came down on to the platform as his duty was. The driver hailed him, "Sailor, have you got anything between here and Fordham. Where's the mail?" That question was never answered: at the moment of asking it the wagon exploded. It blew the engine's tender to pieces, killed the signalman and the fireman, and Gimbert himself recovered consciousness lying on the far platform badly injured. Virtually every window in Soham was smashed and the station itself completely wrecked. The crater underneath the wagon was fifteen feet deep and sixty-six feet wide. For this the driver and fireman received the George Cross, the fireman, alas, posthumously; and there is of course no doubt at all that their courage and resource saved the town of Soham, for had that whole train exploded, as it must have done if the blazing wagon had not been uncoupled and drawn well away from the rest, there could have been nothing left of the town. One hardly knows what to admire more, the courage or the coolness, but—as what has already been said shows—there was hardly any driver who would not under the same circumstances have acted in exactly the same way. To-day the new Soham station carries a memorial plaque in honour of Fireman Nightall and Driver Gimbert, with the inscription, "The devotion to duty of these brave men saved the town of Soham from grave destruction."

ROGER LLOYD
from S. LEGG (ed.),
The Railway Book (1952)

Return to the front. Victoria Station, London,
during the First World War.

THE SEND-OFF

Down the close, darkening lanes they sang their way
To the siding-shed,
And lined the train with faces grimly gay.

Their breasts were stuck all white with wreath and spray
As men's are, dead.

Dull porters watched them, and a casual tramp
Stood staring hard,
Sorry to miss them from the upland camp.
Then, unmoved, signals nodded, and a lamp
Winked to the guard.

So secretly, like wrongs hushed-up, they went.
They were not ours:
We never heard to which front these were sent.

Nor there if they yet mock what women meant
Who gave them flowers.

Shall they return to beatings of great bells
In wild train-loads?
A few, a few, too few for drums and yells,
May creep back, silent, to still village wells
Up half-known roads.

WILFRED OWEN

CRASHES

Therapeutic benefits of a crash . . .

It is a curious fact that, in at least two known instances, railway accidents have exercised a directly curative effect. The Rev. W. Woods, formerly of Leicester, assured the writer that a collision in which he had the good fortune to be had an immediate and most salutary influence upon his nervous system. Similarly a gentleman who wrote in November, 1869, to the *Times*, stated that a few days before he had been threatened "with a violent attack of rheumatic fever; in fact," he said, "my condition so alarmed me, and my dread of a sojourn in a Manchester hotel bed for two or three months was so great, that I resolved to make a bold *sortie* and, well wrapped up, start for London by the 3.30 P.M. Midland fast train. From the time of leaving that station to the time of the collision, my heart was going at express speed; my weak body was in a profuse perspiration; flashes of pain announced that the muscular fibres were under the tyrannical control of rheumatism, and I was almost beside myself with toothache. . . . From the moment of the collision to the present hour no ache, pain, sweat, or tremor has troubled me in the slightest degree, and instead of being, as I expected, and indeed intended, in bed, drinking *tinct. aurantii*, or absorbing through my pores oil of horse-chestnut, I am conscientiously bound to be at my office bodily sound." The writer humorously adds, "Don't print my name and address, or the Midland Company may come down on me for compensation."

ANON

Social benefits of a crash . . .

One of the effects, we will not say advantages, of travelling in
a long car may be to promote sociability. "An American," says
a St. Louis paper, in an article on native politeness, "may not be
so elegant at a dinner party, but he will not ride half a day in a
railway car without speaking to the fellow-passenger at his el-
bow, as the Englishman will." "No," remarks an American
critic, "indeed he will not: 'fore George he will not. How often,
oh, how often, have we wished that he would! But he won't. He
will pounce upon a stranger whom he has never seen before in
all his life, and talk him deaf, dumb, and blind in fifty miles.
Catch an American holding his mouth shut when he has a
chance to talk to some man who doesn't want to be talked to."

But sociability in Pullman cars may, especially under certain circumstances, take more demonstrative forms. "I have
never," observes another traveller, "got so well acquainted with
the passengers on the train as I did the other day on the Mil-
waukee and St. Paul Railroad. We were going at the rate of
about thirty miles an hour, and another train from the other
direction telescoped us. We were all thrown into each other's
society, and brought into immediate social contact, so to speak.
I went over and sat in the lap of a corpulent lady from Mani-
toba, and a girl from Chicago jumped over nine seats and sat
down on the plug hat of a preacher from La Crosse, with so
much timid, girlish enthusiasm that it shoved his hat clear
down over his shoulders. Everybody seemed to lay aside the
usual cool reserve of strangers, and we made ourselves entirely
at home. A shy young man, with an emaciated oil-cloth valise,
left his own seat and went over and sat down in a lunch basket,
where a bridal couple seemed to be wrestling with their first
picnic. Do you suppose that reticent young man would have
done such a thing on ordinary occasions? Do you think if he had
been at a celebration at home that he would have risen impetuously and gone where those people were eating by themselves,
and sat down in the cranberry jelly of a total stranger? I should
rather think not. Why, one old man, who probably at home led

the class-meeting, and who was as dignified as Roscoe Conkling's father, was eating a piece of custard pie when we met the other train, and he left his own seat and went over to the other end of the car and shot that piece of custard pie into the ear of a beautiful widow from Iowa. People travelling somehow forget the austerity of their home lives, and form acquaintances that sometimes last through life."

ANON

Preventative measures in a crash . . .

Many concussions give no warning of their approach, while others do, the usual premonitory symptoms being a kind of bouncing or leaping of the train. It is well to know that the bottom of the carriage is the safest place, and, therefore, when a person has reason to anticipate a concussion, he should, without hesitation, throw himself on the floor of the carriage. It was by this means that Lord Guillamore saved his life and that of his fellow passengers some years since, when a concussion took place on one of the Irish railways. His Lordship feeling a shock, which he knew to be the forerunner of a concussion, without more ado sprang upon the two persons sitting opposite to him, and dragged them with him to the bottom of the carriage; the astonished persons first imagined that they had been set upon by a maniac, and commenced struggling for their liberty, but in a few seconds they but too well understood the nature of the case; the concussion came, and the upper part of the carriage in which Lord Guillamore and the other two persons were was shattered to pieces, while the floor was untouched, and thus left them lying in safety; while the other carriages of the train presented nothing but a ghastly spectacle of dead and wounded.

ANON
from S. LEGG (ed.),
The Railway Book (1952)

A curious encounter
between two John Perkins

In March, we had another instance of the unwisdom of allowing lines of railway to cross each other at right angles on the level— "at grade," to give the American expression. The accident took place at Bedford, where the Midland Company's Line from Bedford to Hitchin, then in use as their main line to London, King's Cross, crossed the Bedford and Bletchley Line, near the London and North-Western Bedford Station. The signals for the London and North-Western driver to cross, were not lowered, and he ought to have stopped clear of the crossing; but, failing to do so, he came into collision with the Midland train, running from Hitchin towards Bedford, for which the signals were lowered. One passenger was killed, and four injured. It was very singular, that both the North-Western driver and the Midland driver had the same name, "John Perkins!" The signals were badly placed originally, and had not been modernized; they had been passed by Colonel Yolland in 1857, who did not relish being reminded of the fact.

ANON

GEORGE ALLEY

Along came the F.F.V., the fastest on the line,
Running along the C & O road, just twenty minutes
    behind.
A-running into Sewell yard, quartered on the line,
Awaiting for strict orders from the station just behind.

And when she blew for Hinton, her engineer was there.
George Alley was his name, with bright and wavy hair;
His fireman, young Jack Dickson, was standing by his
    side,
Awaiting for strict orders and in the cab to ride.

George Alley said to his fireman, "Jack, a little more
    steam;
I intend to run old number 4, the fastest ever seen;
So over this road I mean to fly, as angels' wings unfold,
And when we see the Big Bend Tunnel, they'll hear my
    whistle blow."

George Alley said to his fireman, "Jack, a rock ahead I
    see,
And I know that death is lurking there, awaiting for you
    and me;
So from this car, dear Jack, you leap, your darling life to
    save,
For I want you to be an engineer, when I'm sleeping in
    my grave."

George Alley's mother came to him with a bucket on her
    arm;
She said, "My darling boy, be careful how you run,
For many a man has lost his life in trying to make lost
    time,
But if you run your engine right, you'll get there just on
    time."

George Alley said, "Dear Mother, you know I'll take
    your heed.
I know my engine, it's all right, I know that she will
    speed.
So over this road I mean to run with a speed unknown to
    all,
And when I blow for Clifton Forge, they'll surely hear
    my call."

Then up the road he hurtled, against the rock he crashed;
The engine it turned over, poor George's chest was
    mashed.
George's head in the firebox lay; the flames were rolling
    high.
"I'm glad I was born for an engineer, on the C & O road
    to die."

George Alley's mother came to him, in sorrow she did
   sigh,
When she looked upon her darling boy and saw that he
   must die.
"Too late, too late, dear Mother! My life is almost done,
And I know that God will let me in when I've finished
   my last run."
The doctor said, "Dear George, my darling boy be still;
Your life may yet be spared, if it is God's precious will."
"Oh no!," said George, "That cannot be. I want to die so
   free,
I want to die on the engine I love, 143."

The doctor said, "George Alley, your life cannot be
   saved.
Murdered upon the railway, to lie in a lonesome grave."
His face was covered up with blood, his eyes they could
   not see;
The very last words George Alley said were "Nearer, my
   God, to Thee."

ANON

Dickens in danger

Gad's Hill Place, Higham by Rochester, Kent.
Tuesday, Thirteenth June, 1865.
MY DEAR MITTON,

   I should have written to you yesterday or the day before, if
I had been quite up to writing.

   I was in the only carriage that did not go over into the
stream. It was caught upon the turn by some of the ruin of the
bridge, and hung suspended and balanced in an apparently
impossible manner. Two ladies were my fellow-passengers, an
old one and a young one. This is exactly what passed. You may
judge from it the precise length of the suspense. Suddenly we
were off the rail, and beating the ground as the car of a half-

emptied balloon might. The old lady cried out "My God!" and the young one screamed. I caught hold of them both (the old lady sat opposite and the young one on my left) and said: "We can't help ourselves, but we can be quiet and composed. Pray don't cry out." The old lady immediately answered: "Thank you. Rely upon me. Upon my soul I will be quiet." We were then all tilted down together in a corner of the carriage, and stopped. I said to them thereupon, "You may be sure nothing worse can happen. Our danger *must* be over. Will you remain here without stirring, while I get out of the window?" They both answered quite collectedly "Yes" and I got out without the least notion what had happened.

The accident at Staplehurst, Kent, in which
Charles Dickens was involved. Ten people were killed
and forty-nine injured.

Fortunately I got out with great caution and stood upon the step. Looking down I saw the bridge gone, and nothing below me but the line of rail. Some people in the two other compartments were madly trying to plunge out of the window, and had no idea that there was an open swampy field fifteen feet down below them, and nothing else! The two guards (one with his face cut) were running up and down on the down side of the bridge (which was not torn up) quite wildly. I called out to them: "Look at me. Do stop an instant and look at me, and tell me whether you don't know me." One of them answered, "We know you very well, Mr Dickens." "Then," I said, "my good fellow, for God's sake give me your key, and send one of those labourers here, and I'll empty this carriage." We did it quite safely, by means of a plank or two, and when it was done I saw all the rest of the train, except the two baggage vans, down in the stream. I got into the carriage again for my brandy flask, took off my travelling hat for a basin, climbed down the brickwork, and filled my hat with water.

Suddenly I came upon a staggering man covered with blood (I think he must have been flung clean out of his carriage), with such a frightful cut across the skull that I couldn't bear to look at him. I poured some water over his face and gave him some drink, then gave him some brandy, and laid him down on the grass, and he said: "I am gone," and died afterwards. Then I stumbled over a lady lying on her back against a little pollard-tree, with the blood streaming over her face (which was lead colour) in a number of distinct little streams from the head. I asked her if she could swallow a little brandy and she just nodded, and I gave her some and left her for somebody else. The next time I passed her she was dead. Then a man, examined at the inquest yesterday (who evidently had not the least remembrance of what really passed), came running up to me and implored me to help him find his wife, who was afterwards found dead. No imagination can conceive the ruin of the carriages, or the extraordinary weights under which the people were lying, or the complications into which they were twisted up among iron and wood, and mud and water.

I don't want to be examined at the inquest and I don't want to write about it. I could do no good either way, and I could only seem to speak about myself, which of course I would rather not do. I am keeping very quiet here. I have a—I don't know what to call it—constitutional (I suppose) presence of mind, and was not in the least fluttered at the time. I instantly remembered that I had the MS. of a number with me and clambered back into the carriage for it. But in writing these scanty words of recollection I feel the shake and am obliged to stop.

Ever faithfully,

CHARLES DICKENS

from *Letters of Charles Dickens*

Collision at Thorpe

A terminus collision took place at Thorpe, between Norwich and Great Yarmouth, on the Great Eastern Railway in England, on the 10th of September, 1874. The line had in this place but a single track, and the mail train from Norwich, under the rule, had to wait at a station called Brundell until the arrival there of the evening express from Yarmouth, or until it received permission by the telegraph to proceed. On the evening of the disaster the express train was somewhat behind its time, and the inspector wrote a dispatch directing the mail to come forward without waiting for it. This dispatch he left in the telegraph office unsigned, while he went to attend to other matters. Just then the express train came along, and he at once allowed it to proceed. Hardly was it under way when the unsigned dispatch occurred to him, and the unfortunate man dashed to the telegraph office only to learn that the operator had forwarded it. Under the rules of the company no return message was required. A second dispatch was instantly sent to Brundell to stop the mail; the reply came back that the mail was gone. A collision was inevitable.

The two trains were of very equal weight, the one consisting of fourteen and the other of thirteen carriages. They were both drawn by powerful locomotives, the drivers of which had reason for putting on an increased speed, believing, as each had cause to believe, that the other was waiting for him. The night was intensely dark and it was raining heavily, so that, even if the brakes were applied, the wheels would slide along the slippery track. Under these circumstances the two trains rushed upon each other around a slight curve which sufficed to conceal their head-lights. The combined momentum must have amounted to little less than sixty miles an hour, and the shock was heard through all the neighbouring villages. The smoke-stack of the locomotive drawing the mail train was swept away as the other locomotive seemed to rush on top of it, while the carriages of both trains followed until a mound of locomotives and shattered cars was formed which the descending torrents alone hindered from becoming a funeral pyre. So sudden was the collision that the driver of one of the engines did not apparently have an opportunity to shut off the steam, and his locomotive, though forced from the track and disabled, yet remained some time in operation in the midst of the wreck. In both trains, very fortunately, there were a number of empty cars between the locomotives and the carriages in which the passengers were seated, and they were utterly demolished; but for this fortunate circumstance the Thorpe collision might well have proved the most disastrous of all railroad accidents. As it was, the men on both the locomotives were instantly killed, together with seventeen passengers, and four other passengers subsequently died of their injuries; making a total of twenty-five deaths, besides fifty cases of injury.

It would be difficult to conceive of a more violent collision than that which has just been described; and yet, as curiously illustrating the rapidity with which the force of the most severe shock is expended, it is said that two gentlemen in the last carriage of one of the trains, finding it at a sudden standstill close to the place to which they were going, supposed it had stopped for some unimportant cause and concluded to take advantage of a happy chance which left them almost at the doors of their homes. They accordingly got out and hurried away in the rain, learning only the next morning of the catastrophe in which they had been unconscious participants.

C. F. ADAMS
from S. LEGG (ed.),
The Railway Book (1952)

The Ashtabula disaster, 1876

A blinding north-easterly snow-storm, accompanied by a heavy wind, prevailed throughout the day which preceded the accident, greatly impeding the movement of trains. The Pacific express over the Michigan Southern & Lake Shore road had left Erie, going west, considerably behind its time, and had been started only with great difficulty and with the assistance of four locomotives. It was due at Ashtabula at about 5.30 o'clock P.M., but was three hours late, and, the days being then at their shortest, when it arrived at the bridge which was the scene of the accident the darkness was so great that nothing could be seen through the driving snow by those on the leading locomotive even for a distance of 50 feet ahead. The train was made up of two heavy locomotives, four baggage, mail and express cars, one smoking car, two ordinary coaches, a drawing-room car and three sleepers, being in all two locomotives and eleven cars, in the order named, containing, as nearly as can be ascertained, 190 human beings, of whom 170 were passengers. Ashtabula bridge is situated only about 1,000 feet east of the station of the same name, and spans a deep ravine, at the bottom of which flows a shallow stream, some two or three feet in depth, which empties into Lake Erie a mile or two away. The bridge was an iron Howe truss of 150 feet span, elevated 69 feet above the bottom of the ravine, and supported at either end by solid masonwork abutments. It had been built some fourteen years. As the train approached the bridge it had to force its way through a heavy snow-drift, and, when it passed on to it, it was moving at a speed of some twelve or fourteen miles an hour. The entire length of the bridge afforded space only for two of the express cars at most in addition to the locomotives, so that when the wheels of the leading locomotive rested on the western abutment of the bridge nine of the eleven cars which made up the train, including all those in which there were passengers, had yet to reach its eastern end. At the instant when the train stood in this position, the engineer of the leading locomotive heard a sudden cracking sound apparently beneath him, and thought he felt the bridge giving way. Instantly pulling the throttle valve wide open, his locomotive gave a spring forward and, as it did so, the bridge fell, the rear wheels of his tender falling with it. The jerk and impetus of the locomotive, however, sufficed to tear out the coupling, and as his tender was dragged up out of the abyss on to the track, though its rear wheels did not get upon the rails, the frightened engineer caught a fearful glimpse of the second locomotive as it seemed to turn and then fall bottom upwards into the ravine. The bridge had given way, not at once but by a slow sinking motion, which began at the point where the pressure was heaviest, under the two locomotives and at the west abutment. There being two tracks, and this train being on the southernmost of the two, the southern truss had first yielded, letting that side of the bridge down, and rolling, as it were, the second locomotive and the cars immediately behind it off to the left and quite clear of a straight line drawn between the two abutments; then almost immediately the other truss gave way and the whole bridge fell, but in doing so swung slightly to the right. Before this took place the entire train with the exception of the last two sleepers had reached the chasm, each car as it passed over falling nearer than the one which had preceded it to the east abutment, and finally the last two sleepers came, and, without being deflected from their course at all, plunged straight down and fell upon the wreck of the bridge at its east end. It was necessarily all the work of a few seconds.

At the bottom of the ravine the snow lay waist deep and the stream was covered with ice some eight inches in thickness.

Upon this were piled up the fallen cars and engine, the latter on top of the former near the western abutment and upside down. All the passenger cars were heated by stoves. At first a dead silence seemed to follow the successive shocks of the falling mass. In less than two minutes, however, the fire began to show itself and within fifteen the holocaust was at its height. As usual, it was a mass of human beings, all more or less stunned, a few killed, many injured and helpless, and more yet simply pinned down to watch, in the full possession of all their faculties, the rapid approach of the flames. The number of those killed outright seems to have been surprisingly small. In the last car, for instance, no one was lost. This was due to the energy and presence of mind of the porter, a negro named Steward, who, when he felt the car resting firmly on its side, broke a window and crawled through it, and then passed along breaking the other windows and extricating the passengers until all were gotten out. Those in the other cars were far less fortunate. Though an immediate alarm had been given in the neighboring town, the storm was so violent and the snow so deep that assistance arrived but slowly. Nor when it did arrive could much be effected. The essential thing was to extinguish the flames. The means for so doing were close at hand in a steam pump belonging to the railroad company, while an abundance of hose could have been procured at another place but a short distance off. In the excitement and agitation of the moment contradictory orders were given, even to forbidding the use of the pump, and practically no effort to extinguish the fire was made. Within half an hour of the accident the flames were at their height, and when the next morning dawned nothing remained in the ravine but a charred and undistinguishable mass of car trucks, brakerods, twisted rails and bent and tangled bridge iron, with the upturned locomotive close to the west abutment.

C. F. ADAMS
from S. LEGG (ed.),
The Railway Book (1952)

CASEY JONES

Come all you rounders for I want you to hear
The story of a brave engineer;
Casey Jones was the fellow's name,
A big eight-wheeler of a mighty fame.
Caller called Casey at half-past four,
He kissed his wife at the station door,
Mounted to the cabin with orders in his hand,
And took his farewell trip to the promised land.
   Casey Jones, he mounted to the cabin,
   Casey Jones, with his orders in his hand!
   Casey Jones, he mounted to the cabin,
   Took his farewell trip into the promised land.

Put in your water and shovel in your coal,
Put your head out the window, watch the drivers roll,
I'll run her till she leaves the rail,
'Cause we're eight hours late with the Western Mail!
He looked at his watch and his watch was slow,
Looked at the water and the water was low,
Turned to his fireboy and said,
"We'll get to 'Frisco, but we'll all be dead!"
   Chorus

Casey pulled up Reno Hill,
Tooted for the crossing with an awful shrill,
Snakes all knew by the engine's moans
That the hogger at the throttle was Casey Jones.
He pulled up short two miles from the place,
Number Four stared him right in the face,
Turned to his fireboy, said "You'd better jump,
'Cause there's two locomotives going to bump!"
   Chorus

Casey said, just before he died,
"There's two more roads I'd like to ride."
Fireboy said, "What can they be?"
"The Rio Grande and the Old S.P."
Mrs. Jones sat on her bed a-sighing,
Got a pink that Casey was dying,
Said, "Go to bed, children; hush your crying,
'Cause you'll get another papa on the Salt Lake line."
    Casey Jones! Got another papa!
    Casey Jones, on the Salt Lake Line!
    Casey Jones! Got another papa!
    Got another papa on the Salt Lake Line!

WALLACE SAUNDERS

A crash in Palestine

An account of a journey from Damascus to Haifa undertaken
in about 1911 by Sir Frederic Treves, serjeant-surgeon to the
King and Surgeon in Ordinary to Queen Alexandra.

Some way farther along the blank road we came to a stock-
ade of posts, where we stopped and, as instructed, got out. This
we were told was the station, although so far as anything visible
was concerned we might as well have been in the centre of the
Sahara. Apparently there is something occult, or even sacred,
about a railway station in Syria, for neither carriages nor other
mean things on wheels are allowed to come within a certain respectful distance of the presence. We stumbled after the dragoman across some very uneven ground in the direction of a solitary light. This light, poor as it was, revealed the corner of a
small, low, stone building precisely like a miner's cottage in
Cornwall. The building was the station. The light came from a
lantern placed on the ground in front of a sleeping man who was

surrounded by a bank or entrenchment of bread. Probably no conception of the railway terminus of the capital of a country could be more remarkable than this. In place of the usual immense fabric and the vast dome of glass and iron was a miner's cottage, with a lantern on the ground by the side of a sleeping man surrounded by bread.

The time was now 4.50 A.M. Further investigation showed an empty train standing derelict at a little distance from the stone cottage. Between the latter and the train was a slope of very bumpy ground such as is met with around houses in course of erection, and this we concluded would be the platform. It was occupied by a number of large bundles which proved to be men wrapped up in blankets and asleep. Similar bundles were propped up, in an unsteady row, against the wall of what we now knew to be the Central Station of Damascus. These sleeping men were pilgrims from Mecca. They were on their way to the coast, as we were, but they were taking no risks as to catching the train. They knew something of oriental railways and their habits, and by sleeping on the platform between the booking-office and the actual carriages they evidently felt that the train could scarcely creep away without their knowledge. The men who were asleep on the ground about the miner's cottage were by no means all the intending travellers by "the early train." Close to the building were a number of tents full of silent human beings whose feet projected here and there from beneath the canvas. There had been a camp fire in the centre of the bivouac, but it had evidently long died out. It was apparent now that the man with the lantern and the bank of bread represented the refreshment-room. The buffet was not yet open, for the baker was still wrapt in his dreams.

Our coming was an event of moment, for we awoke the slumbering station. But for us the passengers, the station-master, the ticket clerk, and the porters might possibly have slept until noon. We woke the first series of men accidentally by falling over them and by treading on their bodies. They arose in panic, dreaming no doubt that the train had gone, and proceeded to rouse their friends and to aimlessly drag their luggage about. In a few minutes we witnessed what was no less than a resurrection scene. We found the terminus in a state of silence and the ground occupied apparently by dead men. Almost immediately these bodies rose from the earth, took up their beds, and walked. In a while out of the camp of tents poured several scores of pilgrims to join the shuffling crowd. All of them seemed confused, as would be a like body of men on the resurrection morning.

It was the train now that afforded a surprise. It consisted of three closed vans—labelled, as we perceived, later on, for eight horses or forty men—a third-class corridor carriage, and a like carriage with first-class compartments. The carriages were in darkness and apparently sealed up. But pilgrims began to beat on the doors of the goods wagons with their hands, when, to my amazement, they opened and out of each poured no fewer than forty sleep muddled Moslems. These devout men were in fact making exceedingly sure of the train by sleeping in it. Some of those who were released from what must have been a chamber of asphyxiation began forthwith to clamour at the doors of the third-class carriage, when, behold, that structure in turn proceeded to give up its dead, for out of its doors stumbled or fell more than enough men to fill it, I should imagine, twice over. The man-producing powers of the place appeared to be now exhausted, for the crowd already amounted—as was afterwards made clear—to over 150 souls. But this was not all, as was proved when an excited man attacked the first-class carriage which had, up to this moment, exhibited no sign of life. He beat violently upon the walls and doors of the same, screaming the while "Aboo-Shihab, Aboo-Shihab." The man who made this onslaught upon the irresponsive carriage was apparently connected with the railway. He not only screamed and kicked the doors with his feet but he thumped the windows with his fist. For a long time there was no response to this vast outburst of noise; but finally a sleepy man, whom I supposed to be Aboo-Shihab, opened the door (which he had locked from the inside) and stepped to the ground like one in a trance. He was followed by many others, all of whom were evidently railway men who, not wishing to miss the starting of the train or to be late to their work, had wisely slept in the field of their labours.

Up to this moment the stone cottage had exhibited no evidence of human occupation. It still remained silent and dark in spite of the fact that the dragoman had been hammering upon the door with an umbrella for some time. Possibly the inhabitants of the building would have remained lost to the world for the rest of the day had it not been for the actively minded man who had awakened Aboo-Shihab. This enthusiast, at 5.15 A.M., seized a bell and rang it like a demented person for a considerable period. The effect produced was marvellous. The pilgrims began to cry aloud and to rush to and fro like people in a burning house. As each man dragged his belongings with him the platform became a place of danger. There was evidently a belief that the train was starting at once, although there was no engine attached to it, nor was there even a sign of one; so they began to climb into the third-class carriage and the vans as if they had but few seconds to spare. The bellringing, however, had an effect upon the little stone house, for in a while a light appeared, and later on bolts were withdrawn and the door opened. I was anxious to have a peep at the station-master, the man upon whose word the rising of the sun depended, but he was as difficult to discover among the buzzing crowd as a queen bee in a swarm. Consequently I never saw him—a circumstance I shall always regret.

After a while the pilgrims became calmer again; they even strolled about, chatted with one another, bought bread of the baker, and generally behaved as people of leisure to whom railway travelling is rather a bore. At 5.30 A.M., however, the awakener of Aboo-Shihab seized the bell again and rang it for his very life. The effect was again astounding. The loitering pilgrims were once more electrified. They once more made a rush for the carriage doors as people rush to the exits of a burning theatre; they blocked the doors, they trampled upon one another, they fought to get in, while those who found any attempt at entry impossible flitted to and fro on the platform as folk deprived of reason.

Near about 6 A.M. the bell was rung for the third time, but the pilgrims had not yet recovered from the last shock, so beyond a general shudder it produced no visible effect. As a matter of fact the platform was deserted, every man was already in his place, the engine had been coupled on, the baker had sold all his bread, had blown out his lamp, and could be seen wending his way towards the city. The dawn was appearing. It would seem as if the ringing of the bell had awakened even the sun. The light fell upon one of the most forlorn-looking railway stations I had ever seen, upon the deserted camp, upon the ashes of the fire, and upon a wide drift of litter that was indescribable. As soon as the bell had ceased, the train, without further ceremony, glided out into the mist, and we knew that the sun was at last at liberty to rise.

It is desirable to note—in connection with what happened later on—that next to the engine came the three closed goods vans, each containing about fifty pilgrims, and that it was followed by the third-class corridor carriage which held no fewer than forty more devotees from Mecca. At the end of the train was the first-class carriage in which we and our dragoman were the sole passengers. The pilgrims were Russian Moslems, men of a marked Mongolian type of face, who were clad in heavy coats, one coat being worn over the other, while the outer garment was peeled off, on occasion, to make a praying carpet. They carried with them a good deal of untidy baggage, varying from battered German trunks and sailors' sea bags to bundles in blankets. With the same were associated such odd articles of luggage as lamps, jugs, and cooking pots, with, above all, the inevitable samovar which they clung to as if it had been a sacred image.

The descent from the tableland to the plain is by a mountain railway of considerable length and of no mean degree of steepness. We came to about the worst part of the incline at 2.30 in the afternoon. The line at this point follows a rocky defile. The road, which is very narrow, is represented by a ledge cut on the side of an almost vertical cliff. Above the line is the precipitous face of the hill, while below, at the foot of the great wall of rock, is the river, converted into a torrent by the recent rains. At this somewhat hair-raising spot the engine was proceeding very slowly, when we suddenly felt a shock which I imagined was due to the carriage being struck by a falling rock. There followed immediately a second blow like to the first, and then I became aware of the fact that the train was off the line. Before I fully realised that there was very little margin for a manoeuvre of this kind we came to a sudden stop. I jumped out and made

my way to the front of the train. On arriving there I was as-
tounded to see that both the engine and the tender were missing,
and, looking down over the cliff, I saw both these vehicles in the
river. Apart from the roar of the stream everything was so quiet
that these essential parts of the train might have been lying in
the water for weeks. The engine was upside down and was almost entirely submerged in the muddy water, the wheels alone
being visible above the flood. The tender was the right way up,
but the water reached to the level of the floor, while it was
empty of every particle of coal. The drop from the line to the
river bed was about forty to fifty feet.

We were relieved to see two men—the driver and the stoker
—crawling out of the river. Their escape from immediate death
was due to the fact that the engine, in turning over in its fall,
had thrown them on to a slope of stones, on to just such an incline as forms the talus at the foot of a mountain. The officials
on the train immediately went to the assistance of their comrades. The approach to the water's edge was difficult, and still
more difficult was the conveying of the injured men up an adjacent slope. The stoker, who was a Turk, was suffering a good
deal from shock, was badly cut about the head and face and
much bruised elsewhere. The engine-driver, a Bulgarian, was
unhappily in a worse plight, for, in addition to superficial injuries, it was evident that one of the abdominal organs had been
ruptured. Both of the men were placed lying down in the compartment next to ours. They were in great pain, but fortunately
I had with me a medicine case and a flask of whisky. After two
doses of morphia they each expressed themselves as much better.
The stoker began to regain his pulse, but the poor engine-driver,
although free from pain, showed no amendment, and it was
evident that, as no operation was possible in this wild ravine,
his case was hopeless.

As to the cause of the accident no light was forthcoming,
but it was quite clear that the carriages had not been struck by
any falling rock as I had supposed. The first of the three goods
vans full of pilgrims was wholly derailed, the front wheels being
within eighteen inches of the edge of the precipice. Had not the
couplings broken the disaster would have been terrible to con-

template. The front part or bogie of the second van had left the rails, but the hind wheels still held to the metals and so saved the whole train, after the couplings had given, from running headlong over the cliff, for the incline of the road was considerable. The third van and the two carriages were not derailed.

The pilgrims turned out of the train in a languid and lethargic mass and crawled vaguely about the line. They contemplated the engine in the river with an air of weariness. They were so little disturbed from their tortoise-like calm that one might have supposed that an episode of this kind was a common occurrence. The journey from Mecca had been to them a succession of wonders, and this was but one of many strange things. If a railway bell had been rung they would have been thrilled and alarmed, but the dropping of an engine with two men into.

The world's first major railway accident. On 8 May 1842 a train from Versailles to Paris was derailed and caught fire. Many passengers were unable to escape, the carriage doors having been locked. Fifty-seven died.

a river was not a matter for emotion. Their first care was to set the samovar going and then to glide down to the river to wash.

I may say that during all this time it was raining hard. It had rained steadily since daylight, and further, I may add that it rained with equal perseverance all night. In due course, namely at 5 P.M., a relief train came up from the direction of Haifa. It consisted of trucks enough to take the pilgrims, and of a guard's van. The process of transferring the baggage was very slow, owing to the narrowness of the way. On the river side the train was within eighteen inches of the edge, so that it was dangerous to pass on that part of the road with heavy trunks; while on what may be termed the land side was a deep, stone-lined trench between the line of rails and the cliff. There was a choice, therefore, between falling into the river on the one side, or into the stone crevasse on the other. A special difficulty arose in connection with the transfer of the injured men. The stoker could be helped along betwen two of his comrades, but the driver was unable to stand. It so happened that on the train was a solitary Bedouin who possessed a very strong and ample cloak. I proposed that the driver should be placed in the cloak and carried between two men along the narrow way as if he were on a stretcher. It was explained to me, however, that he was a Moslem and that he could not be carried lying down because it would be "unlucky" and a portent of death. He must be carried, his co-religionists decided, upon a man's back. I protested earnestly against this inhuman procedure. I appealed to the patient as well as to his friends, but all was in vain; so I witnessed the horrible spectacle of a heavy man with a ruptured intestine being carried along a very shaky road on another man's back, while he was held precariously in place by a third. I made the poor fellow as comfortable as I could on the floor of the guard's van, on a bed of coats and cloaks, and was gratified to find that he slept a little before we came to the journey's end. He was a man of admirable fortitude and courage, who never uttered a sound of complaint, and was only distressed by the fear that he was giving trouble.

We left the scene of the accident at 5.30 P.M. As there was no available carriage on the train my wife and I rode in the guard's van, sitting on bags on the floor. It was a very dreary journey, for we were destined not to reach Haifa until 2 A.M. on the following morning. The hours seemed to be interminable. I never looked at my watch without being convinced that it had stopped. The night was not only dark but very cold, while the pattering of rain on the roof of the van made for melancholy. To increase the dreariness of the situation there was no light in the van until a candle was obtained from the pilgrims. It was stuck in a bottle and placed on the floor. It gave a sorry illumination to a sorry scene—a bare van with people sitting or lying on the floor in company with a dying man and another who was grievously injured. I am inclined to think that we should have been better without the candle, for there is a negative relief in absolute darkness.

When we were two or three hours distant from Haifa a passenger carriage was attached to the train in which we completed the journey. It was at this point that we met certain prominent officials of the line who were on their way to the scene of the disaster. There were some six of them—all, I believe, Turks. They very courteously came to see me in the guard's van, and civilities and cards were exchanged through the medium of the dragoman. I was wishing that I could speak direct to these gentlemen, when one of them came towards me, and, holding out his hand, observed with fervour, "Oh, what a bally country!" It was a somewhat unusual introductory remark, but, assuming that the adjective employed had a condemnatory meaning, it was not entirely out of place, for the night was dark and cold, it was pouring with rain, we were without food or the possibility of obtaining any. I was, however, so delighted to meet a person who spoke English that I grasped this gentleman very warmly by the hand and told him how pleased I was to meet some one I could talk to. To this he replied, "Oh, what a bally country!" I agreed with his views as to the immediate country, but, wishing to change the subject, said, "This has been a most unfortunate accident." To which he answered, "Oh, what a bally country!" I then tried simpler sentences, such as "Good evening," "Are you not wet?" but on each occasion he replied with the criticism, "Oh, what a bally country!" I then found that, with the exception of this curious sentence, he did not know a single word or syllable of English. I am convinced that he had not the faintest idea of the meaning of his speech. I imagine that he had been at one time associated with an English railway engineer who had given vent to this expression so frequently that this courteous, well-intending Turk had learnt it like a parrot. As he stepped out of the guard's van into the rain I said, "I am afraid you will have a very trying journey," to which he answered, with a smile and a polite bow, "Oh, what a bally country!" Thus we parted without further exchange of ideas.

We reached Haifa at 2 A.M. and got to bed at 3 A.M., having been "up" exactly twenty-four hours. The engine-driver was removed to the excellent and admirably equipped German hospital in the town. I went to see him early next morning. He was conscious, but quite free from pain, and was rapidly nearing the end. His wife was with him. He smiled, as an old friend would smile, when we shook hands, for there was this bond between us—that I had been with him on the train. He nodded as I went out of the room. It was to show that he knew that he was really saying good-bye. He died a little while after I left the ward.

SIR FREDERICK TREVES,
The Land That Is Desolate

The Trans-Siberian takes a purler

There is no more luxurious sensation than what may be described as the End of Term Feeling. The traditional scurrilities of

> This time to-morrow where shall I be?
> Not in this academee

have accompanied delights as keen and unqualified as any that most of us will ever know. As we left Baikal behind and went lurching through the operatic passes of Buriat Mongolia, I felt very content. To-morrow we should reach the frontier. After to-morrow there would be no more of that black bread, in consistency and flavour suggesting rancid peat: no more of that equally alluvial tea: no more of a Trappist's existence, no more days entirely blank of action. It was true that I did not know what I was going to do, that I had nothing very specific to look forward to. But I knew what I was going to stop doing, and that, for the moment, was enough.

I undressed and got into bed. As I did so, I noticed for the first time that the number of my berth was thirteen.

For a long time I could not go to sleep. I counted sheep, I counted weasels (I find them much more efficacious, as a rule. I don't know why). I recited in a loud, angry voice soporific passages from Shakespeare. I intoned the names of stations we had passed through since leaving Moscow: Bui, Perm, Omsk, Tomsk, Kansk, Krasnoyarsk. (At one a low-hung rookery in birch trees, at another the chattering of swifts against a pale evening sky, had made me home-sick for a moment.) I thought of all the most boring people I knew, imagining that they were in the compartment with me, and had brought their favourite subjects with them. It was no good. My mind became more and more active. Obviously I was never going to sleep. . . .

It was the Trooping of the Colour, and I was going to be late for it. There, outside, in the street below my window, was my horse; *but it was covered with thick yellow fur!* This was awful! Why hadn't it been clipped? What would they think of me, coming on parade like that? Inadequately dressed though I was, I dashed out of my room and down the moving staircase. And then (horror of horrors!) the moving staircase broke. It lurched, twisted, flung me off my feet. There was a frightful jarring, followed by a crash. . . .

I sat up in my berth. From the rack high above me my heaviest suitcase, metal-bound, was cannonaded down, catching me with fearful force on either knee-cap. I was somehow not particularly surprised. This is the end of the world, I thought, and in addition they have broken both my legs. I had a vague sense of injustice.

My little world was tilted drunkenly. The window showed me nothing except a few square yards of goodish grazing, of which it offered an oblique bird's eye view. Larks were singing somewhere. It was six o'clock. I began to dress. I now felt very much annoyed.

But I climbed out of the carriage into a refreshingly spectacular world, and the annoyance passed. The Trans-Siberian Express sprawled foolishly down the embankment. The mail van and the dining-car, which had been in front, lay on their sides at the bottom. Behind them the five sleeping-cars, headed by my own, were disposed in attitudes which became less and less grotesque until you got to the last, which had remained, primly, on the rails. Fifty yards down the line the engine, which had parted company with the train, was dug in, snorting, on top of the embankment. It had a truculent and naughty look; it was defiantly conscious of indiscretion.

It would be difficult to imagine a nicer sort of railway accident. The weather was ideal. No one was badly hurt. And the whole thing was done in just the right Drury Lane manner, with lots of twisted steel and splintered woodwork and turf scarred deeply with demoniac force. For once the Russians had carried something off.

The air was full of agonizing groans and the sound of breaking glass, the first supplied by two attendants who had been winded, the second by passengers escaping from a coach in which both the doors had jammed. The sun shone brightly. I began to take photographs as fast as I could. This is strictly forbidden on Soviet territory, but the officials had their hands full and were too upset to notice.

The staff of the train were scattered about the wreckage, writing contradictory reports with trembling hands. A charming German consul and his family—the only other foreigners on the train—had been in the last coach and were unscathed. Their small daughter, aged six, was delighted with the whole affair, which she regarded as having been arranged specially for her entertainment; I am afraid she will grow up to expect too much from trains.

Gradually I discovered what had happened, or at least what was thought to have happened. As a rule the Trans-Siberian

Expresses have no great turn of speed, but ours, at the time when disaster overtook her, had been on top of her form. She had a long, steep hill behind her, and also a following wind; she was giving of her best. But, alas, at the bottom of that long, steep hill the signals were against her, a fact which the driver noticed in the course of time. He put on his brakes. Nothing happened. He put on his emergency brakes. Still nothing happened. Slightly less rapidly than before, but still at a very creditable speed, the train went charging down the long, steep hill.

The line at this point is single track, but at the foot of the hill there is a little halt, where a train may stand and let another pass. Our train, however was in no mood for stopping: it looked as if she was going to ignore the signals and try conclusions with a west-bound train, head on. In this she was thwarted by a pointsman at the little halt, who summed up the situation and switched the runaway neatly into a siding. It was a long, curved siding, and to my layman's eye appeared to have been designed for the sole purpose of receiving trains which got out of control on the hill above it. But for whatever purpose it was designed, it was designed a very long time ago. Its permanent way had a more precarious claim to that epithet than is usual even in Russia. We were altogether too much for the siding. We made matchwood of its rotten sleepers and flung ourselves dramatically down the embankment.

But it had been great fun: a comical and violent climax to an interlude in which comedy and violence had been altogether too lacking for my tastes. It was good to lie back in the long grass on a little knoll and meditate upon that sprawling scrap-heap, that study in perdition. There she lay, in the middle of a wide green plain: the crack train, the Trans-Siberian Luxury Express. For more than a week she had bullied us. She had knocked us about when we tried to clean our teeth, she had jogged our elbows when we wrote, and when we read she had made the print dance tiresomely before our eyes. Her whistle had arbitrarily curtailed our frenzied excursions on the wayside platforms. Her windows we might not open on account of the dust, and when closed they had proved a perpetual attraction to small, sabotaging boys with stones. She had annoyed us in a hundred little ways: by spilling tea in our laps, by running out of butter, by regulating her life in accordance with Moscow time, now six hours behind the sun. She had been our prison, our Little Ease. We had not liked her.

Now she was down and out. We left her lying there, a broken buckled toy, a thick black worm without a head, awkwardly twisted: a thing of no use, above which larks sang in an empty plain.

If I know Russia, she is lying there still.

PETER FLEMING,
One's Company

The Tay Bridge disaster

The train moved on and, at thirteen minutes past seven, it reached the beginning of the bridge. At this point, before entering upon the single line of rails over the bridge, it slowed down opposite the signal cabin, to allow the baton to be passed. Without this exchange it was not permitted to proceed, and, still filled by a sense of misgiving, Denis again lowered his window and looked out, to observe that everything was correct. The force of the gale almost decapitated him but, in the red glare cast by the engine, he discerned, stretching dimly into the distance, the massive girders of the bridge, like the colossal skeleton of an enormous reptile, but of steel, strong and adamantine. Then, all at once, he saw the signalman descend the steps from his box with consummate care, clutching the rail tightly with one hand. He surrendered the baton to the stoker, and, when he had accomplished this, he climbed back into his cabin with the utmost difficulty, fighting the wind and being assisted up the last few steps by the hand of a friend held out to him from within.

And now the train moved off again, and entered the bridge. Denis raised his window and sank back in his seat composedly, but, as he was carried past the signal-box, he received the fleeting impression of two pale, terrified faces looking at him from out of it, like ghostly countenances brushing past him in the blackness.

The Tay Bridge Disaster, 1880. On a wild and stormy night at the end of 1879 a train started to cross Scotland's newly completed Tay Bridge—then the longest bridge in the world—from the southern shore. When it was halfway across, the girders were unable to withstand the pressure of the wind. They collapsed; and the train and its engine fell headlong into the waters of the Firth of Tay, a hundred feet below. Seventy-five people died.

The violence of the gale was now unbounded. The wind hurled the rain against the sides of the train with the noise of a thousand anvils, and the wet snow again came slobbering upon the window panes, blotting out all vision. The train rocked upon the rails with a drunken, swaying oscillation, and although it proceeded slowly, cautiously, it seemed, from the fury and rush of the storm, to dash headlong upon its course. Thus, as it advanced, with the blackness, the noise of the wheels, the tearing rush of the wind, and the crashing of the waves upon the pier of the bridge below, there was developed the sensation of reckless, headlong acceleration.

As Denis sat alone, in the silent, cabined space of his compartment, tossed this way and that by the jactation, he felt suddenly that the grinding wheels of the train spoke to him. As they raced upon the line he heard them rasp out, with a heavy, despairing refrain: "God help us! God help us! God help us!"

Amidst the blare of the storm this slow, melancholy dirge beat itself into Denis' brain. The certain sense of some terrible disaster began to oppress him. Strangely, he feared, not for himself, but for Mary. Frightful visions flashed through the dark field of his imagination. He saw her, in a white shroud, with sad, imploring eyes, with dank, streaming hair, with bleeding feet and hands. Fantastic shapes oppressed her which made her shrink into the obliterating darkness. Again he saw her grimacing, simpering palely like a sorry statue of the Madonna and holding by the hand the weazened figure of a child. He shouted in horror. In a panic of distress he jumped to his feet. He desired to get to her. He wanted to open the door, to jump out of this confining box which enclosed him like a sepulchre. He would have given, instantly, everything he possessed to get out of the train. But he could not.

He was imprisoned in the train, which advanced inexorably, winding in its own glare like a dark, red serpent twisting sinuously forward. It had traversed one mile of the bridge and had now reached the middle span, where a mesh of steel girders formed a hollow tube through which it must pass. The train entered this tunnel. It entered slowly, fearfully, reluctantly, juddering in every bolt and rivet of its frame as the hurricane assaulted, and sought to destroy, the greater resistance now offered to it. The wheels clanked with the ceaseless insistence of the tolling of a passing-bell, still protesting, endlessly: "God help us! God help us! God help us!"

Then, abruptly, when the whole train lay enwrapped within the iron lamellae of the middle link of the bridge, the wind elevated itself with a culminating, exultant roar to the orgasm of its power and passion.

The bridge broke. Steel girders snapped like twigs, cement crumbled like sand, iron pillars bent like willow wands. The middle span melted like wax. Its wreckage clung around the tortured train, which gyrated madly for an instant in space. Immediately, a shattering rush of broken glass and wood descended upon Denis, cutting and bruising him with mangling violence. He felt the wrenching torsion of metal, and the grating of falling masonry. The inexpressible desolation of a hundred human voices, united in a sudden, short anguished cry of mingled agony and terror, fell upon his ears hideously, with the deathly fatality of a coronach. The walls of his compartment whirled about him and upon him, like a winding-sheet, the floor rushed over his head. As he spun round, with a loud cry he, too, shouted: "God help us!" then, faintly, the name: "Mary!"

Then the train with incredible speed, curving like a rocket, arched the darkness in a glittering parabola of light, and plunged soundlessly into the black hell of water below, where, like a rocket, it was instantly extinguished—for ever obliterated! For the infinity of a second, as he hurtled through the air, Denis knew what had happened. He knew everything, then instantly he ceased to know. At the same instant as the first faint cry of his child ascended feebly in the byre at Levenford, his mutilated body hit the dark, raging water and lay dead, deep down upon the bed of the firth.

A. J. CRONIN,
Hatter's Castle

FICTION

A cargo of cheeses

I remember a friend of mine buying a couple of cheeses at Liverpool. Splendid cheeses they were, ripe and mellow, and with a two hundred horse-power scent about them that might have been warranted to carry three miles, and knock a man over at two hundred yards. I was in Liverpool at the time, and my friend said that if I didn't mind he would get me to take them back with me to London, as he should not be coming up for a day or two himself, and he did not think the cheeses ought to be kept much longer.

"Oh, with pleasure, dear boy," I replied, "with pleasure."

I called for the cheeses, and took them away in a cab. It was a ramshackle affair, dragged along by a knock-kneed, broken-winded somnambulist, which his owner, in a moment of enthusiasm, during conversation, referred to as a horse. I put the cheeses on the top, and we started off at a shamble that would have done credit to the swiftest steam-roller ever built, and all went merry as a funeral bell, until we turned the corner. There, the wind carried a whiff from the cheeses full on to our steed. It woke him up, and, with a snort of terror, he dashed off at three miles an hour. The wind still blew in his direction, and before we reached the end of the street he was laying himself out at the rate of nearly four miles an hour, leaving the cripples and stout old ladies simply nowhere.

It took two porters as well as the driver to hold him in at the station; and I do not think they would have done it, even then, had not one of the men had the presence of mind to put a handkerchief over his nose, and to light a bit of brown paper.

I took my ticket, and marched proudly up the platform, with my cheeses, the people falling back respectfully on either side. The train was crowded, and I had to get into a carriage where there were already seven other people. One crusty old gentleman objected, but I got in, notwithstanding; and, putting my cheeses upon the rack, squeezed down with a pleasant smile, and said it was a warm day. A few moments passed, and then the old gentleman began to fidget.

"Very close in here," he said.

"Quite oppressive," said the man next him.

And then they both began sniffing, and, at the third sniff, they caught it right on the chest, and rose up without another word and went out. And then a stout lady got up, and said it was disgraceful that a respectable married woman should be harried about in this way, and gathered up a bag and eight parcels and went. The remaining four passengers sat on for a while, until a solemn-looking man in the corner who, from his dress and general appearance, seemed to belong to the undertaker class, said it put him in mind of a dead baby; and the other three passengers tried to get out of the door at the same time, and hurt themselves.

I smiled at the black gentleman, and said I thought we were going to have the carriage to ourselves; and he laughed pleasantly and said that some people made such a fuss over a little thing. But even he grew strangely depressed after we had started, and so, when we reached Crewe, I asked him to come and have a drink. He accepted, and we forced our way into the buffet, where we yelled, and stamped, and waved our umbrellas for a quarter of an hour; and then a young lady came and asked us if we wanted anything.

"What's yours?" I said, turning to my friend.

"I'll have half-a-crown's worth of brandy, neat, if you please, miss," he responded.

And he went off quietly after he had drunk it and got into another carriage, which I thought mean.

From Crewe I had the compartment to myself, though the train was crowded. As we drew up at the different stations, the people, seeing my empty carriage, would rush for it. "Here y' are, Maria; come along, plenty of room." "All right, Tom; we'll get in here" they would shout. And they would run along, carrying heavy bags, and fight round the door to get in first. And one would open the door and mount the steps and stagger back into the arms of the man behind him; and they would all come and have a sniff, and then droop off and squeeze into other carriages, or pay the difference and go first.

From Euston I took the cheeses down to my friend's house. When his wife came into the room she smelt round for an instant. Then she said:

"What is it? Tell me the worst."

JEROME K. JEROME,
Three Men in a Boat

The coming of the milk-girl

Sunrise is a necessary concomitant of long railway journeys, just as are hard-boiled eggs, illustrated papers, packs of cards, rivers upon which boats strain but make no progress. At a certain moment, when I was counting over the thoughts that had filled my mind, in the preceding minutes, so as to discover whether I had just been asleep or not (and when the very uncertainty which made me ask myself the question was to furnish me with an affirmative answer), in the pale square of the window, over a small black wood I saw some ragged clouds whose fleecy edges were of a fixed, dead pink, not liable to change, like the colour that dyes the wing which has grown to wear it, or the sketch upon which the artist's fancy has washed it. But I felt that, unlike them, this colour was due neither to inertia nor to caprice but to necessity and life. Presently there gathered behind it reserves of light. It brightened; the sky turned to a crimson which I strove, glueing my eyes to the window, to see more clearly, for I felt that it was related somehow to the most intimate life of Nature, but, the course of the line altering, the train turned, the morning scene gave place in the frame of the window to a nocturnal village, its roofs still blue with moonlight, its pond encrusted with the opalescent nacre of night, beneath a firmament still powdered with all its stars, and I was lamenting the loss of my strip of pink sky when I caught sight of it afresh, but red this time, in the opposite window which it left at a second bend in the line, so that I spent my time running from one window to the other to reassemble, to collect on a single canvas the intermittent, antipodean fragments of my fine, scarlet, ever-changing morning, and to obtain a comprehensive view of it and a continuous picture.

The scenery became broken, abrupt, the train stopped at a little station between two mountains. Far down the gorge, on the edge of a hurrying stream, one could see only a solitary watch-house, deep-planted in the water which ran past on a level with its windows. If a person can be the product of a soil the peculiar charm of which one distinguishes in that person, more even than the peasant girl whom I had so desperately longed to see appear when I wandered by myself along the Méséglise way, in the woods of Roussainville, such a person must be the big girl whom I now saw emerge from the house and, climbing a path lighted by the first slanting rays of the sun, come towards the station carrying a jar of milk. In her valley from which its congregated summits hid the rest of the world, she could never see anyone save in these trains which stopped for a moment only. She passed down the line of windows, offering coffee and milk to a few awakened passengers. Purpled with the glow of morning, her face was rosier than the sky. I felt in her presence that desire to live which is reborn in us whenever we become conscious anew of beauty and of happiness. We invariably forget that these are individual qualities, and, substituting for them in our mind a conventional type at which we arrive by striking a sort of mean amongst the different faces that have taken our fancy, the pleasures we have known, we are left with mere abstract images which are lifeless and dull because they are lacking in precisely that element of novelty, different from anything we have known, that element which is proper to beauty and to happiness. And we deliver on life a pessimistic judgment which we suppose to be fair, for we believed that we were taking into account when we formed it happiness and beauty, whereas in fact we left them out and replaced them by syntheses in which there is not a single atom of either. So it is that a well-read man will at once begin to yawn with boredom when anyone speaks to him of a new "good book," because he imagines a sort of composite of all the good books that he has read and knows already, whereas a good book is something special, something incalculable, and is made up not of the sum of all previous masterpieces but of something which the most thorough assimilation of every one of them would not enable him to discover, since it exists not in their sum but beyond it. Once he has become acquainted with this new work, the well-read man, till then apathetic, feels his interest awaken in the reality which it depicts. So, alien to the models of beauty which my fancy was wont to sketch when I was by myself, this strapping girl gave me at once the sensation of a certain happiness (the sole form, always different, in which we may learn the sensation of happiness), of a happiness that

Trains in the Snow (Claude Monet, 1875)

would be realised by my staying and living there by her side. But in this again the temporary cessation of Habit played a great part. I was giving the milk-girl the benefit of what was really my own entire being, ready to taste the keenest joys, which now confronted her. As a rule it is with our being reduced to a minimum that we live, most of our faculties lie dormant because they can rely upon Habit, which knows what there is to be done and has no need of their services. But on this morning of travel, the interruption of the routine of my existence, the change of place and time had made their presence indispensable. My habits, which were sedentary and not matutinal, played me false, and all my faculties came hurrying to take their place, vieing with one another in their zeal, rising, each of them, like waves in a storm, to the same unaccustomed level, from the basest to the most exalted, from breath, appetite, the circulation of my blood to receptivity and imagination. I cannot say whether, so as to make me believe that this girl was unlike the rest of women, the rugged charm of these barren tracts had been added to her own, but if so she gave it back to them. Life would have seemed an exquisite thing to me if only I had been free to spend it, hour after hour, with her, to go with her to the stream, to the cow, to the train, to be always at her side, to feel that I was known to her, had my place in her thoughts. She would have initiated me into the delights of country life and of the first hours of the day. I signalled to her to give me some of her coffee. I felt that I must be noticed by her. She did not see me; I called to her. Above her body, which was of massive build, the complexion of her face was so burnished and so ruddy that she appeared almost as though I were looking at her through a lighted window. She had turned and was coming towards me; I could not take my eyes from her face which grew larger as she approached, like a sun which it was somehow possible to arrest in its course and draw towards one, letting itself be seen at close quarters, blinding the eyes with its blaze of red and gold. She fastened on me her penetrating stare, but while the porters ran along the platform shutting doors the train had begun to move. I saw her leave the station and go down the hill to her home; it was broad daylight now; I was speeding away from the dawn. Whether my exaltation had been produced by this girl or had on the other hand been responsible for most of the pleasure that I had found in the sight of her, in the sense of her presence, in either event she was so closely associated with it that my desire to see her again was really not so much a physical as a mental desire, not to allow this state of enthusiasm to perish utterly, not to be separated for ever from the person who, although quite unconsciously, had participated in it. It was not only because this state was a pleasant one. It was principally because (just as increased tension upon a cord or accelerated vibration of a nerve produces a different sound or colour) it gave another tonality to all that I saw, introduced me as an actor upon the stage of an unknown and infinitely more interesting universe; that handsome girl whom I still could see, while the train gathered speed, was like part of a life other than the life that I knew, separated from it by a clear boundary, in which the sensations that things produced in me were no longer the same, from which to return now to my old life would be almost suicide. To procure myself the pleasure of feeling that I had at least an attachment to this new life, it would suffice that I should live near enough to the little station to be able to come to it every morning for a cup of coffee from the girl. But alas, she must be for ever absent from the other life towards which I was being borne with ever increasing swiftness, a life to the prospect of which I resigned myself only by weaving plans that would enable me to take the same train again some day and to stop at the same station, a project which would have the further advantage of providing with subject matter the selfish, active, practical, mechanical, indolent, centrifugal tendency which is that of the human mind; for our mind turns readily aside from the effort which is required if it is to analyse in itself, in a general and disinterested manner, a pleasant impression which we have received. And as, on the other hand, we wish to continue to think of that impression, the mind prefers to imagine it in the future tense, which while it gives us no clue as to the real nature of the thing, saves us the trouble of recreating it in our own consciousness and allows us to hope that we may receive it afresh from without.

MARCEL PROUST,
Remembrance of Things Past
Within a Budding Grove
(trans. C. M. Scott-Moncrieff)

FAINTHEART IN A RAILWAY TRAIN

At nine in the morning there passed a church,
At ten there passed me by the sea,
At twelve a town of smoke and smirch,
At two a forest of oak and birch,
    And then, on a platform, she:

A radiant stranger, who saw not me.
I said, "Get out to her do I dare?"
But I kept my seat in my search for a plea,
And the wheels move on. O could it but be
    That I had alighted there!

THOMAS HARDY

Death of a hobo

Mac went down to the water tank beyond the yards to wait for a chance to hop a freight. The old man's hat and his ruptured shoes were ashen grey with dust; he was sitting all hunched up with his head between his knees and didn't make a move until Mac was right up to him. Mac sat down beside him. A rank smell of feverish sweat came from the old man. "What's the trouble daddy?"

"I'm through, that's all . . . I been a lunger all my life an I guess it's got me now." His mouth twisted in a spasm of pain. He let his head droop between his knees. After a minute he raised his head again, making little feeble gasps with his mouth like a dying fish. When he got his breath he said, "It's a razor a' slicin' off my lungs every time. Stand by, will you kid." "Sure I will," said Mac.

"Listen kid, I wanna go west to where there's trees an' stuff . . . You got to help me into one o' them cars. I'm too weak for the rods . . . Don't let me lay down . . . I'll start bleedin' if I lay down, see." He choked again.

"I got a coupla bucks. I'll square it with the brakeman maybe."

"You don't talk like no vag."

"I'm a printer. I wanto make San Francisco soon as I can."

"A workin' man. I'll be a son of a bitch. Listen here kid . . . I ain't worked in seventeen years."

The train came in and the engine stood hissing by the water-tank.

Mac helped the old man to his feet and got him propped in the corner of a flatcar that was loaded with machine parts covered with a tarpaulin. He saw the fireman and the engineer looking at them out of the cab, but they didn't say anything.

When the train started the wind was cold. Mac took off his coat and put it behind the old man's head to keep it from jiggling with the rattling of the car. The old man sat with his eyes closed and his head thrown back. Mac didn't know whether he was dead or not. It got to be night. Mac was terribly cold and huddled shivering in a fold of tarpaulin in the other end of the car.

In the grey of dawn Mac woke up from a doze with his teeth chattering. The train had stopped on a siding. His legs were so numb it was some time before he could stand on them. He went to look at the old man, but he couldn't tell whether he was alive or not. It got a little lighter and the east began to glow like the edge of a piece of iron in a forge. Mac jumped to the ground and walked back along the train to the caboose.

The brakeman was drowsing beside his lantern. Mac told him that an old tramp was dying in one of the flatcars. The brakeman had a small flask of whiskey in his good coat that hung on a nail in the caboose. They walked together up the track again. When they got to the flatcar it was almost day. The old man had flopped over on his side. His face looked white and grave like the face of a statue of a civil war general. Mac opened his coat and the filthy torn shirts and underclothes and put his hand on the old man's chest. It was cold and lifeless as a board. When he took his hand away there was sticky blood on it.

"Hemorrhage," said the brakeman, making a perfunctory clucking noise in his mouth.

The brakeman said they'd have to get the body off the train. They laid him down flat in the ditch beside the ballast with his hat over his face. Mac asked of the brakeman if he had a spade so that they could bury him, so that the buzzards wouldn't get him, but he said no that the mandywalkers would find him and bury him. He took Mac back to the caboose and gave him a drink and asked him all about how the old man had died.

JOHN DOS PASSOS,
42nd Parallel

On the trail of the thief

Emil woke up just as the train was pulling out of a station, and found himself on the floor, feeling very frightened. He must have been asleep, he thought, and slipped off the seat. Now, for some reason, his heart was beating like a sledgehammer. He could not remember where he was at first, then gradually it all came back to him. Of course, he was in a train, going to Berlin, in a compartment with a man in a bowler hat—and he had fallen asleep too.

The man in the bowler hat! That brought Emil's wits back. He sat up and rubbed his eyes. The man was gone. Emil got slowly to his feet, feeling quite shaky. Then, from sheer force of habit, he began to brush the dust off his trousers and jacket—and that reminded him of the money. Was it safe? He could not bear to feel for it in case it was gone. He leaned against the door, too anxious to raise a finger, just staring at the seat where that man called Grundeis had been sitting, and had gone to sleep, and snored. Now Grundeis was gone.

It was silly to take the worst for granted like this, just because the man had left the train while Emil himself was asleep. Naturally the passengers would not all be going as far as the Friedrich Street station where he was to get out. Of course not. And he had pinned the money in its envelope securely on to the lining of his jacket, so surely it must be safe. He had only to put his hand into that inner pocket on the right-hand side . . . His hand went slowly towards it . . . and felt about in it.

The pocket was empty! The money had gone.

He felt right into the corners of that pocket, and searched frantically through all his other pockets too. He ran his hands over the outside of his jacket—but there was nothing there to crackle. The notes were gone. He gave one last frantic rummage round the inner pocket, and cried out. The pin was still there, and had run into his finger. It stuck in, and left a bead of red blood when he pulled it out.

He wound his handkerchief round the finger, and a tear trickled down the side of his nose—not because of the pinprick, of course. He did not cry for such trifles. Why, a fortnight ago he ran into a lamp post so hard that he almost knocked it over. He still had the bruise on his forehead, and even that hadn't made him cry.

No, it was the money, and because of his mother. You can understand that. It had taken his mother months to save that seven pounds to take him to Berlin. He knew all about that—yet he had fallen asleep as soon as he was in the train! And while he was having that crazy dream, that pig of a man was actually stealing the money. It was enough to make anyone cry. What was to be done about it? Had he got to go on to Berlin and say to his grandmother, "I've come, but I may as well tell you right away that I haven't brought any money, and I'm afraid you'll even have to give me some to buy my return ticket when I go home again."

He could not do that. But the money was gone and Grandma would not get a penny of it. How could he go and stay there after that? But he couldn't go home again either. And all because of a low, mean chap who offered you chocolate, and then pretended to be asleep so that he could steal your money. It really was a terrible thing to have happened.

But Emil soon sniffed back the tears and looked about him. He might pull the communication cord, and the train would stop and the guard come along to find out what was wrong.

"What's the matter?" he'd ask, and Emil would tell him:

"My money's been stolen."

But as like as not, the guard would only say, "Well, better take care of it next time!" Then he'd be sure to ask for Emil's name and address.

"We shall have to write to your mother," he'd say. "Penalty for improper use of the communication cord—five pounds. She'll have to pay up, you know. Now get back into the train—quick."

Express trains have corridors so that passengers can walk from one end to the other. If Emil had been on one of those, he could have gone along to the guard's van straight away and reported the theft. But his was a slow train. It had no corridor, and there was nothing he could do until it stopped at the next station. By that time the man in the bowler hat might be miles away. Emil had no idea when he had left the train. He began to wonder what the time was, and how soon they would reach Berlin.

Out of the window he could see blocks of flats and houses with flower gardens, and then a lot of dirty red chimney stacks. Perhaps it was Berlin. He would go and find the guard at the next station, and tell him what had happened—oh, but then of course they would report it to the police.

Oh dear! The police! If he got mixed up with the police now, Sergeant Jeschke would be bound to hear about it and bring up that matter of the statue. "Ah," he'd say, "I have my suspicions about that boy, Emil Tischbein. First he defaces a fine statue here in Neustadt with chalks, then he says he's been robbed of seven pounds on the way to Berlin. How are we to know that he ever had seven pounds? In my experience anyone capable of defacing a monument is quite equal to making up a story like that. He has probably buried the money somewhere, or even swallowed it. Don't waste your time looking for a thief. If there ever was one, it was probably Emil Tischbein himself. I advise you to arrest him at once, Inspector!"

It was horrible. He could not even go to the police for help.

Emil dragged his suitcase down from the rack, and put on his cap. He stuck the pin carefully back in the lapel of his coat, and was ready to get out. He had no idea what to do next, but he could not bear to stay in that compartment any longer. The train slowed down, and through the window he saw rows and rows of shining rails. There were a lot of platforms, too, and he saw porters running along beside the carriages, ready to help people with their luggage. Then the train stopped.

Out on the platform the name of the station was written up in large letters, ZOOLOGICAL GARDENS. Carriage doors flew open and a lot of people got out. Some had friends waiting for them, and they waved and called to one another.

Emil leaned out of the window of his carriage to look for the guard. Then suddenly, a little distance away in the stream of departing passengers, he saw a bowler hat. At once he thought—*"Ah! Mr Grundeis!"* Had he not left the train after all, but only skipped out of one compartment and into another while the train stopped and Emil was asleep? Without another thought, Emil was out on the platform. He forgot the flowers on the luggage rack, but just had time to scramble back after them, dashing in and out of the train as quickly as he could. Then, flowers in one hand and suitcase in the other, he scurried off towards the exit. People leaving the train were packed tight near the barrier, and could hardly move. In the crush, Emil found he had lost sight of the bowler hat, but he blundered on, stumbling round people's legs and bumping into them with his suitcase; but he kept doggedly on till he saw it again. But then, all at once there were two bowler hats.

The suitcase was so heavy it slowed Emil down terribly, but it might get stolen if he put it down somewhere so that he could run after his man. He just had to plunge on, and at last came nearly level with the bowler hats. But which was the right one? One man seemed too short. Emil twisted in and out of the crowd after the other, like a Red Indian on the trail, and was just in time to see his man push through the barrier, evidently in a great hurry.

"Just you wait, you dirty rotten thief," he thought to himself, "I'll catch you yet."

He gave up his ticket, changed the suitcase to his other hand, wedged the flowers firmly under his right arm, and ran down the stairs.

"Now for it!" he thought.

ERICH KASTNER,
Emil and the Detectives
(trans. Eileen Hall)

Mr. Boot and Mr. Salter

After an early luncheon, William went to say goodbye to his grandmother. She looked at him with doleful, mad eyes. "Going to London, eh? Well I hardly suppose I shall be alive when you return. Wrap up warm, dear." It was eternal winter in Mrs. Boot's sunny bedroom.

All the family who had the use of their legs attended on the steps to see William off; Priscilla bathed in tears of penitence. Nannie Bloggs sent him down three golden sovereigns. Aunt Anne's motor car was there to take him away. At the last moment Uncle Theodore attempted to get in at the off side, but was detected and deterred. "Just wanted to see a chap in Jermyn Street about some business," he said wistfully.

It was always a solemn thing for a Boot to go to London; solemn as a funeral for William on this afternoon. Once or twice on the way to the station, once or twice as the train stopped on the route to Paddington, William was tempted to give up the expedition in despair. Why should he commit himself to this abominable city merely to be railed at and, for all he knew of Lord Copper's temperament, physically assaulted? But sterner counsels prevailed. He might bluff it out. Lord Copper was a townsman, a provincial townsman at that, and certainly did not know the difference between a badger and a great crested grebe. It was William's word against a few cantankerous correspondents and people who wrote to the newspapers were proverbially unbalanced. By the time he reached Westbury he had sketched out a little scene for himself, in which he stood resolutely in the board room defying the doctrinaire zoology of Fleet Street; every inch a Boot, thrice descended from Ethelred the Unready, rightful 15th Baron de Butte, haughty as a chieftain, honest as a peasant. "Lord Copper," he was saying. "No man shall call me a liar unchastised. The great crested grebe *does* hibernate."

He went to the dining-car and ordered some whiskey. The steward said "We're serving teas. Whiskey after Reading." After Reading he tried again. "We're serving dinners. I'll bring you one to your carriage." When it came, William spilled it down his tie. He gave the steward one of Nannie Blogg's sovereigns in mistake for a shilling. It was contemptuously refused and everyone in the carriage stared at him. A man in a bowler hat said, "May I look? Don't often see one of them nowadays. Tell you what I'll do, I'll toss you for it. Call."

William said "Heads."

"Tails it is," said the man in the bowler hat, putting it in his waistcoat pocket. He then went on reading his paper and everyone stared harder at William. His spirits began to sink; the mood of defiance passed. It was always the way; the moment he left the confines of Boot Magna he found himself in a foreign and hostile world. There was a train back at ten o'clock that night. Wild horses would not keep him from it. He would see Lord Copper, explain the situation fully and frankly, throw himself upon his mercy and, successful or defeated, catch the train at ten. By Reading he had worked out this new and humble policy. He would tell Lord Copper about Priscilla's tears; great men were proverbially vulnerable in appeals of that kind. The man opposite him looked over the top of his paper. "Got any more quids?"

"No," said William.

"Pity."

At seven he reached Paddington and the atrocious city was all around him.

*   *   *

That evening, some time after the advertised hour, Mr. Salter alighted at Boot Magna Halt. An hour earlier, at Taunton, he had left the express, and changed into a train such as he did not know existed outside the imagination of his Balkan correspondents; a single tram-like, one-class coach, which had pottered in a desultory fashion through a system of narrow, underpopulated valleys. It had stopped eight times, and at every station there had been a bustle of passengers succeeded by a long, silent pause, before it started again; men had entered who, instead of slinking and shuffling and wriggling themselves into corners and decently screening themselves behind newspapers,

as civilized people should when they travelled by train, had sat
down squarely quite close to Mr. Salter, rested their hands on
their knees, stared at him fixedly and uncritically and suddenly
addressed him on the subject of the weather in barely intelli-
gible accents; there had been very old, unhygienic men and
women, such as you never saw in the Underground, who ought
long ago to have been put away in some public institution; there
had been women carrying a multitude of atrocious little baskets
and parcels which they piled on the seats; one of them had put a
hamper containing a live turkey under Mr. Salter's feet. It had
been a horrible journey.

EVELYN WAUGH,
Scoop

Train without driver

A few days passed. Jacques had returned to his engine, avoid-
ing his comrades, sunk back into his former savage gloom. War
had just been declared, following stormy sessions in the Chamber. There had already been an advance-guard skirmish, which
had turned out well, they said. For a week the transportation of
troops wore down the railroad personnel with fatigue. A continual flow of unscheduled trains made the regular ones fearfully late, not to mention that the best engineers had been
called to assist in the mobilization and concentration of the
armies. And so, one night, instead of his usual express, Jacques
took out of Le Havre a long train of eighteen cars, packed with
soldiers.

That night, Pecqueux arrived at the engine-house very
drunk. The day after he had surprised Philomene and Jacques,
he had resumed his work as fireman on Engine 608 with the
latter again. And he made no allusion to the incident, but remained dark and somber, as though he dared not look at the
engineer. But the latter felt that he was more and more in revolt;
he refused to obey orders, answered them with a low growl. At
last they stopped talking altogether. The platform that had carried them together, so friendly and united, was now no more

than a dangerous and narrow plank on which their rivalry met. Their hatred increased, and, flying at top speed, they were ready to murder each other on these few square feet, from which the least shock might have precipitated them. That night, seeing Pecqueux drunk, Jacques was alarmed; for he knew he was too sly to quarrel sober, and that only wine unleashed the beast in him.

The train, which was to have left at six o'clock, was delayed. It was already night when the soldiers were loaded like sheep into the cattle-cars. Planks had been nailed across for benches, and the soldiers were piled in until it seemed impossible the cars would hold them. They sat on each other, some stood up, so tightly squeezed they could not move their arms. At Paris, another train waited for them, to take them to the Rhine. They were already crushed with fatigue, in the excitement of their departure. But they had been given brandy, and many of them had spent the time before they embarked in the taverns, so that they had a sort of heated, brutal gaiety, their faces were red, their eyes started from their heads. And as the train started out of the station, they began to sing.

Jacques looked at the sky, hidden by stormy clouds. It would be a black night. Not a breath of breeze stirred the burning-hot air. The wind made by their speed, usually fresh, was warm tonight. No light showed on the black horizon but the signals, like live coals. He increased the pressure to make the heavy grade from Harfleur to Saint-Romain. In spite of his several weeks of experimenting with Engine 608, he was not yet its master. It was too new, and its whims and childish pranks constantly surprised him. That night it seemed especially unmanageable, whimsical, ready to overturn on account of a few pieces of coal too many. His hand on the throttle, he kept an eye on the fires, as he grew more and more anxious over his fireman's appearance. The little light that illumined the water-gauge left the platform in a penumbra of darkness, purple from the red-hot fire-box door. He could hardly make out Pecqueux; he had twice felt something brush his legs, as though fingers were practicing to take hold of them. But he decided that must have been drunken clumsiness, for he could hear him, over the engine's roar, chuckling aloud, breaking coal with unnecessarily heavy blows. Every minute, he opened the door, and threw coal on the grate, in unreasonable amounts.

"That's enough!" cried Jacques.

The other pretended not to hear or understand, but continued to throw in shovelful after shovelful. The engineer took him by the arm, and he turned threateningly, in drunken, increasing fury, with the quarrel he sought, at last at hand.

"Let me go, or I'll batter you! I like to go fast."

The train now ran at full speed over the plateau between Bolbec and Motteville. It was to proceed direct to Paris, without a stop except to take water. The huge mass of eighteen cars loaded, crammed, with human cattle, pounded and roared over the black countryside. And the men who were being carried to the slaughter were singing, so clamorously that the sound of it was louder than that of the rumbling wheels.

Jacques kicked the door closed. Then, moving the injector, still controlling himself:

"There's too much fire. Go to sleep, if you're drunk."

Pecqueux reopened the door and piled on more and more fuel, as though he were trying to burst the boilers. It was revolt, orders disregarded, frenzied passion that forgot completely all the human lives behind. Jacques leaned over to lower the bar of the grate, to diminish the draft at least. But the fireman took hold of him, tried to shove him suddenly off the engine.

"You bastard! So that's what you wanted! Then you could say I fell! You bastard!"

He had caught hold of the edge of the tender. They were both slipping. The struggle continued on the little iron platform that danced and jumped. Teeth clenched, they no longer spoke, but concentrated each on throwing the other through the narrow opening which had only a single iron bar across it. But it wasn't easy. The engine sped on and on. Barentin was passed, and the train plunged into Malaunay tunnel. They were still struggling, thrown down on the coal, their heads now and then striking against the water tanks. Both avoided the red-hot fire-box door, which burned their legs each time they came close to it.

For a moment, Jacques thought that if he could get up, he would close the throttle, and be able to call for help, to rid himself of this drunken maniac, mad with wine and jealousy. He was weakening, and began to despair of having the strength to throw him off; he was already beaten, and felt the terror of the fall prickling his scalp. He made a supreme effort, feeling with his hand, and the other understood, stiffened himself, and picked him up like a child.

"Oh, so you want to stop! . . . Oh, so you took my woman! . . . Come on, you've got to pay, now!"

The engine sped on and on. The train had left the tunnel with a roar, and continued on its mad course across the dark, empty countryside. They passed through the station of Malaunay so fast that the assistant station-master, standing on the platform, did not even glimpse the two men murdering each other in the engine-cab.

With a final effort, Pecqueux threw Jacques off, and Jacques feeling himself fall, terror-struck, clung to his neck so tight he dragged him with him. There were two terrible screams that seemed like one, then died away. The two men, falling together, dragged under the wheels by the action of the train's speed, were cut and sliced, in their horrible embrace. They had lived for so long like brothers. They were found headless, without feet, two bloody trunks still holding each other in a murderous hug.

And the engine, free of control, flew on and on. At last the irresponsible, rebellious engine could yield to the caprice of its youth, like an unbroken colt, escaped from its master's hands, and galloping over the fields. There was water in the boiler, the coal that had been piled on the grate was turning red. For half an hour the pressure rose madly, as the speed madly increased. The conductor had no doubt fallen asleep. The soldiers, whose drunkenness was greater for the crowding, cheered the increasing speed, sang louder. The train went through Maromme with lightning speed. There was no whistling at signals or stations. It was a steady gallop, a beast with silent head low to the ground, brooking no obstacle. It sped and sped on endlessly, as though maddened and infuriated by the strident shrieking of its own breath.

At Rouen, they were to take on water; and the station was chilled with terror when the train passed, a streak of smoke and flame, its engine without engineer or fireman, its cattle-cars filled with troops howling patriotic airs. They were going to war, speeding to the banks of the Rhine. The employees stared, waving their arms. Suddenly everyone cried out. That abandoned, masterless train could never get through the Sotteville station, where there was always a clutter of manoeuvering engines and coaches. The telegraph clicked. At Sotteville, a freight train which was on the line was side-tracked. The roar of the escaped monster came from the distance. It had plunged through the two tunnels close to Rouen, and was arriving at a mad gallop, like a prodigious, irresistible force which there was no hope of stopping. It burned through Sotteville station, sped between all obstacles, and plunged into the darkness again, where the roar of its passage slowly died away.

Now every telegraph instrument along the line clicked, every heart beat, with the news of a phantom train that had just gone through Sotteville and Rouen. Everyone trembled. An express, ahead on the same line, would surely be caught up with. Like a boar through the woods, the train sped on without regard for red lights or cracker signals. At Oissel, it narrowly missed striking a shunting-engine. Pont-de-l'Arche was terror-struck, for its speed did not seem diminished. Disappearing again it sped, and roared into the black night, no one knew where, ahead.

And what did they matter, the victims crushed on the road by the locomotive? Was it not going into the future, careless of spilt blood? Without a master, through the blackness, a blind, deaf beast, unleashed with death, it sped on, and on, loaded with cannon-fodder, with soldiers stupid with exhaustion, drunk, singing.

ÉMILE ZOLA,
The Hungry Beast
(trans. Louis Colman)

THE LITTLE BLACK TRAIN
(Suggested by a folk song)

Who hears that whistle blowing?
Who hears that hellish din?
Not the living—but they will.
   Ah, where is it going?
   And where has it been?
Ask the darkness that falls on the hill.

Behind—a ghost smoke flowing;
   Ahead—that quiet inn
Which all may enter—but none come back.
   Ah, where are they going?
   And where have they been?
Ask the thistles that bloom on the track.

The cabman is all-knowing
(They say), and at peace within;
But it must be lonely at night.
   Ah, where is he going?
   And where has he been?
Ask the millions who wait without light.

Black roses need no sowing,
And the soul is born in sin
(We're told)—fouled by that ancient pair.
   Ah, where is it going?
   And where has it been?
Ask the star that touches your loved one's hair.

And now the train is slowing,
And the passengers they grin,
As well they might—a little sly.
   Ah, where are they going?
   And where have they been?
Ask the lanterns that swing in the sky.

KENNETH PATCHEN

Holmes and Moriarty:
The Final Problem

I had often admired my friend's courage, but never more than
now, as he sat quietly checking off a series of incidents which
must have combined to make up a day of horror.

"You will spend the night here?" I said.

"No, my friend, you might find me a dangerous guest. I have
my plans laid, and all will be well. Matters have gone so far
now that they can move without my help as far as the arrest
goes, though my presence is necessary for a conviction. It is obvious, therefore, that I cannot do better than get away for the few
days which remain before the police are at liberty to act. It
would be a great pleasure to me, therefore, if you could come on
to the Continent with me."

"The practice is quiet," said I, "and I have an accommodat-
ing neighbour. I should be glad to come."

"And to start to-morrow morning?"

"If necessary."

"Oh yes, it is most necessary. Then these are your instruc-
tions, and I beg, my dear Watson, that you will obey them to
the letter, for you are now playing a double-handed game with
me against the cleverest rogue and the most powerful syndicate
of criminals in Europe. Now listen! You will despatch whatever
luggage you intend to take by a trusty messenger unaddressed
to Victoria to-night. In the morning you will send for a hansom,
desiring your man to take neither the first nor the second which
may present itself. Into this hansom you will jump, and you will
drive to the Strand end of the Lowther Arcade, handing the
address to the cabman upon a slip of paper, with a request that
he will not throw it away. Have your fare ready, and the instant
that your cab stops, dash through the Arcade, timing yourself
to reach the other side at a quarter-past nine. You will find a
small brougham waiting close to the curb, driven by a fellow

with a heavy black cloak tipped at the collar with red. Into this you will step, and you will reach Victoria in time for the Continental express."

"Where shall I meet you?"

"At the station. The second first-class carriage from the front will be reserved for us."

The most famous detective in the world, with his almost equally famous companion (Sidney Paget, 1892)

"The carriage is our rendezvous, then?"

"Yes."

It was in vain that I asked Holmes to remain for the evening. It was evident to me that he thought he might bring trouble to the roof he was under, and that that was the motive which impelled him to go. With a few hurried words as to our plans for the morrow he rose and came out with me into the garden, clambering over the wall which leads into Mortimer Street, and immediately whistling for a hansom, in which I heard him drive away.

In the morning I obeyed Holmes's injunctions to the letter. A hansom was procured with such precautions as would prevent its being one which was placed ready for us, and I drove immediately after breakfast to the Lowther Arcade, through which I hurried at the top of my speed. A brougham was waiting with a very massive driver wrapped in a dark cloak, who, the instant that I had stepped in, whipped up the horse and rattled off to Victoria Station. On my alighting there he turned the carriage, and dashed away again without so much as a look in my direction.

So far all had gone admirably. My luggage was waiting for me, and I had no difficulty in finding the carriage which Holmes had indicated, the less so as it was the only one in the train which was marked "Engaged." My only source of anxiety now was the non-appearance of Holmes. The station clock marked only seven minutes from the time when we were due to start. In vain I searched among the groups of travellers and leave-takers for the lithe figure of my friend. There was no sign of him. I spent a few minutes in assisting a venerable Italian priest, who was endeavouring to make a porter understand, in his broken English, that his luggage was to be booked through to Paris. Then, having taken another look round, I returned to my carriage, where I found that the porter, in spite of the ticket, had given me my decrepit Italian friend as a travelling companion. It was useless for me to explain to him that his presence was an intrusion, for my Italian was even more limited than his English, so I shrugged my shoulders resignedly, and continued to look out anxiously for my friend. A chill of fear had come over me, as I thought that his absence might mean that some blow had fallen during the night. Already the doors had all been shut and the whistle blown, when—

"My dear Watson," said a voice, "you have not even condescended to say good-morning."

I turned in uncontrollable astonishment. The aged ecclesiastic had turned his face towards me. For an instant the wrinkles were smoothed away, the nose drew away from the chin, the lower lip ceased to protrude and the mouth to mumble, the dull eyes regained their fire, the drooping figure expanded. The next the whole frame collapsed again, and Holmes had gone as quickly as he had come.

"Good heavens!" I cried; "how you startled me!"

"Every precaution is still necessary," he whispered. "I have reason to think that they are hot upon our trail. Ah, there is Moriarty himself."

The train had already begun to move as Holmes spoke. Glancing back, I saw a tall man pushing his way furiously through the crowd, and waving his hand as if he desired to have the train stopped. It was too late, however, for we were rapidly gathering momentum, and an instant later had shot clear of the station.

"With all our precautions, you see that we have cut it rather fine," said Holmes, laughing. He rose, and throwing off the black cassock and hat which had formed his disguise, he packed them away in a hand-bag.

"Have you seen the morning paper, Watson?"

"No."

"You haven't seen about Baker Street, then?"

"Baker Street?"

"They set fire to our rooms last night. No great harm was done."

"Good heavens, Holmes! this is intolerable."

"They must have lost my track completely after their bludgeon-man was arrested. Otherwise they could not have imagined that I had returned to my rooms. They have evidently taken the precaution of watching you, however, and that is what has brought Moriarty to Victoria. You could not have made any slip in coming?"

"I did exactly what you advised."

"Did you find your brougham?"

"Yes, it was waiting."

"Did you recognise your coachman?"

"No."

"It was my brother Mycroft. It is an advantage to get about in such a case without taking a mercenary into your confidence. But we must plan what we are to do about Moriarty now."

"As this is an express, and as the boat runs in connection with it, I should think we have shaken him off very effectively."

"My dear Watson, you evidently did not realise my meaning when I said that this man may be taken as being quite on the same intellectual plane as myself. You do not imagine that if I were the pursuer I should allow myself to be baffled by so slight an obstacle. Why, then, should you think so meanly of him?"

"What will he do?"

"What I should do."

"What would you do, then?"

"Engage a special."

"But it must be late."

"By no means. This train stops at Canterbury; and there is always at least a quarter of an hour's delay at the boat. He will catch us there."

"One would think that we were the criminals. Let us have him arrested on his arrival."

"It would be to ruin the work of three months. We should get the big fish, but the smaller would dart right and left out of the net. On Monday we should have them all. No, an arrest is inadmissible."

"What then?"

"We shall get out at Canterbury."

"And then?"

"Well, then we must make a cross-country journey to New-haven, and so over to Dieppe. Moriarty will again do what I should do. He will get on to Paris, mark down our luggage, and wait for two days at the depot. In the meantime we shall treat ourselves to a couple of carpet-bags, encourage the manufactures of the countries through which we travel, and make our way at our leisure into Switzerland, *via* Luxembourg and Basle."

At Canterbury, therefore, we alighted, only to find that we should have to wait an hour before we could get a train to Newhaven.

I was still looking rather ruefully after the rapidly disappearing luggage-van which contained my wardrobe, when Holmes pulled my sleeve and pointed up the line.

"Already, you see," said he.

Far away, from among the Kentish woods there rose a thin spray of smoke. A minute later a carriage and engine could be seen flying along the open curve which leads to the station. We had hardly time to take our place behind a pile of luggage when it passed with a rattle and a roar, beating a blast of hot air into our faces.

"There he goes," said Holmes, as we watched the carriage swing and rock over the points. "There are limits, you see, to our friend's intelligence. It would have been a *coup-de-maître* had he deduced what I would deduce and acted accordingly."

"And what would he have done had he overtaken us?"

"There cannot be the least doubt that he would have made a murderous attack upon me. It is, however, a game at which two may play. The question now is whether we should take a premature lunch here, or run our chance of starving before we reach the buffet at Newhaven."

ARTHUR CONAN DOYLE,
The Adventures of Sherlock Holmes

The very silent traveller

The squat funnel of the engine gave a choking, gurgling sound. It spat myriads of fiery sparks into the pitch-coloured night. The comet's tail of the sparks was like a woman's mane, spreading along the length of the clattering train—a wavering, fading and recurrent magic carpet, broken and reunited as the rush of the coaches created an irregular slipstream, now narrowing at the curves, now spreading out again on the straight stretches. Behind the train the sparks settled on the black soil, blinked briefly and then died one by one as they touched the cool earth.

A row of lights appeared in the night. The train began to slow down, brakes bit on wheels, the roaring and panting became less strident. The three-toned whistle gave a long shriek as the glimmer of the second set of signals streaked by.

The engine pulled up, pulsating and burbling steam, at a small station on the edge of the vast Argentine plains. The station was marked by half-a-dozen apple-trees; the name of it, on a faded and battered piece of corrugated iron, was scarcely visible. The sheet of iron had been fastened with wire between two of the trees to secure it against the violent winter storms. There was no platform, no hut, no telegraphist's shack. Apart from the sign wired to the trees and a few forlorn oil-lamps there was nothing to signify a stop. The nearest station on the line with a permanent staff was at least thirty miles away.

The halt was brief; little more than three minutes. The engine spewed forth another column of fiery sparks, emitting a cloud of steam. Then the wheels began to turn again; the choking, gurgling, panting sounds were repeated and the shrill whistle pierced the night.

In this brief interval one passenger boarded the train. Or rather, he was helped up the steep iron steps by three others who were evidently seeing him off. They supported him along the corridor and placed him in an empty compartment. Then, without any goodbyes or last-minute talk, they jumped from the train. The wheels were already moving and they barely had time to regain the ground before the train pulled out. It would seem a case of bad manners—yet the three men had a good excuse for not lingering.

Transporting dead bodies in the Argentine used to be an extremely costly and difficult business. Red tape indeed made it almost impossible; it needed six different kinds of permits, a dozen declarations, a pile of documents. All this became even more difficult in districts where the simple ranches, the scattered *estancias*, were fifty or a hundred miles from the nearest town. Not even the fastest horse could carry the messengers to collect the necessary permits within the two or three days during which a corpse could be preserved. And if, by some lucky chance, the permits were forthcoming, the railway company charged ten times as much for a dead traveller as for a living one—not to mention the expense of the coffin and the ticket of the attendant who, under the company rules, had to accompany such a consignment. Many of the ranchers lived well without having more than a small fund of cash; more than one would have been ruined by such a heavy expenditure. Yet they were loath to bury their relatives on their own farms, especially if there was a family mausoleum in Buenos Aires.

But luckily there was still some ingenuity and enterprise left in these parts, and the traveller who boarded the train at the wayside halt was making his trip because of such ingenuity. He was very dead indeed; but his pious and grief-stricken relatives simply smuggled him on to the express. They wrapped him up well and pushed his sombrero over his forehead; by supporting him closely, they made any possible observer believe that he was

First Class—the Meeting (Abraham Solomon, 1854)

an invalid or maybe a little drunk. One of them then settled the
price of the ticket with the conductor, tipping him well so that
the "poor invalid" should be left undisturbed and in sole possession of the compartment.

As soon as the train had pulled out, another of the three men
jumped on a horse and rode off post-haste to the nearest telegraph office, twenty miles away. There he sent a telegram to the
dead man's uncle in Buenos Aires, giving him the number of the
coach and compartment in which the corpse was travelling.
Uncle Felipe was to meet the train at the terminus and take care
of the rest.

The other two men remained standing near the track, staring after the rapidly-disappearing red tail-lights. They felt very
solemn—but also considerably relieved.

At the next stop—a much bigger one—Captain Grodeck boarded
the train.

The Captain had started life in the Imperial German Army
but owing to some slight misunderstanding over cards (a fifth
ace had unaccountably got into the pack) he was obliged to
resign his commission. He had had some hard times after that,
but later found his perfect niche in promoting revolutions. They
needed little promoting in South and Central America—except
that the captain was organizing them strictly for the benefit of
his employers, a large and prosperous armaments group.

Just now he was on his way back from Paraguay, after a
very profitable stay. He had a lot of baggage which he had to
lug down the corridor himself. By the time he had finished the
chore he was bathed in sweat, his scarred face glistening with it;
and he was in a vile temper. Cursing, panting and shouting, he
expressed most unflattering opinions about the Argentinian railway system in general and the lack of porters in particular. He
dwelt with venomous intensity on the high steps of the carriages
and the time-table of the only southbound express train that
made a night journey inevitable.

He continued his loud outburst outside each crowded compartment. He was forced to drag his suitcase, boxes and rugs
along the swaying narrow corridors—there was nowhere an
empty seat.

Finally he reached the compartment in which the silent traveller was ensconced in solitary splendour. He was sitting in the darkest corner, huddled up, limp. The broadbrimmed black sombrero had slipped down on the tip of his nose. The blue-shaded reading lamp threw a pale circle of light upon him. He seemed to be sleeping soundly, lost in a happier world of dreams.

"Do you mind, señor?" asked Captain Grodeck.

There was no answer. He pushed his way into the compartment, distributing his luggage with considerable noise; then switched on the central light and, sitting down, inspected his fellow-traveller.

The huddled passenger sat modestly and quietly in his corner. There was little to be seen of his face—except that he had not shaved for some time. His cloak reached to the ground, enveloping his body: both hands were buried in the large patch pockets. The rhythmic shaking of the train made the body tremble and sway gently.

Captain Grodeck took the seat opposite. As he had become quite wrought-up with his passionate denunciations, he knew he couldn't sleep. So he decided to have some intelligent conversation—or just conversation.

Politely he asked a number of questions in his execrable Spanish. When he received no reply, he tried other languages—Portuguese, French, English, even his native German. But this linguistic effort proved all unavailing. His travelling companion sat there, stubbornly silent, clumsily immobile.

Captain Grodeck was a persistent man. He produced his pigskin cigar-case, selected the finest, speckled Havana and held it out invitingly. He praised its quality, its aroma; he hoped that the señor would accept it as a token of friendship.

There was no answer.

The captain made two other attempts to make the silent traveller speak. But it was all in vain. Neither polite remarks, nor friendly questions nor offers of cigar and cigarette brought any response.

And now Captain Grodeck discovered that though he had a mass of luggage and was equipped with every convenience for a long journey, he had failed to provide himself with the simplest necessity. He had no matches: his lighter was empty. A cigar between his thick lips, he felt himself all over, reaching into every pocket—but he did not find a single match.

He turned to his companion. "Could I trouble you for a light?" he asked. But there was no reply.

This final discourtesy made Captain Grodeck see red. He jumped up, bent over the silent stranger and started to shake him with all his might. The lifeless head was knocked several times against the back of the seat, the captain shouting and cursing at him.

Under the powerful grip of the German's hands, the huddled man slid sideways. His sombrero slipped back until it was barely clinging to the back of his head. His hands emerged from the deep pockets; then his whole body suddenly jerked forward, and like a bag of sand it dropped heavily on to the floor of the compartment. The hat rolled away and Grodeck needed no second glance to tell him that the traveller was dead.

Startled and horrified, he stared at the body. He knew his own hot, ungovernable temper and had cursed it a thousand times whenever it got him into a scrape. But he had not expected *this*. After all, he had just given the man a good shaking and knocked his silly head a few times against the wall. . . .

But his hesitation only lasted a few moments. With a sudden decision, he bent down and lifted the corpse from the floor. He dragged it to the window and propped it up while he opened the sliding glass. Then, with a mighty heave, he let it drop into the pitch-dark night.

The train rattled on, unconcerned, its wheels devouring the miles.

Early in the morning the express arrived in Buenos Aires.

Uncle Felipe had been waiting for the last hour. Excited and anxious, he elbowed his way through the large crowd until he found the carriage which had been indicated in the telegram.

His plan was all ready. He would board the train, enter the compartment, "discover" the dead man and shout for help. . . . But, of course, it would be too late: his poor, dear nephew had died somewhere on the way.

But he searched in vain: there was no trace of his relative in the compartment nor in the whole carriage. Thinking that he had made a mistake, he explored the other carriages. They were all empty now—except for one man with a scarred face and a military bearing who was still lugging some of his heavy suitcases down to the platform. He was just collecting the last piece —from the very compartment in which Uncle Felipe's nephew was supposed to have travelled.

"Excuse me, sir," Uncle Felipe addressed him. "Did you have a fellow-passenger in this compartment?"

"Oh yes," replied Captain Grodeck with a completely expressionless face.

"And?" Uncle Felipe waited breathlessly.

"Oh, he got off about three stations back," the captain answered and, picking up his last suitcase, descended from the carriage. He made his way along the platform, unconcerned and self-assured while Uncle Felipe crossed himself three times and collapsed in a dead faint.

PAUL TABORI,
The Very Silent Traveller

The workman and the wet-nurse

The train had just left Genoa, in the direction of Marseilles, and was following the rocky and sinuous coast, gliding like an iron serpent between the sea and the mountains, creeping over the yellow sand edged with silver waves and entering suddenly into the black-mouthed tunnels like a beast into its lair.

In the last carriage, a stout woman and a young man sat opposite each other. They did not speak, but occasionally they would glance at each other. She was about twenty-five years old. Seated by the window, she silently gazed at the passing landscape. She was from Piedmont, a peasant, with large black eyes, a full bust and fat cheeks. She had deposited several parcels under the wooden seat and she held a basket on her knees.

The man might have been twenty years old. He was thin and sunburned, with the dark complexion that denotes work in the open. Tied up in a handkerchief was his whole fortune; a pair of heavy boots, a pair of trousers, a shirt and a coat. Hidden under the seat were a shovel and a pickaxe tied together with a rope.

He was going to France to seek work.

The sun, rising in the sky, spread a fiery light over the coast; it was toward the end of May and delightful odours floated in the air and penetrated through the open windows of the railway carriage. The blooming orange and lemon-trees exhaled a heavy, sweet perfume that mingled with the breath of the roses which grew in profusion everywhere along the line, in the gardens of the wealthy, in front of cottage doors, and even wild.

Roses are at home along this coast! They fill the whole region with their dainty and powerful fragrance and make the atmosphere taste like a delicacy, something better than wine, and as intoxicating.

The train was going at slow speed as if loath to leave behind this wonderful garden. It stopped every few minutes at small stations, at clusters of white houses, then went on again leisurely, emitting long whistles. Nobody got in. One would have thought that all the world had gone to sleep, unable to stir, on that sultry spring morning. The plump peasant woman from time to time closed her eyes, but opened them suddenly as her basket began to slide from her lap. She would catch it, replace it, look out of the window a little while and then doze off again. Tiny beads of perspiration covered her brow and she breathed with difficulty, as if suffering from a painful oppression.

The young man had let his head fall on his breast and was sleeping the sound sleep of the labouring man.

All of a sudden, just as the train left a small station, the peasant woman woke up and opening her basket, drew forth a piece of bread, some hard-boiled eggs, and a flask of wine and some fine, red plums. She began to eat.

The man had also wakened and he watched the woman, watched every morsel that travelled from her knees to her lips. He sat with his arms folded, his eyes set and his lips tightly compressed.

The woman ate like a glutton, with relish. Every little while she would take a swallow of wine to wash down the eggs and then she would stop for breath.

Everything vanished, the bread, the eggs, the plums and the wine. As soon as she finished her meal, the man closed his eyes.

Then, feeling ill at ease, she loosened her blouse and the man suddenly looked at her again.

She did not seem to mind and continued to unbutton her dress.

The pressure of her flesh causing the opening to gape, she revealed a portion of white linen chemise and a portion of her skin.

As soon as she felt more comfortable, she turned to her fellow-traveller and remarked in Italian: "It's too hot to breathe."

He answered, in the same tongue and with the same accent: "Fine weather for travelling."

She asked: "Are you from Piedmont?"

"From Asti."

"And I'm from Casale."

They were neighbours. They began to talk.

They exchanged the commonplace remarks that working people repeat over and over and which are sufficient for their slow-working and narrow minds. They spoke of their homes. They had mutual acquaintances.

They quoted names and became more and more friendly as they discovered more and more people they knew. Short, rapid words, with sonorous endings and the Italian cadence, gushed from their lips.

After that, they talked about themselves. She was married and had three children whom she had left with her sister, for she had found a situation as nurse, a good situation with a French lady at Marseilles.

He was going to look for work.

He had been told that he would be able to find it in France, for they were building a great deal, he had heard.

They then fell silent.

The heat was becoming terrible; it beat down like fire on the roof of the railway carriage. A cloud of dust flew behind the train and entered through the window, and the fragrance of the roses and orange-blossoms had become stronger, heavier and more penetrating.

The two travellers went to sleep again.

They awakened almost at the same time. The sun was nearing the edge of the horizon and shed its glorious light on the blue sea. The atmosphere was lighter and cooler.

The nurse was gasping. Her dress was open and her cheeks looked flabby and moist, and in an oppressed voice, she breathed:

"I have not nursed since yesterday; I feel as if I were going to faint."

The man did not reply; he hardly knew what to say.

She continued: "When a woman has as much milk as I she must nurse three times a day or she'll feel uncomfortable. It feels like a weight on my heart, a weight that prevents my breathing and just exhausts me. It's terrible to have so much milk."

He replied: "Yes, it's bad. It must hurt you."

She really seemed ill and almost ready to faint. She murmured: "I only have to press and the milk flows out like a fountain. It is really interesting to see. You wouldn't believe it. In Casale, all the neighbours came to see it."

He replied: "Ah! really."

"Yes, really. I would show you, only it wouldn't help me. You can't make enough come out that way."

And she paused.

The train stopped at a station. Leaning on a fence was a woman holding a crying infant in her arms. She was thin and in rags.

The nurse watched her. Then she said in a compassionate tone: "There's a woman I could help. And the baby could help me, too. I'm not rich; I'm leaving my home, my people and my baby to take a place, but still, I'd give five francs to have that child and be able to nurse it for ten minutes. It would quiet him, and me too, I can tell you. I think I would feel as if I were being born again."

She paused again. Then she passed her hot hand several times across her wet brow and moaned: "Oh! I can't stand it any longer. I believe I shall die." And with an unconscious motion, she opened her dress altogether.

Her right breast appeared all swollen and stiff, with its brown teat, and the poor woman gasped: "Ah! gracious Heaven! What shall I do?"

The train had left the station and was running on, while the flowers breathed out their penetrating fragrance on the warm evening air.

Sometimes they saw a fishing-boat, which seemed asleep on the blue sea with its motionless white sail, which was reflected in the water as though another boat were there, head down.

The young man, embarrassed, stammered: "But—madam—I—might perhaps be—be able to help you."

In an exhausted whisper, she replied: "Yes, if you will be so kind, you'll do me a great favour. I can't stand it any longer, really I can't."

He got on his knees before her; and she leaned over to him with a motherly gesture as if he were a child. In the movement she made to draw near to the man, a drop of milk appeared on her breast. He absorbed it quickly, and, taking this heavy breast in his mouth like a fruit, he began to drink regularly and greedily.

He had passed his arms around the woman's waist and pressed her close to him in order not to lose a drop of the nourishment. And he drank with slow gulps, like a baby.

All of a sudden she said: "That's enough, now the other side!" Docilely, he took the other.

She had placed both hands on his back and now was breathing happily, freely, enjoying the perfume of the flowers carried on the breeze that entered the open windows.

"What a lovely smell," she said.

He made no reply and drank on at the living fountain of her breast, closing his eyes as though to savour it better.

But she gently pushed him from her.

"That's enough. I feel much better now. It has put life into me again."

He rose and wiped his mouth with the back of his hand.

While she replaced her breasts inside her dress, she said:

"You did me a great favour. I thank you very much!"

And he replied in a grateful tone:

"It is I who thank you, for I hadn't eaten a thing for two days!"

GUY DE MAUPASSANT,
An Idyll
(trans. Boyd)

JOURNEY

Oh the wild engine! Every time I sit
In any train I must remember it.
The way it smashes through the air; its great
Petulant majesty and terrible rate:
Driving the ground before it, with those round
Feet pounding, beating, covering the ground;
The piston using up the white steam so
You cannot watch it when it come or go;
The cutting, the embankment; how it takes
The tunnels, and the clatter that it makes;
So careful of the train and of the track,
Guiding us out, or helping us go back;
Breasting its destination: at the close
Yawning, and slowly dropping to a doze.

We who have looked each other in the eyes
This journey long, and trundled with the train,
Now to our separate purposes must rise,
Becoming decent strangers once again.
The little chamber we have made our home
In which we so conveniently abode,
The complicated journey we have come,
Must be an unremembered episode.
Our common purpose made us all like friends.
How suddenly it ends!
A nod, a murmur, or a little smile,
Or often nothing, and away we file.

I hate to leave you, comrades. I will stay
To watch you drift apart and pass away.
It seems impossible to go and meet
All those strange eyes of people in the street.
But, like some proud unconscious god, the train
Gathers us up and scatters us again.

Harold Monro

Farewell to the Light Brigade (Robert Collinson, 1855)

Train to Johannesburg

From Ixopo the toy train climbs up into other hills, the green rolling hills of Lufafa, Eastwolds, Donnybrook. From Donnybrook the broad-gauge runs to the great valley of the Umkomaas. Here the tribes live, and the soil is sick, almost beyond healing. Up out of the valley it climbs, past Hemu-hemu to Elandskop. Down the long valley of the Umsindusi, past Edendale and the black slums to Pietermaritzburg, the lovely city. Change here to the greatest train of all, the train for Johannesburg. Here is a white man's wonder, a train that has no engine, only an iron cage on its head, taking power from metal ropes stretched out above.

Climb up to Hilton and Lion's River, to Balgowan, Rosetta, Mooi River, through hills lovely beyond any singing of it. Thunder through the night, over battlefields of long ago. Climb over the Drakensberg, on to the level plains.

Wake in the swaying coach to the half-light before the dawn. The engine is steaming again, and there are no more ropes overhead. This is a new country, a strange country, rolling and rolling away as far as the eye can see. There are new names here, hard names for a Zulu who has been schooled in English. For they are in the language that was called Afrikaans, a language that he had never yet heard spoken.

—The mines, they cry, the mines. For many of them are going to work in the mines.

Are these the mines, those white flat hills in the distance? He can ask safely, for there is no one here who heard him yesterday.

—That is the rock out of the mines, umfundisi.* The gold has been taken out of it.

—How does the rock come out?

—We go down and dig it out, umfundisi. And when it is hard to dig, we go away, and the white men blow it out with the firesticks. Then we come back and clear it away; we load it on to the trucks; and it goes up in a cage, up a long chimney so long that I cannot say it for you.

—How does it go up?

* Man of the church (Zulu).

—It is wound up by a great wheel. Wait, and I shall show you one.

He is silent, and his heart beats a little faster, with excitement and fear.

—There is the wheel, umfundisi. There is the wheel.

A great iron structure rearing into the air, and a great wheel above it, going so fast that the spokes play tricks with the sight. Great buildings, and steam blowing out of pipes, and men hurrying about. A great white hill, and an endless procession of trucks climbing upon it, high up in the air. On the ground, motor cars, lorries, buses, one great confusion.

—Is that Johannesburg? he asks.

But they laugh confidently. Old hands some of them are.

—That is nothing, they say. In Johannesburg there are buildings, so high—but they cannot describe them.

—My brother, says one, you know the hill that stands so, straight up, behind my father's kraal. So high as that.

The other man nods, but Kumalo does not know that hill.

And now the buildings are endless, the buildings, and the white hills, and the great wheels, and streets without number, and cars and lorries and buses.

—This surely is Johannesburg? he says.

But they laugh again. They are growing a little tired. This is nothing, they say.

Railway-lines, railway-lines, it is a wonder. To the left, to the right, so many that he cannot count. A train rushes past them, with a sudden roaring of sound that makes him jump in his seat. And on the other side of them, another races beside them, but drops slowly behind. Stations, stations, more than he has ever imagined. People are waiting there in hundreds, but the train rushes past, leaving them disappointed.

The buildings get higher, the streets more uncountable. How does one find one's way in such a confusion? It is dusk, and the lights are coming on in the streets.

One of the men points for him.

—Johannesburg, umfundisi.

He sees great high buildings; there are red and green lights on them, almost as tall as the buildings. They go on and off. Water comes out of a bottle, till the glass is full. Then the lights go out. And when they come on again, lo the bottle is full and upright, and the glass empty. And there goes the bottle over again. Black and white, it says, black and white, though it is red and green. It is too much to understand.

He is silent, his head aches, he is afraid. There is this railway station to come, this great place with all its tunnels under the ground. The train stops, under a great roof, and there are thousands of people. Steps go down into the earth, and here is the tunnel under the ground. Black people, white people, some going, some coming, so many that the tunnel is full. He goes carefully that he may not bump anybody, holding tightly on to his bag. He comes out into a great hall, and the stream goes up the steps, and here he is out in the street. The noise is immense. Cars and buses one behind the other, more than he has ever imagined. The stream goes over the street, but remembering Mpanza's son, he is afraid to follow. Lights change from green to red, and back again to green. He has heard that. When it is green, you may go. But when he starts across, a great bus swings across the path. There is some law of it that he does not understand, and he retreats again. He finds himself a place against the wall, he will look as though he is waiting for some purpose. His heart beats like that of a child, there is nothing to do or think to stop it. *Tixo*, watch over me, he says to himself. *Tixo*, watch over me.

ALAN PATON,
Cry, the Beloved Country

———◆———

The great race east

Harvey Cheyne, a multi-millionaire living in San Diego, California, believes that his only son Harvey has drowned in the North Atlantic after falling off an ocean liner. When, months later, he receives a telegram from his son that he has arrived safely in Gloucester, Massachusetts (having been picked up by a Grand Banks fishing boat), he hires a special train for himself and his wife to go to him.

It was a busy week-end among the wires; for, now that their anxiety was removed, men and cities hastened to accommodate.

Los Angeles called to San Diego and Barstow that the Southern California engineers might know and be ready in their lonely round-houses; Barstow passed the word to the Atlantic and Pacific; and Albuquerque flung it the whole length of the Atchison, Topeka, and Santa Fe management, even into Chicago. An engine, combination-car with crew, and the great and gilded "Constance" private car were to be "expedited" over those two thousand three hundred and fifty miles. The train would take precedence of one hundred and seventy-seven others meeting and passing; despatchers and crews of every one of those said trains must be notified. Sixteen locomotives, sixteen engineers, and sixteen firemen would be needed—each and every one the best available. Two and one-half minutes would be allowed for changing engines; three for watering and two for coaling. "Warn the men, and arrange tanks and chutes accordingly; for Harvey Cheyne is in a hurry, a hurry—a hurry," sang the wires. "Forty miles an hour will be expected, and division superintendents will accompany this special over their respective divisions. From San Diego to Sixteenth Street, Chicago, let the magic carpet be laid down. Hurry! oh, hurry!"

"It will be hot," said Cheyne, as they rolled out of San Diego in the dawn of Sunday. "We're going to hurry, mamma, just as fast as ever we can; but I really don't think there's any good of your putting on your bonnet and gloves yet. You'd much better lie down and take your medicine. I'd play you a game o' dominoes, but it's Sunday."

"I'll be good. Oh, I *will* be good. Only—taking off my bonnet makes me feel as if we'd never get there."

"Try to sleep a little, mamma, and we'll be in Chicago before you know."

"But it's Boston, father. Tell them to hurry."

The six-foot drivers were hammering their way to San Bernardino and the Mohave wastes, but this was no grade for speed. That would come later. The heat of the desert followed the heat of the hills as they turned east to the Needles and the Colorado River. The car cracked in the utter drouth and glare, and they put crushed ice to Mrs. Cheyne's neck, and toiled up the long, long grades, past Ash Fork, towards Flagstaff, where the forests and quarries are, under the dry, remote skies. The needle of the

speed indicator flicked and wagged to and fro; the cinders rattled on the roof, and a whirl of dust sucked after the whirling
wheels. The crew of the combination sat on their bunks, panting
in their shirt-sleeves, and Cheyne found himself among them
shouting old, old stories of the railroad that every trainman
knows, above the roar of the car. He told them about his son,
and how the sea had given up its dead, and they nodded and
spat and rejoiced with him; asked after "her, back there," and
whether she could stand it if the engineer "let her out a piece,"
and Cheyne thought she could. Accordingly, the great fire-
horse was "let out" from Flagstaff to Winslow till a division
superintendent protested.

But Mrs. Cheyne, in the boudoir state-room, where the
French maid, sallow-white with fear, clung to the silver door-
handle, only moaned a little and begged her husband to bid
them "hurry." And so they dropped the dry sands and moon-
struck rocks of Arizona behind them, and grilled on till the
crash of the couplings and the wheeze of the brake-hose told
them they were at Coolidge by the Continental Divide.

Three bold and experienced men—cool, confident, and dry
when they began; white, quivering, and wet when they finished
their trick at those terrible wheels—swung her over the great
lift from Albuquerque to Glorietta and beyond Springer, up
and up to the Raton Tunnel on the State line, whence they
dropped rocking into La Junta, had sight of the Arkansaw, and
tore down the long slope to Dodge City, where Cheyne took
comfort once again from setting his watch an hour ahead.

There was very little talk in the car. The secretary and
typewriter sat together on the stamped Spanish leather cushions by the plate-glass observation window at the rear end,
watching the surge and ripple of the ties crowded back behind
them, and, it is believed, making notes of the scenery. Cheyne
moved nervously between his own extravagant gorgeousness
and the naked necessity of the combination, an unlit cigar in
his teeth, till the pitying crews forgot that he was their tribal
enemy, and did their best to entertain him.

At night the bunched electrics lit up that distressful palace
of all the luxuries, and they fared sumptuously, swinging on
through the emptiness of abject desolation. Now they heard the

swish of a water-tank, and the guttural voice of a Chinaman, the clink-clink of hammers that tested the Krupp-steel wheels, and the oath of a tramp chased off the rear-platform; now the solid crash of coal shot into the tender; and now a beating back of noises as they flew past a waiting train. Now they looked out into great abysses, a trestle purring beneath their tread, or up to rocks that barred out half the stars. Now scaur and ravine changed and rolled back to jagged mountains on the horizon's edge, and now broke into hills lower and lower, till at last came the true plains.

At Dodge City an unknown hand threw in a copy of a Kansas paper containing some sort of an interview with Harvey, who had evidently fallen in with an enterprising reporter, telegraphed on from Boston. The joyful journalese revealed that it was beyond question their boy, and it soothed Mrs. Cheyne for a while. Her one word "hurry" was conveyed by the crews to the engineers at Nickerson, Topeka, and Marceline, where the grades are easy, and they brushed the continent behind them. Towns and villages were close together now, and a man could feel here that he moved among people.

"I can't see the dial, and my eyes ache so. What are we doing?"

"The very best we can, mamma. There's no sense in getting in before the Limited. We'd only have to wait."

"I don't care. I want to feel we're moving. Sit down and tell me the miles."

Cheyne sat down and read the dial for her (there were some miles which stand for records to this day), but the seventy-foot car never changed its long steamer-like roll, moving through the heat with the hum of a giant bee. Yet the speed was not enough for Mrs. Cheyne; and the heat, the remorseless August heat, was making her giddy; the clock hands would not move, and when, oh, when would they be in Chicago?

It is not true that, as they changed engines at Fort Madison, Cheyne passed over to the Amalgamated Brotherhood of Locomotive Engineers an endowment sufficient to enable them to fight him and his fellows on equal terms for evermore. He paid his obligations to engineers and firemen as he believed they deserved, and only his bank knows what he gave the crews who had sympathized with him. It is on record that the last crew took entire charge of switching operations at Sixteenth Street, because "she" was in a doze at last, and Heaven was to help any one who bumped her.

Now the highly-paid specialist who conveys the Lake Shore and Michigan Southern Limited from Chicago to Elkhart is something of an autocrat, and he does not approve of being told how to back up to a car. None the less he handled the "Constance" as if she might have been a load of dynamite, and when the crew rebuked him, they did it in whispers and dumb show.

"Pshaw!" said the Atchison, Topeka, and Santa Fe men, discussing life, later; "we weren't runnin' for a record. Harvey Cheyne's wife, she were sick back, an' we didn't want to jounce her. Come to think of it, our runnin' time from San Diego to Chicago was 57.54. You can tell that to them Eastern way-trains. When we're tryin' for a record, we'll let you know."

To the Western man (though this would not please either city), Chicago and Boston are cheek by jowl, and some railroads encourage the delusion. The Limited whirled the "Constance" into Buffalo, and the arms of the New York Central and Hudson River (illustrious magnates with white whiskers and gold charms on their watch-chains boarded her here to talk a little business to Cheyne), who slid her gracefully into Albany, where the Boston and Albany completed the run from tide-water to tide-water—total time, eighty-seven hours and thirty-five minutes, or three days, fifteen hours and one-half. Harvey was waiting for them.

RUDYARD KIPLING,
Captains Courageous (1897)

———◆———

The story-teller

It was a hot afternoon, and the railway carriage was correspondingly sultry, and the next stop was at Templecombe, nearly an hour ahead. The occupants of the carriage were a small girl, and a smaller girl, and a small boy. An aunt belonging to the children occupied one corner seat, and the further corner seat on the opposite side was occupied by a bachelor who was a stranger to their party, but the small girls and the small boy emphatically occupied the compartment. Both the aunt and the children were conversational in a limited, persistent way, reminding one of the attentions of a housefly that refused to be discouraged. Most of the aunt's remarks seemed to begin with "Don't," and nearly all of the children's remarks began with "Why?" The bachelor said something out loud.

"Don't, Cyril, don't," exclaimed the aunt, as the small boy began smacking the cushions of the seat, producing a cloud of dust at each blow.

"Come and look out of the window," she added.

The child moved reluctantly to the window. "Why are those sheep being driven out of that field?" he asked.

"I expect they are being driven to another field where there is more grass," said the aunt weakly.

"But there is lots of grass in that field," protested the boy; "there's nothing else but grass there. Aunt, there's lots of grass in that field."

"Perhaps the grass in the other field is better," suggested the aunt fatuously.

"Why is it better?" came the swift, inevitable question.

"Oh, look at those cows!" exclaimed the aunt. Nearly every field along the line had contained cows or bullocks, but she spoke as though she were drawing attention to a rarity.

"Why is the grass in the other field better?" persisted Cyril.

The frown on the bachelor's face was deepening to a scowl. He was a hard, unsympathetic man, the aunt decided in her mind. She was utterly unable to come to any satisfactory decision about the grass in the other field.

The smaller girl created a diversion by beginning to recite "On the Road to Mandalay." She only knew the first line, but she put her limited knowledge to the fullest possible use. She repeated the line over and over again in a dreamy but resolute and very audible voice; it seemed to the bachelor as though some one had had a bet with her that she could not repeat the line aloud two thousand times without stopping. Whoever it was who had made the wager was likely to lose his bet.

"Come over here and listen to a story," said the aunt, when

the bachelor had looked twice at her and once at the communi-cation cord.

The children moved listlessly towards the aunt's end of the carriage. Evidently her reputation as a story-teller did not rank high in their estimation.

In a low, confidential voice, interrupted at frequent intervals by loud, petulant questions from her listeners, she began an un-enterprising and deplorably uninteresting story about a little girl who was good, and made friends with every one on account of her goodness, and was finally saved from a mad bull by a number of rescuers who admired her moral character.

"Wouldn't they have saved her if she hadn't been good?" demanded the bigger of the small girls. It was exactly the ques-tion that the bachelor had wanted to ask.

"Well, yes," admitted the aunt lamely, "but I don't think they would have run quite so fast to her help if they had not liked her so much."

"It's the stupidest story I've ever heard," said the bigger of the small girls, with immense conviction.

"I didn't listen after the first bit, it was so stupid," said Cyril.

The smaller girl made no actual comment on the story, but she had long ago recommenced a murmured repetition of her favourite line.

"You don't seem to be a success as a story-teller," said the bachelor suddenly from his corner.

The aunt bristled in instant defence at this unexpected attack.

"It's a very difficult thing to tell stories that children can both understand and appreciate," she said stiffly.

"I don't agree with you," said the bachelor.

"Perhaps *you* would like to tell them a story," was the aunt's retort.

"Tell us a story," demanded the bigger of the small girls.

"Once upon a time," began the bachelor, "there was a little girl called Bertha, who was extraordinarily good."

The children's momentarily-aroused interest began at once to flicker; all stories seemed dreadfully alike, no matter who told them.

"She did all that she was told, she was always truthful, she kept her clothes clean, ate milk puddings as though they were jam tarts, learned her lessons perfectly, and was polite in her manners."

"Was she pretty?" asked the bigger of the small girls.

"Not as pretty as any of you," said the bachelor, "but she was horribly good."

There was a wave of reaction in favour of the story; the word horrible in connection with goodness was a novelty that commended itself. It seemed to introduce a ring of truth that was absent from the aunt's tales of infant life.

"She was so good," continued the bachelor, "that she won several medals for goodness, which she always wore, pinned on to her dress. There was a medal for obedience, another medal for punctuality, and a third for good behaviour. They were large metal medals and they clicked against one another as she walked. No other child in the town where she lived had as many as three medals, so everybody knew that she must be an extra good child."

"Horribly good," quoted Cyril.

"Everybody talked about her goodness, and the Prince of the country got to hear about it, and he said that as she was so very good she might be allowed once a week to walk in his park, which was just outside the town. It was a beautiful park, and no children were ever allowed in it, so it was a great honour for Bertha to be allowed to go there."

"Were there any sheep in the park?" demanded Cyril.

"No," said the bachelor, "there were no sheep."

"Why weren't there any sheep?" came the inevitable question arising out of that answer.

The aunt permitted herself a smile, which might almost have been described as a grin.

"There were no sheep in the park," said the bachelor, "because the Prince's mother had once had a dream that her son would either be killed by a sheep or else by a clock falling on him. For that reason the Prince never kept a sheep in his park or a clock in his palace."

The aunt suppressed a gasp of admiration.

"Was the Prince killed by a sheep or by a clock?" asked Cyril.

"He is still alive, so we can't tell whether the dream will come true," said the bachelor unconcernedly; "anyway, there were no sheep in the park, but there were lots of little pigs running all over the place."

"What colour were they?"

"Black with white faces, white with black spots, black all over, grey with white patches, and some were white all over."

The story-teller paused to let a full idea of the park's treasures sink into the children's imaginations; then he resumed:

"Bertha was rather sorry to find that there were no flowers in the park. She had promised her aunts, with tears in her eyes, that she would not pick any of the kind Prince's flowers, and she had meant to keep her promise, so of course it made her feel silly to find that there were no flowers to pick."

"Why weren't there any flowers?"

"Because the pigs had eaten them all," said the bachelor promptly. "The gardeners had told the Prince that you couldn't have pigs and flowers, so he decided to have pigs and no flowers."

There was a murmur of approval at the excellence of the Prince's decision; so many people would have decided the other way.

"There were lots of other delightful things in the park. There were ponds with gold and blue and green fish in them, and trees with beautiful parrots that said clever things at a moment's notice, and humming birds that hummed all the popular tunes of the day. Bertha walked up and down and enjoyed herself immensely, and thought to herself: 'If I were not so extraordinarily good I should not have been allowed to come into this beautiful park and enjoy all that there is to be seen in it,' and her three medals clinked against one another as she walked and helped to remind her how very good she really was. Just then an enormous wolf came prowling into the park to see if it could catch a fat little pig for its supper."

"What colour was it?" asked the children, amid an immediate quickening of interest.

"Mud-colour all over, with a black tongue and pale grey eyes that gleamed with unspeakable ferocity. The first thing that it saw in the park was Bertha; her pinafore was so spotlessly white and clean that it could be seen from a great distance. Bertha saw the wolf and saw that it was stealing towards her, and she began to wish that she had never been allowed to come into the park. She ran as hard as she could, and the wolf came after her with huge leaps and bounds. She managed to reach a shrubbery of myrtle bushes and she hid herself in one of the thickest of the bushes. The wolf came sniffing among the branches, its black tongue lolling out of its mouth and its pale grey eyes glaring with rage. Bertha was terribly frightened, and thought to herself: 'If I had not been so extraordinarily good I should have been safe in the town at this moment.' However, the scent of the myrtle was so strong that the wolf could not sniff out where Bertha was hiding, and the bushes were so thick that he might have hunted about in them for a long time without catching sight of her, so he thought he might as well go off and catch a little pig instead. Bertha was trembling very much at having the wolf prowling and sniffing so near her, and as she trembled the medal for obedience clinked against the medals for good conduct and punctuality. The wolf was just moving away when he heard the sound of the medals clinking and stopped to listen; they clinked again in a bush quite near him. He dashed into the bush, his pale grey eyes gleaming with ferocity and triumph, and dragged Bertha out and devoured her to the last morsel. All that was left of her were her shoes, bits of clothing, and the three medals for goodness."

"Were any of the little pigs killed?"

"No, they all escaped."

"The story began badly," said the smaller of the small girls, "but it had a beautiful ending."

"It is the most beautiful story that I ever heard," said the bigger of the small girls, with immense decision.

"It is the *only* beautiful story I have ever heard," said Cyril.

A dissentient opinion came from the aunt.

"A most improper story to tell to young children! You have undermined the effect of years of careful teaching."

"At any rate," said the bachelor, collecting his belongings preparatory to leaving the carriage, "I kept them quiet for ten minutes, which was more than you were able to do."

"Unhappy woman!" he observed to himself as he walked down the platform of Templecombe station; "for the next six months or so those children will assail her in public with demands for an improper story!"

SAKI,
The Story-Teller

INCIDENT IN AUGUST

When the Circle train was held up by a signal
    Between Gloucester Road and High Street (Ken)
In the battering dog-day heat of August
    We sweated and mopped our brows. And then
We saw in the cutting, amid the loosestrife
    And butterflies looping through bindweed trails,
A boy who lay drinking, straight from the bottle,
    When, of course, he was paid to look after the rails.

High stood the sun and the heat-haze shimmered,
    The crickets shrilled to the burnished tracks;
But our minds and the motors throbbed together,
    Insisting "You're late. You mustn't relax,
You mustn't look backward, you mustn't look . . .
    Southward?"
    (Oh, the linemen stood by in the hills of Var
And leaned on their spades as the trains went past them
    And swigged red wine from a great stone jar.)

Now, the boy in the sunlight was drinking water—
    Or beer at the best. It might have been Beaune
Or Chateauneuf, but a London embankment
    Was not the slopes of the Côtes-du-Rhône.
Still, a Mistral blew out of dry Vaucluse,
    A Mistral blew over South-West Ten . . .
Till the train pulled out from Mondragon-sur-Lez
    As the points changed back towards High Street
    (Ken).

BRYAN MORGAN

Ethel and Mr Salteena
go to Rickamere Hall

When the great morning came Mr Salteena did not have an egg for his brekfast in case he should be sick on the jorney.

What top hat will you wear asked Ethel.

I shall wear my best black and my white alpacka coat to keep off the dust and flies replied Mr Salteena.

I shall put some red ruge on my face said Ethel because I am very pale owing to the drains in this house.

You will look very silly said Mr Salteena with a dry laugh.

Well so will you said Ethel in a snappy tone and she ran out of the room with a very superier run throwing out her legs behind and her arms swinging in rithum.

Well said the owner of the house she has a most idiotick run.

Presently Ethel came back in her best hat and a lovly velvit coat of royal blue. Do I look nice in my get up she asked.

Mr Salteena survayed her. You look rather rash my dear your colors dont quite match your face but never mind I am just going up to say goodbye to Rosalind the housemaid.

Well dont be long said Ethel. Mr S. skipped upstairs to Rosalinds room. Goodbye Rosalind he said I shall be back soon and I hope I shall enjoy myself.

I make no doubt of that sir said Rosalind with a blush as Mr Salteena silently put 2/6 on the dirty toilet cover.

Take care of your bronkitis said Mr S. rarther bashfully and he hastilly left the room waving his hand carelessly to the housemaid.

Come along cried Ethel powdering her nose in the hall let us get into the cab. Mr Salteena did not care for powder but he was an unselfish man so he dashed into the cab. Sit down said Ethel as the cabman waved his whip you are standing on my luggage. Well I am paying for the cab said Mr S. so I might be allowed to put my feet were I like.

They traveled 2nd class in the train and Ethel was longing to go first but thought perhaps least said soonest mended. Mr Salteena got very excited in the train about his visit. Ethel was

calm but she felt excited inside. Bernard has a big house said
Mr S. gazing at Ethel he is inclined to be rich.

Oh indeed said Ethel looking at some cows flashing past the
window. Mr S. felt rarther disheartened so he read the paper
till the train stopped and the porters shouted Rickamere station.
We had better collect our traps said Mr Salteena and just then
a very exalted footman in a cocked hat and olive green uniform
put his head in at the window. Are you for Rickamere Hall he
said in impressive tones.

Well yes I am said Mr Salteena and so is this lady.

Very good sir said the noble footman if you will alight I will
see to your luggage there is a convayance awaiting you.

Oh thankyou thankyou said Mr S. and he and Ethel stepped
along the platform. Outside they found a lovely cariage lined
with olive green cushons to match the footman and the horses
had green bridles and bows on their manes and tails. They got
gingerly in. Will he bring our luggage asked Ethel nervously.

I expect so said Mr Salteena lighting a very long cigar.

Do we tip him asked Ethel quietly.

Well no I don't think so not yet we had better just thank him
perlitely.

Just then the footman staggered out with the bagage. Ethel
bowed gracefully over the door of the cariage and Mr S. waved
his hand as each bit of luggage was hoisted up to make sure it
was all there. Then he said thankyou my good fellow very
politely. Not at all sir said the footman and touching his cocked
hat he jumped actively to the box.

I was right not to tip him whispered Mr Salteena the thing
to do is to leave 2/6 on your dressing table when your stay is
over.

Does he find it asked Ethel who did not really know at all
how to go on at a visit. I beleeve so replied Mr Salteena anyhow
it is quite the custom and we cant help it if he does not. Now my
dear what do you think of the scenery.

DAISY ASHFORD (aged 9),
The Young Visitors

Love on the Orient Express

When Coral left the doctor she began to run, as fast as was possible with a suitcase in a lurching train, so that she was out of breath and almost pretty when Myatt saw her pulling at the handle of his door. He had put away the correspondence from Mr. Eckman and the list of market prices ten minutes ago, because he found that always, before the phrases or the figures could convey anything to his mind, he heard the girl's voice: "I love you."

What a joke, he thought, what a joke.

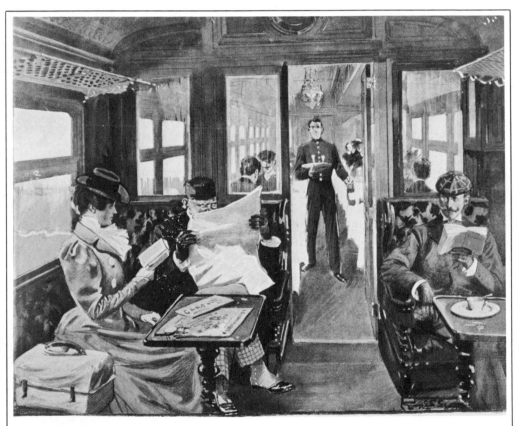

Interior of the Orient Express. The gentleman on the right looks hopeful of his chances. With a five-day journey ahead he has every reason to be.

He looked at his watch. No stop now for seven hours and he had tipped the guard. He wondered whether they got used to this kind of affair on long-distance trains. When he was younger he used to read stories of kings' messengers seduced by beautiful countesses travelling alone and wonder whether such good fortune would ever happen to him. He looked at himself in the glass and pressed back his oiled black hair. I am not bad-looking, if my skin were not so sallow; but when he took off his fur coat, he could not help remembering that he was growing fat and that he was travelling in currants and not with a portfolio of sealed papers. Nor is she a beautiful Russian countess, but she likes me and she has a pretty figure.

He sat down, and then looked at his watch, and got up again. He was excited. You fool, he thought, she's nothing new; pretty and kind and common, you can find her any night on the Spaniards road, and yet in spite of these persuasions he could not but feel that the adventure had in it a touch of freshness, of unfamiliarity. Perhaps it was only the situation: travelling at forty miles an hour in a berth little more than two feet across. Perhaps it was her exclamation at dinner; the girls he had known were shy of using that phrase; they would say "I love you" if they were asked, but their spontaneous tribute was more likely to be "You're a nice boy." He began to think of her as he had never thought before of any woman who was attainable: she is dear and sweet, I should like to do things for her. It did not occur to him for several moments that she had already reason for gratitude.

"Come in," he said, "come in." He took the suitcase from her and pushed it under the seat and then took her hands.

"Well," she said with a smile. "I'm here, aren't I?" In spite of her smile he thought her frightened and wondered why. He loosed her hands in order to pull down the blinds of the corridor windows, so that they seemed suddenly to become alone in a small trembling box. He kissed her and found her mouth cool, soft, uncertainly responsive. She sat down on the seat which had become converted into a berth and asked him, "Did you wonder whether I'd come?"

"You promised," he reminded her.

"I might have changed my mind."

"But why?" Myatt was becoming impatient. He did not want to sit about and talk; her legs, swinging freely without touching the floor, excited him. "We'll have a nice time." He took off her shoes and ran his hands up her stockings. "You know a lot, don't you?" she said. He flushed. "Do you mind that?"

"Oh, I'm glad," she said, "so glad. I couldn't bear it if you hadn't known a lot." Her eyes large and scared, her face pale under the dim blue globe, first amused him, then attracted him. He wanted to shake her out of aloofness into passion. He kissed her again and tried to slip her frock over her shoulder. Her body trembled and moved under her dress like a cat tied in a bag; suddenly she put her lips up to him and kissed his chin. "I do love you," she said, "I do."

The sense of unfamiliarity deepened round him. It was as

The Orient Express quickly acquired a risqué reputation;
hence this poster advertising a bawdy Parisian musical.

if he had started out from home on a familiar walk, past the gas works, across the brick bridge over the Wimble, across two fields, and found himself not in the lane which ran uphill to the new road and the bungalows, but on the threshold of a strange wood, faced by a shaded path he had never taken, running God knew where. He took his hands from her shoulders and said without touching her, "How sweet you are," and then with astonishment, "How dear." He had never felt lust rising in him and yet checked and increasing because of the check; he had always spilt himself into new adventures with an easy excitement.

"What shall I do? Shall I take off my clothes?" He nodded, finding it hard to speak, and saw her rise from the berth and go into a corner and begin to undress slowly and very methodically, folding each garment in turn, the blouse, the skirt, the bodice, the vest, and laying it in a neat pile on the opposite seat. He was conscious as he watched her calm absorbed movements of the inadequacy of his body. He said: "You are very lovely," and his words stumbled a little with an unfamiliar excitement. When she came across the carriage to him he saw that he had been deceived; her calm was like a thin skin tightly drawn; her face was flushed with excitement and her eyes were scared; she looked uncertain whether to laugh or cry. But they came together simply in the narrow space between the seats. "I wish the light would go right out," she said. She stood close against him while he touched her with his hands, both swaying easily to the motion of the train. "No," he said, "I'd like to turn it full on."

"It would be more becoming," she said and began to laugh quietly to herself. Her laughter lay, an almost imperceptible pool of sound, beneath the pounding and the clatter of the express, but when they spoke, instead of whispering, they had to utter the intimate words loudly and clearly.

The sense of strangeness survived even the customary gestures; lying in the berth she proved awkward in a mysterious innocent fashion which astonished him. Her laughter stopped, not coming gradually to an end, but vanishing so that he wondered whether he had imagined the sound or whether it had been a trick of the glancing wheels. She said suddenly and urgently: "Be patient. I don't know much," and then she cried out with pain. He could not have been more startled if a ghost had passed through the compartment dressed in an antique wear which antedated steam. He would have left her if she had not held him to her with her hands, while she said in a voice of which snatches only escaped the sound of the engine: "Don't go. I'm sorry. I didn't mean . . ." Then the sudden stopping of the train lurched them apart. "What is it?" she said. "A station." She protested with pain, "Why must it now?"

Myatt opened the window a little way and leant out. The dim chain of lights lit the ground for only a few feet beside the line. Snow already lay inches thick; somewhere in the distance a red spark shone intermittently, like a revolving light between the white gusts. "It isn't a station," he said. "Only a signal against us." The stilling of the wheels made the night very quiet with one whistle of steam to break it; here and there men woke and put their heads out of windows and spoke to each other. From the third-class carriages at the rear of the train came the sound of a fiddle. The tune was bare, witty, mathematical, but in its passage through the dark and over the snow it became less determinate, until it picked from Myatt's mind a trace of perplexity and regret: "I never knew. I never guessed." There was such warmth in the carriage now between them that, without closing the window, he knelt beside the berth and put his hand to her face, touching her features with curious fingers. Again he was overwhelmed with the novel thought, "How sweet, how dear." She lay quiet, shaken a little by quick breaths of pain or excitement.

Somebody in the third-class carriages began to curse the fiddler in German, saying that he could not sleep for the noise. It seemed not to occur to him that he had slept through the racket of the train, and that it was the silence surrounding the precise slow notes which woke him. The fiddler swore back and went on fiddling, and a number of people began to talk at once, and someone laughed.

"Were you disappointed?" she said. "Was I awfully bad at it?"

"You were lovely," he said. "But I never knew. Why did you come?"

She said in a tone as light as the fiddle's, but equally able to absorb another's sense of bewilderment: "A girl's got to learn some time." He touched her face again. "I hurt you."

"It wasn't a picnic," she said.

"Next time," he began to promise, but she interrupted with a question which made him laugh by its gravity: "There'll be another time? Did I pass all right?"

"You want another time?"

"Yes," she said, but she was thinking not of his embrace, but of the flat in Constantinople and her own bedroom and going to bed at ten.

GRAHAM GREENE,
Stamboul Train